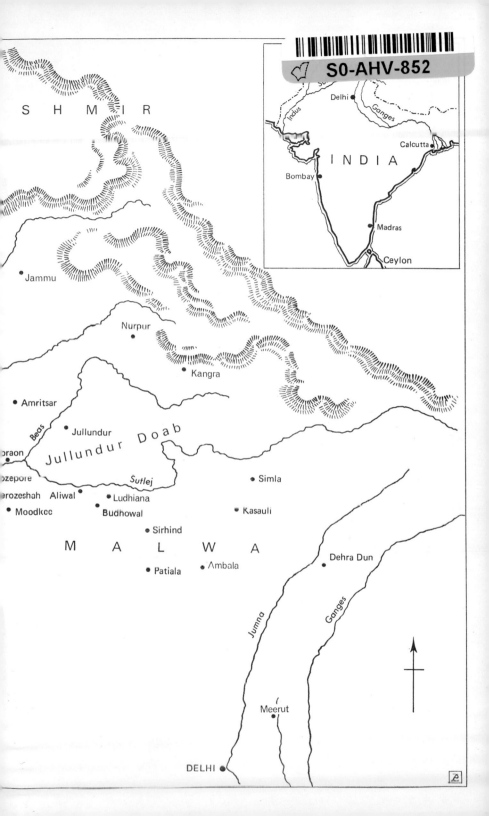

S0-AHV-852

K A S H M I R

INDIA

Delhi

Indus

Ganges

Calcutta

Bombay

Madras

Ceylon

Jammu

Nurpur

Kangra

Amritsar

Beas

Jullundur

Jullundur Doab

raon

Sutlej

Simla

zepore

erozeshah   Aliwal   Ludhiana

Moodkee   Budhowal   Kasauli

Sirhind

M A L W A

Patiala   Ambala

Dehra Dun

Jumna

Ganges

Meerut

DELHI

Fernald Library
Colby - Sawyer College
New London, New Hampshire

Presented by

MR. AND MRS. WILLIAM RUTTER

The
Sikh
Wars

The Sikh Wars
THE BRITISH ARMY
IN THE PUNJAB
1845 - 1849

by
HUGH COOK

LEO COOPER · LONDON

FERNALD LIBRARY
COLBY-SAWYER COLLEGE
NEW LONDON, N.H. 03257

DS
477.1
C66

First published in Great Britain 1975
by LEO COOPER LTD
196 Shaftesbury Avenue, London WC2H 8JL

Copyright © 1975 by Hugh Cook

ISBN 0 85052 164 5

88504

Made and printed in Great Britain by
The Garden City Press Limited
Letchworth, Hertfordshire
SG6 1JS

CONTENTS

MAPS

6

ILLUSTRATIONS

The author and publishers would like to thank the following for permission to reproduce the above illustrations: The National Army Museum, Nos 5, 7, 8, 11, 14, 16, 18 and 19, The Mansell Collection, Nos 2, 9, 12, 17, and 20, The United Service and Royal Aero Club, No 1, RMA Sandhurst, No 3, and The Parker Gallery No 21.

7

INTRODUCTION AND ACKNOWLEDGMENTS

The two Sikh Wars should, for a number of reasons, have a special fascination both for the military historian and for anyone interested in the story of British rule in India. They were no comparative walk-over, with the climate and terrain providing more real opposition than the enemy, as was the case in a number of Britain's colonial campaigns; but a hard-fought contest against a well-trained army composed of first class fighting men. They completed the conquest of British India and they were the last campaigns fought by the armies of the old East India Company on Indian soil before everything was changed by the Mutiny of 1857. When the Mutiny came, within a decade of the final Sikh surrender, the losers proved to be the staunchest supporters of the British 'Raj' and thereafter the Punjab was the main reservoir from which the Indian Army was recruited. The hard-fought battles of both wars were decided primarily by the discipline and tenacity of the European troops. The ordinary English Line Regiments, the bedrock of the British Army, have seldom been given the publicity accorded to their more glamorous counterparts from elsewhere in Britain; and in these wars every one of the Queen's Regiments was English.

Most of the accounts written during the last century tend to be somewhat partisan, a particular victim being the much maligned British Commander-in-Chief, Lord Gough. I have tried to present a fair picture. Some British accounts, too, convey the impression that the Sikhs were little better than semi-civilized tribesmen, which was far from being the case. I have where possible endeavoured to give something of the story from the Sikh side and in doing so I hope I have done justice to the soldiers of the Khalsa.

9

Since the real heroes of the struggle on both sides were the regimental soldiers, I have, while consulting most of the recognized published works on the subject, set out to get as much information as possible from regimental sources, and particularly from unpublished contemporary accounts. This has, I hope, helped me to give some idea of the men who fought in these campaigns and the conditions with which they had to contend. I have been in touch with the Regimental Headquarters of all the descendants of the British regiments involved and visited most of them. I would like to express my sincere gratitude to all the Regimental secretaries and Museum Curators concerned for their universal helpfulness and for allowing me access to their archives. Unfortunately, while some regiments have very full records, in other cases the cupboards have proved to be very nearly bare. I am also most grateful for the help and courtesy extended to me by the staffs of the Ministry of Defence (War Department) Library, the RUSI Library, the Archives Room of the Army Museum and the India Office Library. Finally I must thank Mrs Elizabeth Charmer who has typed and retyped my drafts and even learned to decipher my writing.

CHAPTER 1

The Rise of the Sikhs

Bʀɪᴛɪꜱʜ soldiers had many a hard fight in India during the two hundred years of the 'Raj', but never did they come up against tougher opposition than they did in the Punjab during the two Sikh Wars, when on one fateful night in particular the Governor-General felt that 'the fate of India trembled in the balance'. The British spoke of their enemy in these campaigns as 'The Sikh Nation'; yet in fact the Sikhs were not, racially speaking, a nation at all, but a religious sect. To understand the course of events one must first know something of the Punjab and its people, the rise of the Sikhs, and the general situation in India at the time.

The Punjab, the 'land of the five rivers', consisted in the days of Sikh rule of an area roughly in the form of an isosceles triangle, with the base formed by the foothills of the Himalayas in the north, the western side by the River Indus and the eastern by its tributary, the Sutlej. The land stretching eastwards from the Sutlej to the Jumna, known as Malwa, was later to be included in the province under British rule. Beyond the Indus were the mountains bordering on Afghanistan. The Sutlej is the most easterly of the 'five rivers', the others being the Beas, the Ravi, the Chenab and the Jhelum in that order. All rise in the Himalayan foothills, the Beas flowing into the Sutlej above the town of Ferozepore, while the Ravi and Jhelum both join the Chenab, which in turn flows into the Sutlej not far from its confluence with the Indus. The term 'doab' signifies the land lying between the two rivers. Thus the district between the Sutlej and the Beas is known as the Jullundur Doab from the principal

11

town in the area, that between the Beas and the Ravi the Bari Doab and so on. Except in the Himalayan foothills in the north, the country is mainly flat, although there are ranges of hills in the north west. The river valleys were well cultivated, but between them there were patches of jungle and sandy waste. The climate is generally hot by day, especially in the period before the rains when the thermometer may read over 100 degrees fahrenheit for days on end, but the winter nights can be bitterly cold.

The earliest recorded communities in the Punjab, part of the civilization based on Mohenjo-Daro, were in existence about 3000 BC, but very little is known of them and the story of Punjabi peoples really starts with the arrival of the Aryan invaders through the Afghan passes some thousand years later. These Aryans were of the same race as those who were then moving into Europe. They differed from most of the later invaders, since they arrived, with their womenfolk, as settlers. They developed the Hindu religion with its rigid caste system based on four main groups, the Brahmins, who were the priests, the Kshatriyas, the warriors, the Vaisyas, peasants and merchants, and the Sudras, who were the serfs. Outside the caste system were the Pariahs or, to use a later term, the Untouchables, who consisted basically of the aboriginal inhabitants. It was a system devised to keep the race pure, an ancient form of apartheid. In modern times, broadly speaking, the Rajput can be said to represent the Kshatriya and the Jat the Vaisya.

After the arrival of the Aryans, India remained isolated from the rest of the world until about 500 BC, when Darius established a satrapy or province of his vast Persian empire to include the Punjab. This lasted roughly a hundred years. The next invader was Alexander the Great, who in 376 BC met and defeated an Indian King, Puri or Porus, in a battle on the banks of the Jhelum almost on the same ground on which the Battle of Chillianwalla was fought in 1849. Alexander's Greeks withdrew, but two hundred years later, Menander, who had succeeded to the throne of the Seleucids, the heirs of the eastern part of Alexander's empire, annexed the Punjab, bringing in many officials of Greek descent. Then from about AD 50 came the Kushans, a tribe who originated in China and who were to rule the Punjab for 250 years. Finally, around AD 500, a wave of White Huns, of the race which Attila was leading westwards, came in through the Afghan passes. Thereafter no invader appeared from the north-west for another five hundred years. Up to this time each successive new race had gradually become assimilated with the existing inhabitants, adopting their customs and religion.

There was now to be a change of pattern. In 1001 Mahmud of Ghazni invaded the Punjab. His Mohammedans, who regarded the Hindu as the worst type of idol-worshipping infidel, destroyed temples and practised forcible conversion on a large scale. It has even been said that the bitterness of feeling between Hindu and Mohammedan in India owes its origins to Mahmud. He did not pursue his conquests beyond the Punjab and it was a hundred years more before Mohammedan rule was extended over most of India. During the next three centuries, except in the extreme south, the Mohammedans ruled India as overlords, setting up a number of independent states, the rulers of which normally exploited their Hindu subjects. In about 1300 the Punjab suffered another invasion when Tamerlane led his Mongols across the Hindu Kush, but this was more in the nature of a major raid. Finally in 1526 Baber, a descendant of Tamerlane, led another Mohammedan army from Samarkand into India to set up the Mogul Empire in Delhi, which was, for the first time since the rule of the Guptas in the fourth century, to establish a hegemony over nearly the whole of the Peninsula. By the time this happened the inhabitants of the Punjab were of pretty mixed ancestry. These origins, and the fact that the original permanent Aryan settlement was based on the area, account for the people of the Punjab and the North West Frontier Province being today fairer skinned and better built than those of the remainder of the Peninsula.

Meanwhile in 1469 a religious reformer named Nanak had been born in the Punjab. Becoming known as the Guru or leader, he set out to try and purify the Hindu religion and established a sect whose members, drawn almost entirely from the Jat community, became known as Sikhs, a word meaning disciples. It was originally a purely religious body, stressing the

13

brotherhood of man. Its members spread over the Punjab proper and into Malwa. Under the tolerant rule of the great Mogul Emperor, Akbar, the contemporary of Queen Elizabeth I, the sect flourished peaceably. It was in his reign that the fourth Guru completed the Sikh holy book, the Granth, and built the golden temple at Amritsar as a centre of what was becoming a new religion. Under Akbar's successors less tolerance was shown to non-Mohammedans and the fourth Guru was put to death on the orders of the Emperor Jehangir. Not unnaturally the Sikhs became increasingly anti-Mohammedan and began to develop into a militant organization, giving military training to their members.

It was under Govind, the tenth Guru, whose father, the ninth Guru, had been summoned to Delhi and had failed to return, probably being murdered by order of the Emperor Aurangzeb, that the final organization of the Sikhs was achieved. He declared himself the last Guru and established the Khalsa, the army of the free, in which all men were equal. Wherever five— the traditional Indian *panchayat*—were gathered together, the spirit of the Guru was present. Govind also laid down certain rules for the Khalsa, the 'five K's', so called from the initial letter of the Punjabi words denoting them. No man was to cut his hair, a comb was always to be carried, short pants were to be worn, with always a steel bangle on the right wrist and a sword or dagger. Smoking was strictly prohibited. The members of the Khalsa adopted the suffix 'Singh', signifying lion, to their name.

Govind Singh was murdered by two Pathans, whose father he had himself slain, in 1708. His successor as leader of the community, Banda Singh, lacked his political skill and became involved in a rebellion against the Mogul power in Malwa. In due course he was captured and put to death, a fate suffered by many of his followers. After this the Sikhs suffered a period of eclipse, and could do little against their Mohammedan overlords. Then in 1738 the Persian Nadir Shah invaded India and took Delhi. He withdrew, but eight years later there followed the first of nine successive Afghan invasions. As the power of the Moguls wilted under these blows, the Sikhs recovered and the Khalsa once more began to be a power in the Punjab. At this

14

stage it was based largely upon groups of feudal cavalry, known as misls, each under its own chief.

By this time another non-Mohammedan power, the Mahratta Confederacy, had arisen in Western and Central India. When the Mahrattas were defeated by the combined Mogul and Afghan forces at Panipat near Delhi in 1761, it must have seemed to many fervent Sikhs that they were fated to become the main power which could resist Mohammedan domination. There was, however, no unified leadership. Individual chiefs were very much a law unto themselves and indeed the Sikh community itself was split, in that the Sikhs of Malwa acknowledged the sovereignty of Delhi and those of the Punjab proper came under the sway of Kabul. Furthermore, despite their check at Panipat, the Mahrattas were, with the withdrawal of the Afghans, able to re-assert their influence at Delhi to dominate the Mogul Emperor.

Another and greater power had also arrived in India and was soon inevitably to come into contact with the Sikhs. The British had originally come to India purely for purposes of trade. The Honourable East India Company established 'factories'—really trading depots—first at Surat on the west coast in 1612, and later at Madras, Calcutta and Bombay. Originally 'John Company', as it came to be called, was loath to be concerned in any way in the internal affairs of the country, but inevitably in the mid-eighteenth century it became involved in the struggle for colonial supremacy between England and France. It was the need to combat French influence which led it into warfare with the French and their native allies in South India and later to intervene in Bengal, where Clive's victory over Surajah Dowlah at Plassey (1757) is popularly regarded as the first real step up the ladder which led to Britain becoming the Paramount Power in India. Eight years after Plassey the Company became Dewan, or collector of revenue, for the area later to be known as the provinces of Bengal, Bihar and Orissa. This virtually meant annexation and, from being a purely trading concern, 'John Company' was now administering a vast tract of country. To ensure peaceful conditions in which trade could flourish it was essential to eliminate hostile neighbours or to ensure that there were strong but well disposed rulers in adjoining states. This

15

led by the beginning of the nineteenth century to the annexation of a wide band of territory along the south bank of the Ganges extending into the 'doab' between the Jumna and the Ganges almost as far as Agra, and to the possession of Rohilkand lying to the north of it. Thus only about 100 miles of Mahratta-controlled territory divided the British from the Punjab. In 1803 the inevitable clash between the British and Mahrattas took place. Following Lord Lake's victories at Laswaree and Delhi, the Mahratta power in the north was broken and the British established themselves in Delhi, becoming effective successors of the old Mogul Empire. Moreover, as Malwa passed under their sway, they were now the actual neighbours of the Sikhs.

Meanwhile, a great leader had come to the fore in the Punjab. Ranjit Singh was born in 1780, the son of a minor chieftain, and at an early age was married for political reasons to the daughter of another chief. He soon came to dominate his own group of clans and before the close of the century he was known throughout the Punjab as the leader of resistance to the Afghans. The Shah of Afghanistan attempted to secure his support by making him his deputy in Lahore, but in 1801 Ranjit showed his hand by declaring himself Maharajah of the Punjab and set out to create a unified independent Sikh state.

Ranjit was an unimpressive looking man with only one eye, having lost the other in childhood. He was quite illiterate, but possessed an enquiring mind, and was gifted with great shrewdness and common sense. He impressed himself on his followers by his strong personality and tremendous powers of leadership. He was a fine horseman and a good judge of horseflesh, qualities which appealed to the horse-loving Sikhs. He was also a great womaniser and loved his drink, and indeed his powers in both these fields became quite legendary and further endeared him to his lusty followers.

He soon became convinced that if he was to achieve his ambitions he needed to do two things—to establish an army based on the European system and to avoid coming into conflict with the British. His first contact with them was when Holkar's Mahratta army withdrew into the Punjab after it had been defeated by Lord Lake. Subsequently he had visited Lake's army at Agra. He had been most impressed by what he saw.

16

* *

A further incident had confirmed him in his views. The Bengal sepoys of the escort of the British envoy to Lahore were attacked by a mob of Akalis (Sikh fanatics) and although heavily outnumbered stood firm and drove off their attackers before Ranjit himself was able to come to their assistance. He knew that only good discipline and sound training could account for the success of a small number of Hindustanis against an attack by determined Sikhs.

His first and most obvious bone of contention with the British was over the Sikh states of Malwa and for a time it seemed that the problem might lead to war. Ranjit would clearly have liked to bring them into the fold, but, headed by Patiala, the Sikhs of Malwa preferred to keep a measure of independence under British sovereignty rather than come under the closer control of Lahore. It suited the British to have a cushion of protected states between the directly ruled territory and that of a strong native power, while at the same time they were glad to have such a power, provided it was friendly, to act as a buffer state between themselves and the turbulent Afghans to the north-west. Ranjit accepted the position and in 1809 a treaty confirmed the British protectorate over the Malwa states, although Ranjit retained his own lands east of the Sutlej. British military stations were established at Ferozepore and Ludhiana near the Sutlej and at Ambala some ninety miles from the river. After the Nepal War of 1814–15, in which a Patiala contingent rendered good service to the British, further military stations were established in the hills of Garhwal to the north.

In organizing his army Ranjit Singh had first to overcome the Sikh preference for fighting on horseback and to build up the prestige of the infantry and artillery. He employed foreign advisers, the more important ones having seen service under Napoleon. Allard, who trained his cavalry, was French, as was Court, an artilleryman. Ventura, who trained the infantry, and Avitible, an artilleryman who became governor of Peshawar, were Italians who had been in French service. The army was trained mainly by French methods and in the artillery all words of command were given in French. Another artillery adviser was Gardner, an American soldier of fortune. Ranjit's own main interest was in the artillery and anyone with a knowledge

17

of guns and gunnery was always welcome. There were large numbers of deserters from John Company's army and Ranjit also employed a few Anglo-Indian officers. The men of the army were by no means all Sikhs. Many Punjabi Mohammedans and Pathans were enlisted and there were even some Gurkhas. In 1833 the Khalsa was formed into brigades on the French system, each with three or four battalions of infantry, an artillery battery and anything from two to six thousand cavalry.

As he began to build up his army Ranjit Singh also set out firmly to consolidate his authority in the Punjab and to extend the dominion of the Lahore Government. He conquered Kashmir to the north and captured Multan in the south, thus extending his territory to the junction of the Sutlej and the Indus. Across the latter river he acquired Peshawar, although for a while he held it as a tributary of Kabul. Later the Amir Dost Mohammed of Afghanistan endeavoured to establish his control over the frontier city, but Ranjit defeated him. Thereafter the governor of Peshawar was appointed directly from Lahore.

When he was fifty Ranjit had a stroke, but he still held a firm grip on his people. His friendship with the British was by no means universally approved by the Sikh sirdars and there was a near crisis when, after establishing himself in Multan, he wished to extend his territory to acquire the Shikarpore district of Sind, but gave up the idea under diplomatic pressure from the British. Many of the sirdars resented this; moreover it seemed obvious to them that the British would inevitably work to extend their conquests, as had every paramount power in India in the past, and they were therefore regarded as a potential enemy with whom a clash must come. When the British decided in 1839 to oust Dost Mahammed from the throne of Afghanistan, Ranjit was their nominal ally, but he would not agree to the expedition using the direct route to Kabul through his territory and the invasion was launched from Sind.

In that same year 'The Lion of the Punjab', as he had come to be called, died. The strong hand was removed from the helm and there was no one capable of steering the ship of state. It did not take long for the Punjab to lapse into a state of near anarchy.

Ranjit Singh had many reputed sons, but the only one he

had always acknowledged as undoubtedly his was Kharak
Singh, who now succeeded him as Maharajah. Unfortunately
Kharak was a very weak character, dominated by a male
favourite. His son, Nao Nihal Singh, was a promising youth, but
the main authority really rested with Dhian Singh, Ranjit's
vizier or prime minister. Dhian was not a Sikh, but a Dogra
Rajput, who ruled the province of Jammu jointly with his
brother Gholab. They were known as the 'Jammu brothers'
and their influence was resented by many of the Sikhs. Before
long the Maharajah's favourite was assassinated and the young
heir apparent became virtually head of State. Then Kharak
Singh died and on the very day of his accession Nao Nihal
Singh met with a fatal accident, which was popularly believed
to have been contrived by the Jammu brothers, who had some
evidence that he intended to oust them. Another reputed son
of Ranjit's, Shere Singh, was placed on the throne.

With the weakening of central authority it was becoming
apparent that the real power was passing into the hands of the
army and as they watched developments in Lahore the men
of the Khalsa began to get restive. The Panchayats became
more and more influential and discipline suffered. It was unfortunate from the British point of view that Major Broadfoot,
the Political Agent at Ferozepore, who crossed the Punjab at
this time in charge of a party of dependants en route to the
British Army of Occupation in Kabul, saw a number of Sikh
units and formed a poor opinion of their efficiency. His reports
were a factor in the underestimation in some quarters of Sikh
military capabilities in the coming struggle.

The British venture in Afghanistan strengthened the hand
of the Anglophobe elements in the Khalsa in two ways. In the
first place the mere fact of the invasion raised fears of a British
intention to encircle the Punjab, while the subsequent disastrous
retreat undoubtedly affected British prestige to an extent which
could not be restored by the victories which followed. Nevertheless General Pollock's 'avenging army' was allowed to cross the
Punjab and Sikh forces co-operated with it in the Khyber Pass.

Meanwhile further intrigues had been taking place in Lahore.
Kharak Singh's widow, Chand Kaur, had put forward a claim
to the throne on behalf of a hypothetical unborn son of Nao

19

Nihal Singh, while Ranjit's young widow, the attractive Rani Jindan, pressed the claims of her small son, Dhuleep Singh, as the legitimate heir of his father. This claim was certainly open to question for, since his stroke, Ranjit's sexual capabilities had been at least suspect and the Rani's morals were such that John Lawrence was to refer to her as the 'Messalina of the Punjab'. It was said that in the absence of her acknowledged lover she used to have four young men detailed to place themselves at her disposal in turn each night. A group known as the Sindhanwalla family now came into the picture. Basically they represented the anti-Jammu faction, but at first they co-operated with Dhian Singh, who favoured the claims of young Dhuleep. Apparently with Dhian's approval they assassinated the Maharajah Shere Singh, but they then came out in their true colours, disposed of Dhian Singh, and proclaimed their support for Chand Kaur. Gholab retired to Jammu.

Dhian Singh had a son, Hira Singh, who now called on the army to support Dhuleep's claims, appealing to its nationalist sentiment on the grounds that the Sindhanwallas had British support. He marched on Lahore, eliminated the Sindhanwallas and set up a government in Dhuleep's name with himself as vizier. Chand Kaur was subsequently beaten to death with slippers by her own slave girls, so whatever her qualities it would seem she was none too popular with her servants.

Despite his success Hira Singh was now in a difficult position. He had aroused the anti-British sentiments of the army to achieve power, and whatever his own feelings had to maintain an Anglophobe front to retain its support; yet distrust of his family was widespread and his own hold on the Sikhs was somewhat tenuous. Moreover the Rani Jindan was ambitious for power and would obviously have liked to rule the country through her lovers. His difficulties were made no easier by his own uncle Suchet Singh, the third of the Jammu brothers, who led a revolt in favour of yet another of Ranjit's reputed sons. He was defeated and slain, but his rebellion was the cause of a further increase in Anglophobia, since one of the Sindhanwalla chiefs, who had taken refuge in British territory, was quite improperly allowed to return to take part, while Suchet himself had considerable property in Malwa, and the British declined to allow it to pass to the Sikh state. They insisted that the laws of inheritance of British India applied, but not unnaturally the Sikh Durbar took a different view.

Hira Singh now found himself with serious financial problems; the treasury at Lahore showed signs of running dry. A prime factor was that, in order to secure their loyalty, the pay of the soldiers of the Khalsa had been greatly increased. Hira Singh assembled the officers of the army and explained that expenses must be cut back. This gave the Rani Jindan her chance. She appealed to the men of the Khalsa over the heads of their officers in the name of her son, accusing Hira Singh of intended treason. The Army rose in her favour, Hira Singh was killed, and the Rani became the dominant figure at the Lahore Court, exerting her influence through her brother Jehawir Singh and her lover Lall Singh.

The British had watched the developments in the Punjab with considerable misgivings, particularly after the Sikhs had made an incursion into Tibet in 1841, which showed the aggressive spirit of the Khalsa. Lord Ellenborough, the Governor-General, was convinced that war was bound to come. When the British invaded and annexed Sind in 1843 there was more fuel for anti-British sentiment, since the Sikhs themselves had had ambitions in that direction. It was fortunate for the British that things had not by then gone so far that they were faced with fighting two simultaneous campaigns. It was even more fortunate that such a situation did not arise in the following year when they were involved in the Gwalior War. Had the Sikhs had a united leadership, intent on reversing the policy of Ranjit Singh, the British could have been in the unpleasant position of being engaged with the Khalsa and the well-trained Gwalior Mahratta army in Northern India at the same time.

Sir Henry Hardinge, who succeeded Lord Ellenborough in July, 1844, had instructions to avoid conflict with the Sikhs if at all possible and he did his best to ensure that nothing was done which could be regarded as provocative. For example he refused to sanction the building of badly-needed barracks for European troops at Ferozepore. He did, however, allow the garrisons there and at Ludhiana and Ambala to be virtually doubled, and he arranged for Broadfoot to establish supply

21

dumps at twenty mile intervals between Meerut and Ferozepore. These measures did not go unnoticed by the Sikhs, who had further cause for complaint when Broadfoot, who shared Lord Ellenborough's views, refused to recognize the Lahore Government's title to Ranjit Singh's estates in Malwa and turned back Sikh police sent to look after them. There were of course a number of British officers who agreed with Lord Ellenborough and Broadfoot that a war with the Sikhs was bound to come, and there must have been talk in messes of the prospect of invading the Punjab at some time in the future. No doubt reports of such conversations, repeated and probably much exaggerated by native servants, were relayed across the Sutlej, and fed the fires of suspicion. Meanwhile the Sikhs, for their part, were active in their attempts to seduce the Bengal sepoys from their loyalty to the Company, their efforts meeting with a certain amount of success, especially as the pay offered was nearly double the sepoy's rate. They were also in touch with potentially subversive elements in various places in India.

By 1845 the Khalsa, which had by now become vehemently anti-British, completely dominated the Government at Lahore. Forces were concentrated near the Sutlej. It is only fair to say that some Sikh authorities claim that this move was purely defensive; but the British certainly did not think so. However, tension eased for a while when the Panchayats became suspicious of Gholab Singh and the troops marched on Jammu. Gholab was brought back to Lahore virtually a prisoner. Then Peshora Singh, another reputed son of Ranjit, rebelled against the régime and the Khalsa used him as a means of pressing their own demands. Peshora was murdered, it was believed by order of Jehawir, who was shortly afterwards assassinated by the Khalsa. The post of Vizier was offered to Gholab Singh, who had managed to slip back to the comparative safety of Jammu. He declined the offer, and shortly afterwards got in touch with the British and offered help in the event of hostilities.

The effective head of Government was now the Rani Jindan's lover, Lall Singh, but there was no love lost between the Court and the Khalsa. It seemed to the Rani and her associates that the only solution was to allow the Khalsa to launch itself against the British. If, as seemed likely, it was defeated, then the Court

22

party would be the only people with whom the British could deal, and Dhuleep Singh, with his mother behind him, would probably be allowed to continue to rule the Punjab. If by any chance the Khalsa was victorious, the Rani and her son would stand forth at the head of Sikh state more powerful than Ranjit Singh ever envisaged.

Towards the end of November fresh reports from Broadfoot led Sir Hugh Gough, the Commander-in-Chief, to warn part of the Meerut garrison to move forward, but Sir Henry Hardinge, who still hoped for peace, overruled him and the 9th Lancers, who had already marched, were sent back to Meerut. Then on 2 December, with the Sikh Army again moving towards the Sutlej, General Littler at Ferozepore called for reinforcements, but Hardinge still declined to sanction any forward movement. Two days later he reported to the Secret Committee that he did not anticipate Sikh aggression. On 8 December, however, fresh information persuaded the Governor-General, who had gone up to Ludhiana with his escort so as to be on the spot to give decisions, to change his mind and the 80th Regiment was ordered to move up to the frontier from Ambala. It had not actually marched when the Sikhs crossed the Sutlej on 12 December. The men of the Khalsa were in good heart, but one would be hard put to it to find in history another case in which an Army went to war with its own government at least half hoping for its defeat and with its principal leaders, as will be seen, at best lukewarm in their support of its cause.

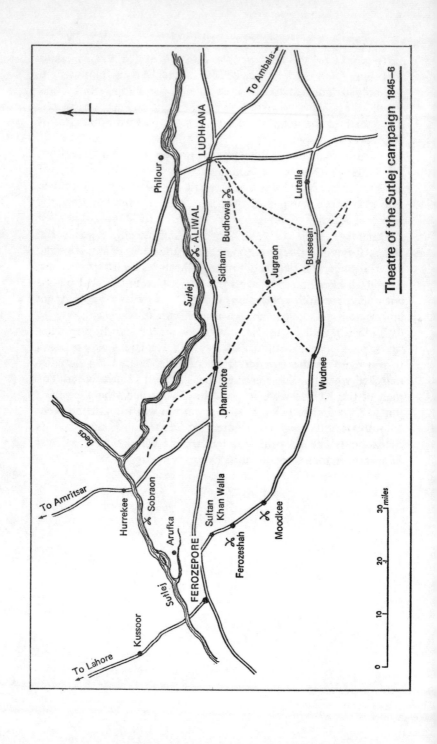

Theatre of the Sutlej campaign 1845–6

To Ambala
LUDHIANA
Philour
Lutalla
Budhowal ✗
Sidham
ALIWAL ✗
Jugraon
Busseean
Sutlej
Wudnee
Dharmkote
Beas
To Amritsar
Hurrekee
Sobraon ✗
Arufka
Sultan
FEROZEPORE
Khan Walla
Ferozeshah ✗
Kussoor
Moodkee ✗
Sutlej
To Lahore

0   10   20   30 miles

CHAPTER 2

The Opposing Forces

————∞∞∞∞∞————

W<small>HEN</small> the Sikhs crossed the Sutlej the main British striking force under Sir Hugh Gough was at Ambala, with two forward detachments in the frontier zone at Ferozepore and Ludhiana, which are some eighty miles apart. The distance from Ambala to Ferozepore is 160 miles and to Ludhiana about eighty miles. The country to be covered was flat and sandy. There were no good roads, few villages and a scarcity of water. The dusty tracks were bad for marching and for wheeled transport. The main supply dump, established at Busseean, was about ninety miles from Ambala.

At Ferozepore, which lay on the main route to Lahore, Sir John Littler, an officer of the Bengal Army who had commanded a division in the Gwalior War, had one regiment of regular and one of irregular native cavalry, two troops of horse artillery and two field batteries, one of each being European and one native, the 62nd (Wiltshire) Regiment and seven regiments of native infantry, in all say 7,000 men and 24 guns. The town lay near the river and there was an open cantonment. The paucity of European troops was due to the lack of suitable barrack accommodation, already mentioned.

At Ludhiana, which lay about ten miles from the river, and where there was a small fort, Brigadier Wheeler had a native cavalry regiment, two troops of horse artillery, the 50th (Queen's Own) Regiment and five native infantry regiments, about 5,000 men and 12 guns. Hugh Wheeler, also an officer of the Bengal Army, was well over sixty, but still very active.

At Ambala, with Major-General Sir Walter Gilbert, another

25

Company officer and incidentally a descendant of Sir Walter Raleigh, were the 3rd Light Dragoons and two native cavalry regiments, three troops of horse artillery and two batteries of field artillery, the 9th (East Norfolk), 31st (Huntingdonshire) and 80th (Staffordshire Volunteers) Regiments, with four regiments of native infantry. The Governor-General's Bodyguard (cavalry) and one native infantry regiment had gone forward as escort to Sir Henry Hardinge and were near Ludhiana. The force could expect to be joined by the 29th (Worcestershire) Regiment and the 1st Bengal European Light Infantry, which were in the hills at Kasauli and Subathu respectively. It would then be about 10,000 strong.

The next station of importance, some 130 miles east of Ambala, was Meerut, where there were about 9,000 troops, including the 9th and 16th Lancers and the 10th (North Lincoln) Regiment. Two Gurkha regiments, the Nasiri and Sirmoor Battalions, which were in the hills near Simla and at Dehra Dun, could also be made available, as could another European regiment, the 53rd (Shropshire), stationed at Agra. The siege train with the heavy guns had been kept back at Delhi for political reasons.

It was the European troops who were fated to bear the brunt of the imminent struggle. Well disciplined, they had a supreme confidence in their own superiority over any native opponent they might meet. The majority of the men were drawn from the labouring classes and were a pretty tough lot. Most of them welcomed a campaign to break the monotony of garrison life in India, where there was little to do in their spare time but drink. They were well led by their regimental officers, drawn largely from the landed gentry, backed up by a steady leavening of experienced sergeants and corporals. Some of the more senior officers were pretty old for active service in India. There were a number of Peninsular and Waterloo veterans who must have been on the wrong side of fifty. One of the majors of the 31st could no longer mount his horse without help. The men were trained in the tactical movements and methods which had been successful in the Peninsula and at Waterloo, and on many fields in India in the past. Some modern commentators have seized on this as a point of criticism; but warfare had changed little and would not do so before the advent of the rifle, and especially the breechloader, forced a change in the system, just as the longer effective ranges of later days compelled the Army to doff its traditional red in favour of khaki. At that time there seemed little point in changing a well-tested system.

The death rate among Europeans in India was appallingly high. The 29th had 147 deaths in 1844, while the 31st lost ninety men from cholera in one month in 1845. When the 50th left Ludhiana to join the main army, three out of thirty-three of their officers and 134 out of 739 men remained in hospital unfit to move. There was always plenty of work for the regimental surgeons.

The cavalry, with regiments organized normally into eight troops, which combined to make four squadrons on active service, had all seen action comparatively recently, the 3rd Light Dragoons in Afghanistan, the 9th Lancers in the Gwalior War and the 16th Lancers in both campaigns. The 3rd Light Dragoons were a particularly well disciplined unit and had the rare distinction for those days of having got through the first six months of 1845 without a single court-martial. Of the infantry regiments, each organized into ten companies, the 9th and the 31st had both served in Afghanistan and the 50th in the Gwalior War, but the 9th had absorbed a draft of 230 men from home earlier in the year. The others had seen no action for some years and the majority of their men were about to smell powder for the first time. Nearly half the 29th were in the 20–25 age bracket. The 80th had only recently arrived in India after a spell guarding convicts in Australia, while the 53rd had not long arrived from Ireland. The 10th had been in India for three years.

All the Regiments involved were English, ancestors of County Regiments of the Line, but many of them contained a high proportion of Irishmen. An officer of the 31st refers to his men giving 'a wild Irish yell' at Moodkee. In the 29th there were 52% English, 43% Irish and 5% Scots. The 62nd and 80th seem to have had a rather lower Irish percentage than the others, the figures for the 80th being 60% English, 32% Irish, 5% Scots and the rest mainly Welsh. Not long before this the Irish proportion had been very much lower, but recently the

27

Regiment had received a big Irish draft. It is of some interest that 34% of the English came from the Midlands and 36% of those from Staffordshire. The high number of Irish in English Regiments was, apart from the Irishman's instinctive desire to get into a fight, due to the fact that regiments tended to recruit where they were stationed, and all English regiments spent part of a home tour in the Emerald Isle.

Although regiments bore subsidiary titles, they seldom served in their own areas; the days of permanent depots were yet to come and a county the size of Huntingdonshire could hardly be expected to fill the ranks of its own regiment. Another factor at this time was the potato famine in Ireland, which could well explain the 80th's big Irish draft. The European troops of the Bengal Army, the Gunners and the 1st Bengal European Light Infantry, many of whom had seen action, also contained a large number of Irish. The figure for the Bengal Horse Artillery, a notoriously hard drinking lot, is given by Gunner Bancroft in his *Reminiscences* as about 80%, with 10% each of English and Scots; but official records show the actual proportion of English and Irish to have been about fifty-fifty. Bancroft may have only been referring to his own troop or possibly it was just that the more extrovert Irish held the stage.

The Bengal Army was the largest of the three Presidency armies of Bengal, Madras and Bombay, into which the regular forces of the East India Company were divided, and it had perhaps an inflated opinion of its own abilities. It was recruited mainly from the Hindustanis of what are now Uttar Pradesh and Bihar, including large numbers from the then independent state of Oudh. In 1842 less than one-fifth were Mohammedans, and of the Hindus, 43% were Rajputs, 33% Brahmins and only 22% lower caste men. The high percentage of Brahmins in particular led to a caste mentality, and to the interests of caste being sometimes put before those of the regiment. This tendency was accentuated by enlistments from the same families. Emphasis on caste could also lead to a lack of respect for the European officers. Sita Ram in his book *From Sepoy to Subedar* laments the growth of this evil and mentions in particular that at Multan the Bengal Sepoys would not dig trenches, which they regarded as work for coolies, while the Bombay regiments dug hard. Sita Ram blames the situation partly on what he calls the '*ma bap*' (mother and father) attitude of the officers, who seemed overindulgent to the whims of their men.

Promotion was by seniority and many of the Indian officers were very long in the tooth. A contemporary report calculates that if a good sepoy enlisted at sixteen, he could hope to be a naik (corporal) at thirty-six, a havildar (sergeant) at forty-five, a jemadar (junior Indian officer) at fifty-four and a subedar at sixty. A risaldar-major (senior native officer) killed at Ramnuggar in the second Sikh War was seventy-eight, and presumably his juniors in the cavalry were ageing in proportion. All this must have led to a live and let live mentality. Hodson, later to be famous as Hodson of Hodson's Horse, joined just before the war and wrote home saying the sepoys were lamentably deficient in discipline and subordination, especially towards native officers and NCOs and that the latter gave more trouble on the march than the men. It is noteworthy that the number of courts-martial had trebled in the previous ten years. Some people held that this was due to the abolition of flogging and indeed Hardinge re-introduced corporal punishment in 1845.

The main cause of the malaise which undoubtedly affected the Bengal Army lay deeper. In former times a commanding officer had had very wide powers, and to his men he represented an all-embracing paternal authority. If a sepoy got involved in the civil courts, his colonel could represent him. But bureaucracy and so-called rationalization had stepped in, such special privileges had been withdrawn, and the powers of commanding officers much curtailed. No longer could the sepoy rely on getting a firm and final decision from his colonel. It might take weeks while higher authority gave a ruling. The sepoy did not understand this and it loosened the bonds. In fact it outdated the old *ma bap* relationship to which Sita Ram refers. Less harm might have been done had the senior regimental officers been younger and more adaptable, but they were nearly all very elderly by modern military standards. There was no fixed retiring age and many of them simply could not afford to retire. Thus they soldiered on, blocking promotion until more often than not they found a final resting place in some corner of a cantonment cemetery. The consequent lack of promotion prospects had a demoralizing effect on their juniors. Many of the best sought staff jobs, joined the political service or took civil appointments. In these fields there were prospects of advancement. The pull to extra-regimental jobs tended to lead to a quick turnover of those serving at regimental duty, so that the sepoys did not get to know their officers really well. Many junior officers, too, found it hard to make both ends meet financially, especially in more expensive stations, and this was a further inducement to go for the higher pay and allowances of extra regimental employment. All this led to a serious shortage of officers. The situation can be illustrated by the parade state of the 47th Bengal Native Infantry not long before war broke out. The Lieutenant-Colonel was present, but his major was in civilian employment. Of seven captains two were present, two attached to irregular units elsewhere, two in civilian employment and one on leave; of nine lieutenants four, including the adjutant, were with the unit, three were on leave, one attached elsewhere and one in civilian employment; of four ensigns two were present and two on leave. Thus only nine of twenty-two officers on the strength were actually with the regiment.

There is no reason to suppose that this was at all an unusual state of affairs. It must be remembered, too, that those on home leave might well be away for about eighteen months. Moreover, those who were left tended to lose interest and become lax. Hodson, who incidentally served in three different native regiments in his first year, mentions that in his first unit the officers were not expected to stay with their men on the march. Sir Henry Hardinge was very shaken on one occasion to find a European officer commanding a guard nicely tucked up in bed and his guard with no written orders. Some did not take the trouble to learn Hindustani (there was no compulsory test then) and one report from the period complains that, whereas once a Bengal officer would have been ashamed to admit that he did not know the names of every sepoy in his company, there were now some who did not even know those of all the native officers. There were of course many good officers serving in the native regiments and many who took a real interest in their men; but the standard was lower than it should have been and the weak links caused far more harm than would have been the case had the overall shortage of officers not been so acute.

In general it can be said that the embers which were to burst into flames in the Mutiny in 1857 were already beginning to smoulder. There had indeed been signs of disaffection among Bengal troops ordered to Sind in 1843. One regiment was disbanded for refusing to march and another mutinied on arrival. Numbers of men in other units under orders asked for their discharge and rather surprisingly were allowed to go. Later there was considerable discontent among Bengal units who served in that campaign, because the financial authorities refused to give them 'batta' (field allowances) despite the great heat and the incidence of malaria in Sind. There had been restiveness among units at Ferozepore as a result of Sikh intrigues. Gubbins, a civilian who was to take a prominent part in the defence of the Residency at Lucknow during the Indian Mutiny, records a conversation with a risaldar who complained that he was drawing only 50 rupees a month, whereas his father had earned 500 rupees a month under Ranjit Singh.

Another factor which was beginning to have some influence on the attitude of the sepoys was the efforts made by some evangelically minded officers to proselytize their men. These enthusiasts were only a small minority, and at least one chaplain of the period complained bitterly that the Company officers would not come to church (it would of course be interesting to know what the officers thought of his sermons), but exaggerated rumours spread easily. Probably, however, the two things which most affected the Bengal sepoys' will to fight were the memories of the disasters in Afghanistan, which had shaken their confidence with practical proof that a 'John Company' army was by no means invincible, and a certain reluctance to see the last great Indian power crushed by the Europeans. Sir Hugh Gough himself was conscious that these feelings existed in some quarters. They may have seemed illogical among soldiers of the Company, but it is understandable if one allows for national pride and the fact that the Sikhs, if not literally co-religionists, were much closer to the mass of sepoys than were their Christian leaders. Furthermore the Sikh, like the Afghan, was known

31

to be a tough opponent and he was likely to offer much more formidable opposition than had most of those whom the Bengal Army had met in the past. The fact that he was as a rule physically a much bigger man than the average Bengal sepoy was not without its influence.

The British horse artillery was armed with 6-pounder guns, which had a range of about 800 yards with shot and little more than 300 yards with grape. Batteries were of six guns each. The field batteries had 9- and 12-pounders of slightly greater range. Gough had tried in vain to get 9-pounders for the horse artillery and to substitute horses for bullocks in the field batteries, but the finance branches had foiled him. A 9-pounder battery at Ambala had in fact been horsed by the outbreak of war, and horses had been sent up for a battery at Ferozepore, but it had to take the field with bullocks as the necessary harness was not sent with them. Bullock-drawn batteries were not only slower on the march but naturally took more time to get into action. The infantry was still armed with the musket popularly known as 'Brown Bess', basically the weapon used at Waterloo, but modified to fire by percussion. It had a range of about 300 yards. It was not an accurate individual weapon and was mainly effective for volley firing. A start had been made in introducing rifle companies armed with the muzzle loading Brunswick in the Bengal Army and the Gurkha Nasiri and Sirmoor Battalions were already armed with this weapon.

The infantry wore scarlet coatees with different coloured facings for each regiment, normally still with the uncomfortable neck-constricting leather stocks, blue trousers and white cross belts. Some units seem to have worn their shakos with a white cover and a flap down the back to cover the neck, but the Queen's regiments wore their flat Kilmarnock caps, also with white covers and flaps. Each regiment carried two Colours, the Queen's, which was the Union flag, and the Regimental, inscribed with its Battle Honours, which was in the colour of the regimental facings. The 3rd Light Dragoons wore blue uniforms and flat caps with white covers, the 9th Lancers blue and the 16th scarlet with blue trousers, both with the flat topped lancer cap, also worn with a white cover. The Bengal artillery wore

1 Viscount Gough in the fighting coat worn by him during the Sikh Wars

2 (*above*)   A Bengal regiment on the march
(*beneath*) The Band and Drums of a Bengal regiment

3 Suchet Singh

blue, with white trousers, the horse gunners being conspicuous with their black metal Roman type helmets with a curved gilded crest, from which streamed scarlet horsehair plumes, earning them the soubriquet of 'the red men'! The regular native cavalry wore French grey, but the dress of the irregulars varied from regiment to regiment. The 2nd for example were clad in green and the 4th in yellow.

The logistical problems of an army in the field in India were complicated by the immense number of native followers, civilians carrying out the administrative and menial tasks for the force. The soldiers were essentially fighting men, but the tail was civilian. An army of 20,000 men might well have some 80,000 followers trailing behind it. The proportion was greater in the cavalry than in the infantry. The 9th Lancers, for example, with a fighting strength of 610, had 3,600 followers when they reached the zone of operations, and the column with which they had marched from Meerut was 3,000 strong with 11,000 followers. One of the factors in the size of the vast array of non-combatants was that every officer took his own personal servants, and owing to the caste system, which limited the tasks each could perform, there could be no question of sharing jobs between them. Lieutenant Colonel Bunbury, who commanded the 80th, marched from Ambala with seventeen. These consisted of a khitmagar, normally the butler; a cook; a dhobi or washerman; a darzi or tailor; two syces or grooms to look after his two chargers; two grass cutters to get forage for the horses; six palanquin bearers; a bhistie or water carrier; a tent pitcher; and a sweeper, the low caste man whose primary responsibility was his master's 'thunder-box'. Junior unmounted officers did not of course expect to take anything like this scale and no doubt many clubbed together, but few could have taken less than three personal followers into the field.

In addition the officers expected to set up a proper mess while the army was halted and this meant additional mess servants and transport with camel or bullock drivers. Units took their mess furniture and it is on record that after the battle of Chillianwalla in the second war the bodies of the dead officers of the 24th Regiment were laid out on the mess table. A solid table designed to seat thirty, even if sectionalized, was a pretty

33

85504

FERNALD LIBRARY
COLBY-SAWYER COLLEGE
NEW LONDON, N.H. 03257

cumbersome load to take into the field. Some elephants were in use as well as many camels and bullock carts. The cavalry tended to live more luxuriously than the infantry and one account of a cavalry regiment moving up from Meerut speaks of each officer having half a dozen camels and two or three bullock carts to carry his requirements.

These details should not be taken to mean that it was only the officers who had luxurious ideas. No doubt the sergeants did their best to emulate them, on a reduced scale, and inevitably every company would have its 'char-wallas', ever ready with tea and buns for the soldiers, as well as its quota of bhisties, sweepers etc. In addition every company had ten doolies—a less exotic form of palanquin—to carry the sick. Each doolie was allowed six bearers, so ten companies made six hundred doolie bearers at full strength.

This vast collection of men and animals presented a difficult feeding problem, particularly as far as forage for the cavalry was concerned. A horse required 10 lb of grain a day, or 8,000 lb for a cavalry regiment at its full strength of 800. Elephants required 30 lb a day, camels and bullocks about 61 lb. With luck the animals could graze, but in sandy country this was not always possible, and reserve fodder had to be carried in bullock carts at a speed of 2 mph. Bullock carts also carried all the reserve ammunition, and it can be realized that in mobile operations the replenishment of stocks with the guns presented a real problem. There was a small amount of transport available in each permanent station, but the vast majority of it had to be requisitioned when an emergency arose. It is to the credit of the Commissariat that the arrangements seem to have gone smoothly and quickly in this case. One thing arising from this vast crowd of animals was the severe fouling of the ground, a serious matter in a hot climate. This explains the constant references to units, especially cavalry, 'changing ground' during static periods.

Medical arrangements were rudimentary. Largely because of the desire not to give provocation by obvious preparations for a campaign, no field hospitals were provided for the force which moved forward from Ambala. Thus only the regimental surgeons and their assistants were available and their means were limited. Apart from battle casualties, nothing was then known of the causes of cholera and typhoid. Water purification was a science of the future.

The British Commander in Chief, Sir Hugh Gough, was an Irishman who had served with distinction in the Peninsular War, when he commanded the 87th Foot. Now aged sixty-six, he had recently enhanced his reputation as commander of the British Expeditionary Force in China, where he brought the campaign, which is sometimes referred to as the 'Opium War', to a successful conclusion. Since becoming Commander-in-Chief he had led the army to victory in the Gwalior campaign, being in personal command at the decisive victory of Maharajpore. Very active and alert for his years, and a fine figure of a man with flowing white hair, he had a reputation as a fighting general. He is on record as saying that in India battles were always won by the infantry, and his alleged predilection for the use of cold steel has been used to build up a rather unfair picture of his abilities. He does not seem to have had particularly good tactical sense, but his strategy was sound. It is fair criticism to say that he did not fully understand and was perhaps a little impatient of the logistical problems facing an army in the field, but the Army of the Sutlej would have been far better prepared to meet the enemy had Gough been able to make his arrangements unhampered by political considerations.

He was not entirely happy in his choice of subordinates and he was none too well served by his staff. Being no staff officer himself, it seems not unlikely that he did not realize the vital importance of efficiency in this respect. There was a good deal of 'interest' and even nepotism in staff appointments, which led to some odd situations. At Sobraon, for example, the Assistant Quartermaster-General of one division was an ensign, hardly a suitable person to represent his commander with a lieutenant-colonel thirty years his senior, even if he was the Quartermaster-General's nephew. That this sort of thing went on in the army must be some reflection on the Commander-in-Chief.

Yet whatever failings Gough may have had, he had one great asset. His men were devoted to him. They knew that he took a real interest in their welfare and they knew that, although he expected a lot of them, he would only ask what he would be prepared to do, and in the past had done, himself. In battle he always wore a white coat over his uniform expressly so that his men could see where he was, and more often than not that was where there was most danger.

Gough faced one difficulty which was almost unique. Not only was his political chief to accompany him in the field, but that chief, Sir Henry Hardinge, was an experienced soldier, himself a Peninsular veteran and a Lieutenant-General on the active list, of the same date but junior to Gough. It is bad enough for a soldier to have his political master constantly looking over his shoulder, but when that master is also expert in his own field, difficulties are almost bound to occur. There were some officers who considered Hardinge a better soldier than Gough and let their views be known, which did not make the Commander-in-Chief's task any easier.

The Sikh forces consisted of the regular army and a number of irregular units, both in the pay of the state, and, behind them, the Jagdiri Fauj, a form of feudal levy which could be called out to follow individual chiefs. The regular army was divided into brigade groups, normally having three or four battalions of infantry, one or two batteries of artillery and a regiment of cavalry, but the actual organization varied considerably. In 1845 there were twelve of these brigade groups with an average strength of rather over 4,000 each. Normally the infantry was organized into regiments, each of two battalions, but by 1845 battalions seem to have operated individually. A battalion was about 900 strong, divided into eight companies. Each battalion had a commandant; a major, who looked after the administration; an adjutant; a paymaster; a writer and a granthi or priest who had a copy of the Granth, the sacred book which was normally kept near the regimental Colour. Each company was commanded by a subedar, who had two other officers (jemadars) and was divided into four sections, each under a havildar (sergeant). The cavalry was organized on much the same lines. The artillery consisted of some thirty-two horse batteries, usually with eight to ten guns, and a number of field batteries, mainly bullock-drawn but sometimes using elephants. There were also numbers of camel-borne swivel guns or zamburaks. In 1845 these were organized into six batteries which appear to have had a maximum strength of about forty zamburaks apiece.

The main irregulars were the Ghorchurras, the cavalry favoured by many of the élite of the Punjab, who were thus able to satisfy in their ranks the Sikhs' love of horses without too many restraints. Some 20% of the Ghorchurras were in a somewhat special category, being paid directly by the Maharajah. The Ghorchurras were better mounted than the regular cavalry. They were organized into derahs or groups, each being sub-divided into a number of the traditional misls. There were seventeen derahs in 1845, while the strength of each misl varied from seventy to fifteen men. The irregular infantry was organized on much the same lines as the regulars, but it was mainly employed in fixed locations as garrison troops.

Estimates of the actual strength of the Sikh forces available at the outbreak of war vary considerably, but there seem to have been about 54,000 regular infantry, 6,200 regular cavalry and 16,000 Ghorchurras, with some 11,000 artillerymen manning about 380 guns of varying calibres, this figure not including static weapons at garrisons in the Punjab. In addition there were about 310 zamburaks. Different sources likewise produce a wide range of figures for the actual strength of the army which crossed the Sutlej, but about 50,000 would seem to be near the mark.

As has already been said, the Khalsa was by no means solidly Sikh, although Sikhs were predominant. Of sixty-two battalions of infantry, fifty-two were Sikh, but the others included Mohammedan, Hindu and Gurkha units. The regular cavalry had about the same proportion, but the Ghorchurras were about 90% Sikh. The Sikh proportion was lowest in the artillery, which contained over 50% Mohammedans, and the commander of all the Sikh artillery was in fact of that faith. The Sikhs included quite a large number of men from Malwa. The Akalis, the Sikh religious fanatics, were to be found only among the Ghorchurras and in the irregular infantry. The Hindus, apart from the Gurkha units, were mainly Dogras from the hills to the north of the Punjab, but there were some Rajputs from the plains, and a number of Poorbeahs, Hindustanis from the British provinces, although this class had been recruited less in recent

37

years. The Mohammedans included Punjabis, Poorbeahs, Ranghars (Mohammedan Rajputs) and Afghans.

Most of the European officers had left since the death of Ranjit Singh. Allard had died in the same year as his master, while Ventura and Avitibile had both departed in 1843. The only important mercenaries actually to take the field against the British were Court, Huebra, a Spanish Engineer, and a Frenchman named Mouton with the cavalry, although Gardner, an American, would have done so had he not been retained by the Rani Jindan as garrison commander at Lahore. Van Cortlandt, the son of a British officer, was still in Sikh service, but when war broke out he was on leave in British territory and he acted as a political officer with the British forces.

The Sikhs' horse artillery had 4- and 6-pounders, while their field batteries had 12- to 15-pounders. In general they out-gunned the British and could bring a bigger strength of metal to bear. The zamburaks fired a 1 lb shot. The infantry were armed with the equivalent of 'Brown Bess'. Although they had bayonets many of them were also armed with tulwars, the curved Sikh sword which they preferred to use. The transport was almost entirely on a pack basis and this enabled a Sikh force to move much faster than a British one of equivalent size. Also they were not impeded by such a vast crowd of followers. The scale of cooks for example was two per company.

The Sikh infantry wore scarlet jackets, looser and longer than the British coatee, and blue linen trousers. Their turbans were of various colours, blue being the most usual, with a loose end to cover the neck and shoulders. They wore cross belts similar to those of the British, but black instead of white. The regular cavalry wore scarlet tunics and turbans with blue trousers, and the artillery black coats and white trousers. The Ghorchurras wore more or less what they liked, as did the Akalis. Senior officers tended to wear more exotic dress. Among the irregulars some wore the traditional Sikh metal spiked helmet, some carried round shields on their left hand and wore quilted coats or razhias.

The morale of the Khalsa, which had little use for the Durbar in Lahore, was extremely high and the vast majority were strongly Anglophobe. Now at last was the opportunity to prove once for all the greatness of the nation Ranjit Singh had built up, to establish it as the most powerful state in India, and to humble for ever the proud British and show them that the Punjab could never be theirs. This spirit, originating with the true Sikhs of the Khalsa, seems to have been absorbed by the other races in the army, despite the fact that to the Punjabi Mohammedans the Sikhs were far from popular overlords. The Sikh soldier was extremely brave and neither gave nor expected quarter. The Army's weakness lay mainly in its leaders. The disappearance of most of the European officers had been followed by a growth of political influence, and the appearance of the Panchayats had seriously weakened the position of the officer corps. The Panchayats decided questions of policy, administration and discipline, and the officer tended to become a figurehead, although he commanded on parade and in battle. Admittedly the Panchayat system was largely put into cold storage under the stress of war, but there was little time to undo its evils. Despite its obvious weaknesses, however, it must be remembered that it was the Panchayat system in particular which had held together the Khalsa and sustained its morale during the period of anarchy. The Sikh regimental officers were mostly illiterate and, brave though they might be, were not worthy of the men they commanded. Neither of the two principal Sikh generals were in fact Sikhs, but were both Brahmins. Lall Singh, who owed his position mainly to the fact that he was the Rani Jindan's lover, was a Dogra by race. His sympathies were obviously with the Durbar rather than the Khalsa and he was much more a courtier than a soldier. Tej Singh was a Poorbeah and although the more soldierly of the two, could hardly be described as filled with burning enthusiasm for the cause for which he was fighting.

CHAPTER 3
Moodkee

As soon as it was clear that the main Sikh Army was crossing the Sutlej, the Governor-General on 13 December issued a formal declaration of war from his camp near Ludhiana. He himself, with his escort, joined up with Brigadier Wheeler's force, which was ordered to leave a garrison with the non-combatants in the fort at Ludhiana, which did not appear to be threatened, and to move to Busseean, where the main supply depot had been set up. His intention was to make contact with the main army, under the Commander-in-Chief, which was setting out from nearby Ambala. In the meantime Wheeler would be able to cover Busseean against Sikh raids. Orders were also sent to the 29th Regiment and 1st European Light Infantry in the hills to start marching towards Ferozepore to join the C-in-C as he reached that area. The garrison at Ferozepore was to stand fast. What happened next would depend on the movements of the Sikhs. Many of the British still underrated their opponents and certainly in the Governor-General's camp there seemed to be an impression that there would be little serious fighting.

At the time it appeared that the main danger was to General Littler at Ferozepore. He was well aware of the fact and for some days his men had been sleeping fully dressed and with their weapons. He still only had his one European regiment, the 62nd, but he had every confidence in his native troops, for although Sikh intrigues had resulted in a few men deserting across the river, the mass of his sepoys had been impervious to Sikh blandishments. On learning that the Khalsa was crossing the Sutlej by boat and ferry some twenty miles up river, he

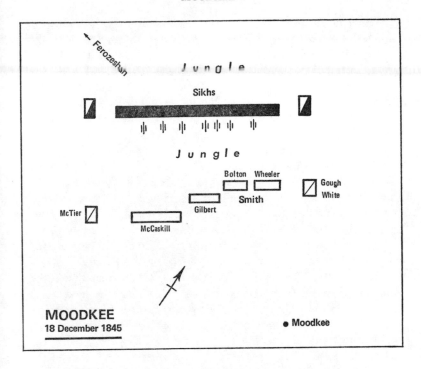

Ferozeshah

J u n g l e

Sikhs

J u n g l e

Bolton Wheeler
Gough
White

Smith

Gilbert

McTier

McCaskill

MOODKEE
18 December 1845

● Moodkee

detailed one native regiment, the 63rd, to hold the cantonment, which had been entrenched and lay some two miles from the native city, while another, the 27th, held the latter. He then moved the rest of his force a short distance to the east and prepared to offer battle in the open field if the Sikhs advanced. In fact on three occasions on the 15th, 16th and 17th forward elements of the Khalsa were reported to be approaching. Each time Littler advanced to meet them and each time they withdrew. Littler has been criticized for not interfering actively with the Sikh crossings; but to do so would have meant a day's march and involved him in the risk of defeat by greatly superior numbers. It was sounder to keep his force intact to co-operate with the main army, which would arrive in a few days time, and it was the Commander-in-Chief's wish that he should do so. As it was, the bold front he exhibited at Ferozepore seems to some degree to have intimidated the Sikh leaders.

There is no question but that the Sikh leadership showed a marked degree of ineptitude during the opening stages of the campaign. The Sikhs were operating in country which contained many sympathizers and they were well acquainted with the British dispositions. One would have thought that they would have at once endeavoured either to seize Ferozepore, with its good crossing over the river, or to mask it and seek to overwhelm Wheeler. Able to move faster than the British, they could even have reached Busseean, which was about fifty miles away, and then forced the main army to fight for its reserve supplies. Even if this involved a distinct element of risk, they might well have used some of their numerous cavalry at least to raid Busseean and destroy the stores. Gough was in fact very concerned lest the Sikh Ghorchurras might open proceedings by making a dash to capture the Governor-General. Fortunately for the British there was no Bedford Forrest in the Khalsa.

Actually the Sikh Army split into two parts, the smaller force under Tej Singh threatening Ferozepore, while the main body remained in the vicinity of the village of Ferozeshah a few miles to the east. One school of thought ascribes this inactivity to deliberate treachery on the part of the Sikh leaders. The argument put forward is that both generals supported the Durbar as opposed to the Khalsa, and hoped to see the latter defeated, when they believed the British would restore the young Maharajah to full authority and they themselves would be powers behind the throne. Therefore, they did not want to overwhelm a detached British force and themselves to be compromised with the ultimate victors. Supporters of this theory point out that Lall Singh actually wrote to Captain Nicholson, whom he knew, later one of the heroes of the Indian Mutiny, and then a commissariat officer with Gough, assuring him of his friendship. This may of course just have been to insure himself for the future; a technique by no means unknown in the East. The evidence of treachery is by no means conclusive and indeed unless the two leaders were able to produce some very convincing reason for their actions, it is difficult to believe that the men of the Khalsa would have allowed them to remain in command. Two other explanations seem possible. The first is that Lall Singh assumed that Wheeler would march to the relief of Ferozepore and the Sikhs could then attack his brigade with overwhelming numbers on ground of their own choosing. The other is simply that Lall Singh, with the Sikhs' faith in the power of their artillery, wished to fight a defensive battle in a well prepared position against the main British force. Knowing Gough's reputation, he assumed he would throw his infantry into the mouths of the Sikh guns, where they would be shattered and he would then launch his Ghorchurras to turn defeat into a rout. Ferozeshah was an ideal spot for his purpose. He would have time to prepare his defences, and Tej Singh, who meanwhile would keep Littler under observation, was quite close at hand and should if required be able to slip away and join him before Littler could possibly join Gough. The reason for Tej Singh's lack of offensive spirit before Ferozepore may simply have been that he wished to retain his freedom of manoeuvre and not to commit himself.

Meanwhile the main British force had set out from Ambala on 12 December. The 80th had actually left two days before, but with its families. It had only gone a few miles when it was halted to await the remainder of the column and the women and children were sent back. The main body covered sixteen miles to Rajpura on the first day, eighteen miles to Sirhind on the next, twenty to Isru on the 14th, about thirty to Luttula on the 15th and another thirty to Wadni on the 16th, picking up Wheeler's Brigade and the Governor-General's party near Busseean en route. This was a fine effort when it is remembered that there were no proper roads and that the troops were often making their way through low thorny jungle, thick sand or ploughed fields. Even on the Grand Trunk Road itself fifteen miles a day was considered very good going and the advance must rank high among the best marching achievements of the British Infantry. The men suffered considerably. It can be very hot in the middle of the day in Northern India, even in the cold weather, and there was often a shortage of water. Their leather stocks added to their discomfort and one unfortunate man of the 31st, who had taken his off and was ordered by his commanding officer to put it on again, shot himself rather than do so. Moreover the men's troubles were not over when they settled into their bivouacs in the evening, for sometimes there was no

43

food and, if there was, the cooking utensils were on the bullock carts lumbering along somewhere behind. The nights were bitterly cold and the men needed their greatcoats, but they were lucky to have them before they went to sleep.

There was a fort at Wadni, which was held by Sikh irregulars, probably local partisans, but Gough, very conscious of the isolated position of Ferozepore, did not want any delay and decided to ignore it. Actually it was evacuated shortly afterwards. It was noticeable that in this part of Malwa the villagers were hostile and there was some risk to stragglers from the main column. An officer who went back to look for some baggage was never seen again.

The men were so exhausted by the time they reached Wadni that Gough gave them virtually a rest day with only a short three mile stretch to Charrack; but the next day the Army pushed on for a further twenty one miles to Moodkee. As the column approached the village, where there was also a fort, the 7th Bengal Irregular Cavalry, patrolling ahead, reported it as occupied by the enemy. The British at once started to form line of battle, but the enemy proved to be only a detachment of Sikh cavalry, who withdrew. Gough now realized he was not far from the Sikh army, but he did not know exactly where it was. He therefore decided to halt at Moodkee for the night, as there were only about three hours of daylight left. The day's march had been particularly trying, and there had been a good deal of straggling. At the penultimate halt the 31st only had fifty men present with the Colours.

Actually the Sikh force in front of Gough was only some two to three miles ahead and moving towards him, but screened by a belt of jungle. Estimates of its number vary widely, but it seems to have consisted of about 10,000 cavalry, 2,300–3,000 infantry and 22 guns. Its task was apparently to delay the British, who had advanced more quickly than the Sikhs had anticipated, to give Lall Singh more time to prepare his chosen position at Ferozeshah, where he intended to fight the decisive battle.

The ground on which the British proposed to camp was open and in front of it stretched about a mile of ploughed land, dotted with some hillocks and scattered trees. Beyond that was the jungle, mostly of a low thorny type, but with a number of

44

largish trees scattered about. The ground was soon being marked out for each unit and, as the weary and thirsty men came up, many must have heaved a sigh of relief that another gruelling march was over and that they would have a good rest before they met the enemy, probably on the morrow. However, not all the troops were in, and the 3rd Light Dragoons had not even dismounted when some of the irregular cavalry, who had been patrolling forward, came galloping back with the news that a large body of Sikhs was advancing through the jungle ahead. Hardly had the alarm sounded when a round shot landed not far away. Gough at once ordered his guns forward to cover the forming-up of his tired infantry, protecting his right flank, where bodies of the Sikh horse came into view, with the 3rd Light Dragoons, the Governor-General's Bodyguard, and the 5th and part of the 4th Bengal Light Cavalry under Brigadiers Gough and White, both of the 3rd Light Dragoons. The same task on the left was given to the 9th Bengal Irregular Cavalry and the rest of the 4th Light Cavalry under Brigadier McTier. The horse batteries pushed forward at once towards the edge of the jungle, being soon joined by the field batteries, thus bringing thirty horse artillery guns and twelve field guns into action against the Sikhs, whose artillery had now opened up along the whole front. Meanwhile the infantry hurriedly formed line. On the right was Sir Harry Smith's Division, with Brigadier Wheeler's Brigade of the 50th Regiment and the 42nd and 48th Bengal Native Infantry on his right and Bolton's Brigade with the 31st Regiment and the 24th and 47th Bengal Native Infantry on his left. Next in line to Smith's Division came Gilbert's, which had no European troops, since its British component, en route from the hills, had not yet joined. It consisted only of the 2nd and 16th Bengal Grenadiers and the 45th Bengal Native Infantry. On the left Brigadier McCaskill had the 9th Regiment and the 26th and 73rd Bengal Native Infantry of his own Division, to which had been added the 80th. He had Brigadier Wallace as his second-in-command. All the infantry was being committed and there was no force reserve.

Two factors to be borne in mind are that the men were all tired and hungry and that the deployment was carried out very hurriedly at a moment when everyone was starting to relax.

45

There had been no time to issue detailed orders and few people knew what was really happening. It is a tribute to good discipline that there was not more confusion. An account from one British regiment tells of men falling in in their shirt sleeves and of some officers with drawn swords and no sword belts. The situation was not improved by the fact that, although the organization into divisions might look tidy on paper, in fact they had been thrown together hurriedly and units had no experience of working together in the field.

Gough had almost at once decided to attack the enemy and he has been seriously criticized in some quarters for his decision, not least by Sir Harry Smith. Had he stood on the defensive, the Sikhs would have had to emerge from the jungle to cross a mile of open country to attack him, and his men would not have been called upon to make yet greater efforts on empty stomachs. Moreover it was nearly the shortest day of the year and darkness would fall in about two hours time, preventing any hope of exploitation, especially in unknown jungle country. If the Sikhs did not come on he could attack in his time after proper reconnaissance and with fresh troops. In his defence it can be argued that he had been caught in the open, he had no time to throw up any defences and in such a situation the longer range of the Sikh artillery would give his enemy a considerable advantage. The main factor, however, was undoubtedly that bold offensive action had nearly always proved the best course against native armies in India and, as the fighting ability of the Khalsa was underrated, there seemed no reason to depart from the normal rule. Besides, this was the first encounter of the campaign and any sign of British hesitancy would do much to boost the morale of the Sikhs. A quick early victory might shorten the whole war.

The artillery duel had now been going on for some time and the heavier Sikh guns were undoubtedly having the better of the exchanges, except perhaps on the right flank, where Brooke's horse battery, supported by two field batteries, seemed to be getting on top. Gough decided the time had come to advance and, as a preliminary, he ordered the cavalry to clear the flanks. Supported by the native regiments on the right wing, the 3rd Light Dragoons charged, the Sikh cavalry falling back without waiting for them. Then came one of the finest feats of the whole campaign. On coming up to the Sikh line the British cavalry led by the 3rd Light Dragoons wheeled left and charged right along its rear, the Light Dragoons overrunning some of the guns and sabreing the gunners. Then they returned, bringing a captured standard with them, and cutting their way through a somewhat ineffective mass of Sikh cavalry who tried to bar their path. On their way back they suffered from snipers perched in trees, whom they engaged not unsuccessfully with their carbines. It was this charge which earned the 3rd Light Dragoons their proud soubriquet 'The Moodkee Wallahs'. The Sikhs had another term—*'Shaitan ke Bachhi'* or 'Children of Satan'. Meanwhile McTier's cavalry on the left flank had also chased the opposing Sikh horse back into the jungle.

By now the infantry was advancing in echelon of brigades from the right. It is a little difficult to see the reasoning behind this method of advance, which was to be used again at Ferozeshah, for it meant the troops on the right flank inevitably drew the main weight of the enemy fire in the early stages and instead of hitting the defenders a simultaneous blow along their front, the brigade attacks came in predictable succession. The only possible argument in favour of this method is that the enemy attention might be drawn towards their left flank, with a consequent weakening of their opposition to the British left; but since the whole line was obviously preparing to advance it seems hardly likely that it would have such an effect. It would seem to have been better to have advanced in line, on a shorter frontage, but with a reserve in hand to exploit success. As it was, nearly all the serious fighting fell to Smith's Division.

By the time the infantry passed through the British gun line the air was so thick with dust that it was often impossible to see more than a few yards. All accounts agree that very few people had the slightest idea of what was going on. The fog of war was well nigh complete. Before reaching the jungle the British suffered some casualties from Sikh snipers who had come forward to climb isolated trees. The 50th on the extreme right early on formed square on seeing a body of Sikh cavalry, probably those endeavouring to impede the return of the triumphant Light Dragoons, but it soon moved forward again, Harry Smith, always in the thick of things, seizing one of its Colours to urge it on. Soon it was in sight of the Sikh guns and on its own, for the native regiments in its brigade had not kept up. They had formed square when the 50th did so and it took them very much longer to get going again. To the left, in Bolton's Brigade, the 31st had much the same experience, and likewise found that it had outdistanced the native regiments, going into the Sikh position without support on either flank. Brigadier Bolton fell at its head early on and both ensigns carrying the Colours were hit. The Regiment came upon and overran a large Sikh battery. Both the 31st and 50th seem to have fired by files before closing with the enemy and then delivered volleys before charging the guns. The Sikh gunners literally fought to the death and their infantry put up a determined resistance. There were some instances of individuals in quilted coats, which were impervious to sword cuts, lying low as the leading troops passed on and then springing to life to try and cut down officers or NCOs. However, in close fighting the British bayonets and discipline were too much for individual bravery and the remaining Sikhs gave way; but by now it was nearly dark and, although the native regiments had come up, no further action was possible.

Some of the native troops in the Division had fought well, but the majority had shown a reluctance to close with the enemy and there had been a good deal of wild firing. Both the 31st and 50th claimed that some of their casualties had been from the fire of the native regiments behind them. Certainly the Europeans had 'carried' the Division and it is noteworthy that the 47th Native Infantry, brigaded with the 31st, had less than 10% of its casualties. Losses in senior officers had been severe, for besides Bolton, who subsequently died of his wounds, Brigadier Wheeler had been wounded, and Sir Robert Sale, hero of the defence of Jellalabad in the Afghan War, and Quarter-master-General in India, who had 'attached himself' to Sir Harry Smith, was killed. Much as one admires Sir Robert's undoubted gallantry, the place of the Quartermaster-General was hardly with the leading infantry in an encounter battle and it is not unreasonable to suggest that there might have been fewer shortcomings in the future in his department had he remained in rear.

4 Sir Henry Hardinge

5 The charge of the 3rd King's Own Light Dragoons at the battle
of Moodkee, 18 December, 1845

6 The 80th (Staffordshire Volunteers) Regiment fighting during the battle of Ferozeshah

7 A night bivouac at Ferozeshah, 21 December, 1845

Gilbert's Division in the centre does not seem to have exerted any very serious pressure on the Sikhs. Hodson, who was with the 2nd Grenadiers, wrote home complaining that his men 'would not come on'. The lack of progress of the whole Division is to some extent confirmed by an account from an officer of the 31st, who refers to seeing the '80th in square on our left'. It is likely that he mistook the 9th for the 80th, for visibility was poor and both had a yellow Regimental Colour; but there should have been three native regiments between the 31st and McCaskill's Division. Gilbert's three regiments had only 120 casualties between them, so probably only small parties closed with the Sikhs.

In McCaskill's Division on the left the fog of war seems to have been even thicker than on the right. The order of deployment from the right was the 9th, the 26th Bengal Native Infantry, the 80th and the 73rd Bengal Native Infantry. Initially the 80th was posted on a small hillock, well protected with thick scrub, and facing along the British line. The 73rd formed square on reports of enemy cavalry and the 80th followed suit, but no cavalry appeared. The Division then advanced, the 80th again forming square a number of times to receive non-existent cavalry as the 73rd on their outer flank continually did so. Eventually the 80th seems to have veered to the right and come up on the left of the 9th, who had been making steady progress, the 26th Native Infantry having apparently been left behind. It was getting dark, bullets were flying about from all directions, and the native units were firing wildly. The Division seems to come to halt without making contact with the main Sikh positions. Colonel Bunbury ordered the 80th to lie down and claims that its low casualty rate was due to this. He himself being mounted was hit in the knee by a bullet which he always insisted came from the 9th. Losses had not been severe; indeed the only officer killed in the Division was Major-General McCaskill himself.

Thus ended one of the most untidy actions the British Army in India had ever fought. An encounter battle always tends to lead to a certain degree of confusion, but rarely can those involved have had so little idea of the general situation as had the British troops at Moodkee. An instance of the confusion

49

even after the firing ceased was provided by Lt-Col Bunbury. As everything seemed to be quiet he handed over to his second-in-command and rode off to get his wound dressed. He suddenly found himself in the middle of a Sikh vedette. Fortunately the Sikhs were as surprised as he was and he was able to get away. However, the soldiers did know that they had met and defeated their enemy, and this at least gave satisfaction to the tired men as they marched back to their bivouacs about Moodkee. Altogether seventeen guns had been taken.

The credit for the success rested mainly with the 3rd Light Dragoons, and the 31st and 50th. These three Regiments also had by far the highest proportion of the total British casualties of 872, the 3rd Light Dragoons losing 23% of their strength. The native infantry regiments had not particularly distinguished themselves. It was notable that even in Smith's Division the total casualties of the four regiments were under 136, whereas the 31st had 175 and the 50th 125. There was some excuse for their poor performance in that they were committed to battle tired and without food, and they had not physically the robustness of their European comrades. There has never been a reliable estimate of the Sikh losses, but they certainly exceeded those of the British.

One unfortunate circumstance was that the Sikhs killed all the wounded they came across, the gallant men who fell in the charge of the 3rd Light Dragoons suffering particularly. The Sikh neither gave nor expected quarter. He would usually fight on as long as he could use a musket. He therefore tended to regard the wounded as potential enemies to be despatched as he would expect to be despatched himself. This philosophy could hardly be appreciated by the British soldier when he found his wounded comrades butchered in this way. From then on he gave no quarter and the 3rd Light Dragoons always went into action with the cry 'Remember Moodkee'.

Death was not the fate of everyone who fell into Sikh hands. A Lieutenant Biddulph of the Bengal Artillery had been captured by a Sikh patrol while on his way up to join his battery in Ferozepore. He was not harmed, although rather brusquely treated, and after being seen by Lall Singh himself, was handed over to the custody of the artillery, whose men it will be remembered were preponderantly Mohammedan. They protected him from harm and after Moodkee he was released and escorted back to the British camp.

The sufferings of the British wounded were considerable. There were no field hospitals with the Army, and it was left to the overworked regimental surgeons to do what they could with their inadequate resources, the wounded being collected in the fort at Moodkee. Even though the force was to remain at Moodkee for two more days there seems to have been no system of clearing the battlefield or burying the dead. Officers were interred under some prominent tree, soldiers where they fell, by their own comrades, if they could be found; but a witness passing the battlefield about a month later wrote of the bodies of British soldiers still lying unburied.

CHAPTER 4

Ferozeshah

ON the day after the Battle of Moodkee the British force remained where it was, although all ranks stood to for some time on rumours that the Sikhs were advancing again. They had in fact retired on Ferozeshah. Meanwhile parties searched the battlefield to collect any wounded who had been missed the night before and had survived the attentions of marauding Sikhs. Towards evening there was a welcome addition of strength when the 29th Regiment and the 1st European Light Infantry marched in from the hills, together with the 11th and 41st Bengal Native Infantry.

Their march had been another splendid effort, for the 29th had covered about 180 miles in nine days with one day's halt and the 1st European Light Infantry some twenty miles more. Both units had received their orders to move on the evening of the 10th and had marched next morning. The column covered over twenty miles each day. The troops marched from 0200 until 0700 hours, halted for breakfast and a rest, and then marched again from 0900 until 1400 hours. On the 18th they could hear the guns of Moodkee and knew that they had missed the first battle. Next morning they were met by elephants and camels sent out by the main force to lift some of the more exhausted men, and later on further animals appeared with much needed water, a blessing for which apparently they could thank the thoughtfulness of Sir Henry Hardinge. As they approached Moodkee they were met by the bands of the regiments which had fought the battle to march them into camp.

The 20th was spent preparing for the battle to come. Gough's

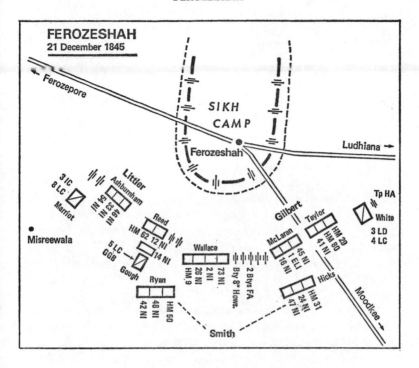

intention was to attack the Sikhs in their position at Ferozeshah before they could be reinforced by Tej Singh but after, he hoped, he had himself been joined by Littler, to whom orders were sent instructing him to slip away with the major part of his Division and join the main army. An alternative suggestion that Gough should move on Ferozepore to make certain of his junction with Littler, and incidentally make that place completely secure, was rejected on the grounds that such a move would inevitably result in the two Sikh armies uniting and would lay open his lines of communication. Each man was issued with sixty rounds and two days' cooked rations and carried a leather-covered water bottle slung over his shoulder. Gough had complete confidence in his European regiments, but must have had reservations about his native units, for the morale of many of his sepoys had been shaken by their experiences at Moodkee.

Having seen what their fate was likely to be if they fell into Sikh hands, Gough was particularly concerned about his wounded. They were all placed within the fort at Moodkee, where two native regiments were left behind as a garrison, each of these regiments being detailed to provide a party under an officer to help look after the casualties. All camp equipment and heavy baggage was also left at Moodkee.

It was on the 20th that Sir Henry Hardinge offered to waive his position as Governor-General and give his services to Gough as his second-in-command. Gough accepted the offer. Most contemporary writers refer to Hardinge's 'noble gesture', but if the Governor-General was actually to be present it was certainly better that he should resume his professional capacity as a soldier rather than remain as the *de jure* commander because of his political appointment. It will be seen, however, that he was quite prepared to exercise his political authority if he thought necessary. It was an incongruous position for the two men.

On the 21st reveille was at 0200 hours, camp was struck an hour later and at 0400 the force moved off. It marched at first in extended line of columns, but after it got light, and it could be seen that the march was unlikely to be opposed, the troops moved in column of route. At about 1030 the column came in sight of the Sikh position and halted to snatch a quick breakfast while Gough made a reconnaissance.

The Sikhs were occupying a rough parallelogram with rounded edges (it has also been described as a horseshoe) around the village of Ferozeshah, with the long sides facing west towards Ferozepore and east towards open country, while the short sides faced north towards the Sutlej and south towards Moodkee. Their batteries were sited on the perimeter, which was protected by abattis of trees. The whole area was covered with scrub jungle as at Moodkee and it was none too easy to pick out details.

Gough decided to attack as soon as possible without waiting for Littler's troops from Ferozepore, who would not be up for at least another three hours. He hoped to open fire about mid-day. He was confident that his men could carry the position and with the experience of Moodkee behind him he was anxious to have plenty of daylight for exploitation. Moreover Littler's Division would be close enough to intervene in the later stages and as yet there was no sign of Tej Singh. The longer Gough delayed the more chance there was that Tej Singh would realize that Littler had moved and be on his way to reinforce Lall Singh. The Commander-in-Chief intended to assault the eastern face. Harry Smith criticizes him for this decision, on the grounds that he should have planned his attack from the western (Ferozepore) side, thus threatening the Sikhs' probable line of retreat and facilitating his junction with Littler. Gough would no doubt have argued that his plan would mean that Littler could threaten the rear of the Sikhs and that any move to the western side might place him between the two Sikh armies. Moreover he would uncover his lines of communication, as he would have done had he moved direct on Ferozepore, which would also endanger his wounded at Moodkee.

However any argument on this score proved academic, for no sooner had Gough given out his plan than Hardinge took him on one side and, assuming again his position as Governor-General, vetoed any attack before Littler's Division had joined. He was no doubt influenced by the unexpectedly tough Sikh resistance at Moodkee and, realizing that the coming battle could be decisive, he felt that the British must be at maximum strength. Gough had no option but to agree. It was an embarrassing position for a Commander-in-Chief to be in, and it is to Gough's credit that, when subsequent events proved him to have been right, he never permitted himself to say 'I told you so'!

As a result of Hardinge's ruling, the whole force moved off in the general direction from which Littler's Division was expected to arrive. The actual junction was made at a place called Misreewala, some 3,000 yards south-west of the Sikh position, at about 1330 hours, Littler himself having come on ahead and arrived an hour and a half previously. His Division had actually marched at 0800, leaving in Ferozepore two native infantry regiments, together with some guns. It is not quite clear why he did not leave earlier. Whatever the reason he was able to slip away without Tej Singh having any idea that he had left. This certainly gives no credit to the Sikh cavalry patrols.

As soon as Littler's Division arrived the army started to deploy, which proved a somewhat complicated business, for Gough's troops and Littler's were moving in opposite directions and it took time to sort them out. When the deployment was completed the troops were facing the south of the Sikh position, lapping round to the eastern side and slightly to the west. It all appears to have been a rather hit and miss affair, for there were complaints that no proper orders were issued and owing to the jungle few of the men had any clear idea of the enemy positions. Harry Smith is particularly critical of the handling of the army and compares Gough to a first-rate battalion commander who should never have been in charge of larger bodies of men. It does also seem that the deployment could have been completed rather more quickly. In fact the battle did not open until nearly 1600 hours, by which time the men were all pretty tired and very thirsty. The men from Moodkee had been on the move for twelve hours and those from Ferozepore for eight.

The army formed up with General Gilbert's Division on the right, Brigadier Wallace's in the centre (he had taken over from McCaskill) and General Littler's on the left, with Sir Harry Smith's Division in reserve. Covering the right flank were the 3rd Light Dragoons and 4th Light Cavalry under Brigadier White, together with a troop of horse artillery. Gilbert had Taylor's Brigade consisting of the 29th and 80th (which had been brought in to replace one of his native regiments left at Moodkee) and the 41st Native Infantry on the right, and McLaran's Brigade, with the 1st European Light Infantry and the 16th and 45th Native Infantry on his left. Then came two troops of horse artillery. The heavy guns, the troop of 8-inch howitzers and two 9-pounder batteries, were positioned between Gilbert and Wallace. Wallace's small Division came next consisting of HM's 9th and the 2nd, 26th and 73rd Native Infantry. Littler had Brigadier Reed's Brigade with HM's 62nd and the 12th and 14th Native Infantry on his right and Ashburnham's Brigade with the 33rd, 46th and 54th Native Infantry on his left. He was supported on his right by two troops of the horse artillery and on his left by two 9-pounder batteries. Brigadier Gough with the Governor-General's Bodyguard and the 5th Light Cavalry was behind Littler's right, while Brigadier Harriott with the 3rd Irregular Cavalry and the 8th Light Cavalry covered the left flank. The two Brigades of Sir Harry Smith's Division were nearly a mile apart, positioned roughly in rear and on either side of Wallace's Division. Brigadier Hicks, with HM's 31st and the 24th and 47th Native Infantry was on the right and Brigadier Ryan with HM's 50th and the 42nd and 48th Native Infantry on the left. Sir Harry Smith also had with him one troop of horse artillery.

Shortly before 1600 hours the British artillery opened fire and the Sikhs replied. It was soon apparent that the latter were getting the best of it. Twice the British batteries moved forward to close the range, and they suffered severely. The superiority of the Sikhs in these exchanges is well illustrated by the fact that not one single Sikh gun bore signs of being hit by British fire after the battle was over. They included 24-, 32- and 36-pounders, pretty serious opposition for the British 6-pounders.

Then, for some reason which has never been properly explained, Littler's Division prematurely launched an attack on the left. There seems to have been a lot of confusion in the deployment on this flank, probably owing to the jungle, and Reed's Brigade appears to have formed up in front of the left wing of Wallace's Division. Littler's Division had started deploying from the right and, as a result, Reed's men were formed up long before Ashburnham had got his troops sorted out. Consequently Reed's Brigade with the 12th Native Infantry on the right, the 62nd, who had removed their white cap covers, on the left and the 14th Native Infantry in second line, advanced against the enemy before Ashburnham was ready. It soon came under heavy fire. About 250 yards from the Sikh position the 62nd came into open ground and was met with a storm of grape shot and canister. In a very few minutes it had suffered a large proportion of its total casualties, which amounted to five officers and ninety-seven other ranks killed, and eleven officers and 186 other ranks wounded. No less than four officers carrying the Colours were shot down. In some cases sergeants were left commanding companies. The advance had been rapid and the 62nd found itself virtually on its own. Only a small portion of the 12th Native Infantry on its right had kept up and the 14th appears to have hung back. Some officers and men tried to

57

work forward and a few individuals seem to have reached the Sikh entrenchments, for there were casualties with sword cuts among the wounded, but the mass of the Regiment halted and could go no further. Apart from the heavy fire the men had been 'blown' by the speed of the advance and were already exhausted and suffering from lack of water. Moreover they had in their ranks many men who were strictly speaking convalescents, some having only recently recovered from cholera. For five or six minutes they stayed where they were, replying to the Sikh fire, but the position was obviously hopeless and Sikh cavalry was threatening their left flank. Brigadier Reed thereupon gave the order to retire and the Regiment drew off in good order, passing back through the ranks of HM's 9th and the 26th Native Infantry who were now behind them. In his subsequent despatch General Littler unfortunately used the word 'panic' to describe the withdrawal of the 62nd, although later he unreservedly withdrew the implication. It is human nature for one regiment to blame another if things go wrong, particularly if its own performance has not been satisfactory, and it must be remembered that Littler was an officer of the Bengal Army and probably tended to listen to the versions of his native regiments too readily. Anyone who has seen a withdrawal under heavy fire will realize that inevitably there are some stragglers who may go to the rear rather faster than their comrades. It is not unlikely that there were a few such individuals in the 62nd that day, and their numbers would inevitably be exaggerated by those anxious to excuse their own actions.

There is every evidence to show that the withdrawal was in fact conducted steadily and it was certainly started as a result of a direct order from the Brigadier. The total casualties in the two native regiments were only a little over half those of the 62nd, a figure which would include some of the 14th, led by their adjutant Lieutenant Paton, who with their Colours joined HM's 9th and took part in the subsequent attack. In Ashburnham's Brigade only the 33rd Native Infantry seem to have got seriously into action at all, while the other regiments hung back. The whole Division withdrew in the direction of Misreewala and took no further part in the fighting, although about fifty of the 33rd under Sandeman joined the 26th Native Infantry in

Wallace's Division. One unfortunate result of the withdrawal was that the batteries covering the Division's flanks were left exposed, and those on the left flank in particular found themselves in a rather tricky situation and were for some time in danger of being cut off. The news of the repulse went quickly round the whole Sikh position and the British troops still waiting to attack heard their enemies cheering boisterously at their success.

The infantry of Gilbert's and Wallace's Divisions had been lying down to avoid casualties, but the order was now given for the main attack to be launched. Gough placed himself in front of Gilbert's Division and Hardinge between Gilbert's and Wallace's. The advance was as at Moodkee in echelon from the right, which meant that the 29th on that flank drew more than its share of the Sikh fire, first round and chain shot, and then grape as the distance closed. The scrub jungle made it difficult to see just what lay ahead. As the 29th moved steadily forward, firing by files as it advanced, it passed through the horse artillery on the right, which was still in action, although most of its guns had been knocked out. As it came into the open ground only about 100 yards from the Sikh position a storm of fire caused the Regiment to hesitate, and for one awful moment the Commanding Officer, Major Congreve, a Peninsular veteran, feared that some of his young soldiers might break; but, impervious himself to shot and shell, he succeeded in steadying them. The delay had allowed the 80th, next in line, to draw level. The two Regiments advanced together, cheering each other on. Pausing to fire a volley at close range, they broke through the abattis of trees with which the Sikhs had protected their position, crossed a deep ditch and rushed the Sikh guns. These were set up on platforms raised about ten feet high, an incline leading to them from the far edge of the ditch. The infantry was drawn up behind them and about six feet below. The gunners fought desperately and quite literally defended their pieces to the last man, but the British bayonets told and the 29th and 80th went through the gun line. As they did so the Sikh infantry opened fire from a kneeling position, but the British overran them and found themselves on the edge of the camp beyond. Brigadier Taylor had meanwhile fallen wounded at the head of his Brigade. There then seems to have been something of a reaction in this sector, as is so often the case after a successful assault. Bunbury of the 80th refers to his men as 'examining the curious workmanship of the Sikh guns' and describes the men of the Native Regiment of the Brigade, the 47th, which had kept up on the left of the 80th and entered the entrenchments, as 'dispersing to find loot'. Certainly it seems to have lost all cohesion after this and does not appear to have functioned as a unit again.

The 29th and 80th were not left long undisturbed to enjoy the fruits of their successful attack. Suddenly a number of Sikhs dressed in chain mail, Akalis who had been lying 'doggo' wrapped in their razhias, appeared in their midst, while numbers of dismounted Ghorchurras came forward from the camp. Some desperate personal combats, sword and bayonet against tulwar, took place, and then came a strong counter-attack by Sikh infantry. Against the 80th the Sikhs were led by a man with a large black flag, around which the fiercest fighting occurred. Two of the company commanders were killed at this time, but the Black Flag was captured by Colour Sergeant Kirkland, fated to be wounded that night and subsequently commissioned for his gallantry. The Black Flag now hangs above the 80th Sikh War Memorial in Lichfield Cathedral. The counter-attack was driven off, leaving the British regiments in undisputed possession of the position they had won. By now darkness had fallen and the situation was made none the easier by a series of explosions, which were thought to be mines, but were almost certainly small dumps of Sikh ammunition going up, while many of the tents in the Sikh camp were on fire.

The British had meanwhile gained further encouragement from another magnificent charge by the 3rd Light Dragoons. They had moved up on Gilbert's right flank, protecting his advance, and as soon as the 29th and 80th had captured the Sikh guns opposite them, the Light Dragoons charged headlong at a battery farther to the right, the guns of which could have swung round to enfilade the infantry. Ignoring round shot and grape alike they rode over the guns, sabreing the gunners, burst through the infantry behind them, and careered on through the

60

camp to rally on the far side. The cost had been high, but the moral effect on the enemy was considerable.

McLaran's Brigade, on the left of the Division, the real punch of which was provided by the 1st European Light Infantry, in which every fifth man carried spikes and a hammer to put the enemy guns out of action, had much the same experience in the assault as did Taylor's regiments, and met with the same success. The 16th Grenadiers on the left kept up with the Europeans, but the 45th Native Infantry hung back, firing volleys at too great a range and certainly inflicting some casualties on the 1st European Light Infantry, which was by then well in front of them. The Europeans do not appear to have had to deal with the fanatical Akalis as did the regiments on their right. Having made good its objective, McLaran's Brigade wheeled left, capturing some more guns and met up with the 9th, which had also broken into the entrenchments. The 1st European Light Infantry was then ordered to make for Ferozeshah village along the axis of the main road through the camp. It had not gone very far when there was a tremendous explosion, one of the main Sikh magazines, which it was just passing, having blown up. There were a number of casualties and the whole Regiment was badly scattered. It took time to gather the men together in the growing darkness but eventually some of them went on towards the village, with one of the Colours, for in the confusion even the Colour Party had been split up, while the major part of the Regiment concentrated back on the line of entrenchments. The detachment which moved on soon found a well and the men were about to slake their thirst when they were fired on by some Sikhs behind a barricade. They made a rush at it, but were repulsed and Ensign Moxon, carrying the Colour, was killed, the Colour itself being left at the foot of the barricade. Lieutenant Greville gallantly dashed forward and recovered it. A second rush was made and the barricade was captured. The party then joined up with Sir Harry Smith near the village.

Wallace's Division, having advanced through thick jungle, had been lying down at the edge of the open ground before the entrenchments. When it moved forward to attack the left hand unit, the 9th, which like the 62nd had removed its white cap covers, was directed on to the south-west angle of the Sikh position, almost on the same ground over which the 62nd had advanced, with the 26th Native Infantry on its right directed on to the south-east angle. The 9th, with which it will be remembered were some of the 14th Native Infantry, was met by a storm of round, chain and grape shot and the left wing of the Regiment, facing the battery which had repulsed the 62nd, was brought to a halt. Colonel Taylor of the 9th, who was commanding the left wing of the Division, was killed and for a while it looked as if the experience of the 62nd was to be repeated, especially as the Sikh cavalry were still hovering to the left. However, part of the right wing of the Regiment, well supported by the 26th Native Infantry, had crossed the entrenchment to the flank of the battery and wheeled inwards. At this moment the left wing, led by Captain Boreton, the senior surviving officer, came on again, and the battery was carried. Some of the 9th, including the Grenadier Company, made for Ferozeshah village, joining up with Sir Harry Smith's Division, which was coming through, and thus becoming separated from the main body of their Regiment, which together with the 26th Native Infantry, pushed ahead to join up with Gilbert's Division. The two native regiments forming the right half of Wallace's Division do not seem to have made a very serious contribution to the attack. Hodson relates that the men of the 2nd Grenadiers simply faded away and soon there were only the officers and about thirty men with the Colours.

When it was seen that Littler's attack had definitely failed, Hardinge ordered Sir Harry Smith to bring up his Division. As already related his two brigades were over a mile apart, so Sir Harry went forward with the left one, Ryan's, leaving Hicks to move independently. He directed his attack to the left of the point which the 9th was assaulting. Smith claims that the advance of the 50th was impeded by stragglers from the 9th, but he almost certainly exaggerates the number involved. As the 50th approached the entrenchments, well in front of the two native regiments in the Brigade, which were hanging back, Broadfoot, the political officer, who was with Smith, reported that he could see a strong force of Avitibile (Regular) Infantry moving forward to counter-attack. The 50th cleared the entrenchments, met the advancing Sikhs head on and drove them back. Broadfoot was killed in the encounter. The 50th pushed on and entered the village, where Sir Harry seized one of its Colours—he seemed to make a habit of this—and planted it on a mud wall. The Sikhs in the village fought fiercely in the narrow streets but it was cleared and the 50th passed through into the camp beyond, where it halted. Sir Harry Smith was joined by detachments of the 9th, the 1st European Light Infantry and a number of native regiments. He formed his men into a semi-circle, but shortly afterwards he had to draw into a tighter formation as a Sikh counter-attack overran the native infantry whom he had placed on his right, an ugly situation being saved by the steadiness of the 50th.

Meanwhile Hicks, whose Brigade had suffered a number of casualties from artillery fire while waiting in reserve, had advanced well to the right of Wallace's Division. An account from HM's 31st, which was the right hand unit, mentions passing wounded not only of the 1st European Light Infantry and the 80th, but of the 29th as well. On reaching the entrenchments the 31st consolidated its position there in the growing darkness.

Night had now fallen and the situation for the British was as confused as it could be. Units were scattered, the fires in the Sikh camp were more extensive and there were continual explosions as the flames caught barrels of gunpowder, explosions which confirmed the impression that there were numerous mines scattered about. Neither Gough nor Hardinge knew what had happened to Sir Harry Smith's Division nor where Littler was. In these circumstances Gough ordered the troops to retire 300 yards from the entrenchment and bivouac for the night. The tired regiments therefore withdrew from the positions they had so dearly won. The night rang with the sound of bugles blowing the numerous regimental calls and everywhere could be heard shouts of men trying to find their comrades. Gradually the regiments concentrated, but they had no water and no chance of a hot meal. It was bitterly cold, there even being a slight frost, and the men had no greatcoats. Attempts to light fires drew unwelcome attentions from the Sikhs, who had manned their entrenchments again and brought some of their guns into action. The European regiments were steady enough, but an increasing

63

number of native troops began slipping away and the artillery soon found that most of the native drivers had made off.

This was the night on which, Hardinge said afterwards, 'the fate of India trembled in the balance'. He and Gough discussed the situation and both were agreed that there could be no question of retreat. They must hang on and attack again in the morning. Hardinge, however, sent away a reluctant Prince Waldemar of Prussia, who had been attached to his staff as an observer since the beginning of the campaign, and despatched to Moodkee Napoleon's sword, which he had with him. He also sent back precise instructions for the burning of State papers, which had been left at Moodkee, in case of a British defeat on the morrow.

Gough and Hardinge would have been happier had they known that the Sikhs were in as bad or even worse confusion than was their own army and that their command structure had virtually broken down. The British commanders could only appreciate that the Sikhs were manning their guns again and there was nothing to tell them that, behind the line of seemingly determined men in the entrenchments, discipline had largely collapsed and bands of Akalis were looting indiscriminately; nor were they to know that during the night Lall Singh abandoned his army and departed with most of his Ghorchurras.

It was about midnight, when things were looking really black, that Hardinge realized that one particularly large Sikh gun was causing a good deal of damage and having a serious effect on the already shaky morale of the native troops. He ordered the 80th to silence it. The Regiment formed up and, with the 1st European Light Infantry in support, advanced steadily and in perfect silence on its objective until it was some seventy yards away, halted briefly to fire a crashing volley, and then charged the battery with what Hodson, the remains of whose Regiment was nearby, described as 'a ringing cheer'. The charge was completely successful and this time the big gun and others in the battery was properly spiked. In fact the 80th had taken the same gun during the afternoon, but had only spiked it with ramrods, which the Sikhs had been able to remove. This time shot wrapped in Kilmarnock caps was rammed down the barrel and proved effective. Having completed its task, the Regiment withdrew as silently as it had advanced and there was no more trouble from the Sikh guns in that sector for the rest of the night. There is little doubt that this attack, at a time when the British prospects looked bleak indeed, had a considerable moral effect, in different ways, on all those who witnessed it. Lord Hardinge had it in mind when, in an account of his meeting the army before Moodkee, he wrote, 'I met again old friends of the 9th, 29th, 31st and 50th and for the first time that Regiment which has since earned itself immortal fame in the annals of the British Army, Her Majesty's 80th.'

While all this was going on Sir Harry Smith had formed the troops who were with him near the village of Ferozeshah into two squares, one of the 50th and the other of the detachments of the various other regiments which had reached the area. It was an eerie situation, lying in the middle of the Sikh position, the night lit up by the glare of burning tents, and not knowing what had happened to the rest of the army. There was no attempt at a concerted attack by the Sikhs, but they seemed to be all around and sniping went on continuously. There could be no rest for anyone, although many men fell asleep from sheer exhaustion and some were actually killed while sleeping. The 50th remained steady, but the native troops in the other square were jumpy in the extreme. At about 0300 Sir Harry decided the time had come for him to get out of his uncomfortable situation and, with the 50th leading, he retired more or less along the route by which he had advanced. He encountered very little opposition and was soon clear of the entrenchments. Seeing some lights ahead he made for them and came upon a large party of wounded men of the 62nd. Here some of his officers advised a withdrawal on Ferozepore, but Smith pointed out that to the best of his belief the Commander-in-Chief was still in the field and that he would almost certainly be renewing the fight on the morrow, when he would need every man he could get. To abandon him in such circumstances was unthinkable. Smith had meanwhile ascertained that Littler's Division was not far off at Misreewala. He therefore directed his troops there and joined up with General Littler, who had assumed that all the British attacks had been repulsed, as had his. Soon after Smith arrived, Captain Lumley, who was acting as Assistant

65

Adjutant-General of the Army, as Colonel Lumley was sick and his deputy, Major Grant, had been wounded at Moodkee, arrived and ordered Smith to move his Division and Littler's to Ferozepore. Smith ascertained that the order had not come from General Gough himself and declined to obey it unless it originated personally from the Commander-in-Chief. Various accounts refer to Lumley, who was to figure in another incident with more serious results before the battle was over, as 'insane'. It seems more likely that it was simply a case of an inexperienced young officer losing his head. It is a sad reflection on the system in force that a junior officer, whose position quite probably resulted from nepotism, should have been virtually acting as chief-of-staff. It was not long after this incident that Captain Christie of the Irregular Cavalry arrived at Misreewala and was able to let Smith and Littler know where General Gough was and give them some idea of the situation elsewhere.

As soon as it was light Gough issued orders for the main body of troops to form up to renew the attack, without waiting for Smith and Littler to rejoin him. Some idea of the confusion of the night may be gleaned from the fact that the 31st, which had entered the battle the previous evening on the left of Gilbert's Division, was now formed up on the extreme right. The men were tired, hungry and thirsty, but the European regiments at least were full of fight. They knew that the issue depended on them, for many of the native infantry regiments had disintegrated.

The British guns, which were by now very short of ammunition, opened fire, but drew little reaction from the Sikhs, those guns which replied firing high, possibly because their trails had sunk into the ground as a result of their heavy firing the previous day. The infantry then advanced steadily on the entrenchments they had captured once already. This time to their surprise there was little opposition. Few of the Sikhs waited for them, the vast majority streaming off north-west towards the jungle. Their morale had cracked. After the hard fighting the previous evening, the apparent collapse of their command structure, the departure of their commander, and the warning given by the night attack that their opponents were by no means finished, the long line of bayonets glistening in the early morning sun was too much.

The British swept through the camp and halted the other side, hardly able to realize that complete victory was apparently theirs. Gough rode along the line to congratulate individual units and everyone cheered him to the echo. By now Smith's and Littler's troops were coming in from the south and the men started to look for water, only to find many of the wells polluted by dead bodies. Then the bugles shrilled out the assembly and mounted scouts came galloping back with the news that a large Sikh force was advancing upon them. Tej Singh had arrived at last. Having defeated one army, the tired British, with depleted ranks and their ammunition nearly exhausted, now had to face a fresh one. It was a grim prospect indeed.

The Sikh army was advancing from the west, while the British troops who had come through the entrenchments were facing north-west. There was a quick change of front and, as there was a mass of cavalry on both Sikh flanks, which showed every sign of advancing, the infantry formed into squares. Then the Sikh artillery opened fire and inflicted a number of casualties. Among others Brigadier Wallace was killed. The troops lay down to save further losses. The British guns came forward to reply to the Sikh fire, but they were desperately short of ammunition and had little effect. Some batteries had managed to find a few rounds in dumps in the camp, but it was mostly of the wrong calibre. At least two British guns were dismounted by Sikh fire. It was at this point that Gough, conspicuous in his white fighting coat, rode out to a flank with one ADC in an endeavour to draw the fire from his infantry. Many of the native followers were now making off and a native cavalry regiment which went forward to protect the guns on the left soon came back and re-assembled in rear of the infantry. It seems too that it was not only native followers who left the field, for Gunner Bancroft, who had been wounded on the previous day and had been put on a vehicle going to Ferozepore, mentions that there were quite a few sepoys headed the same way, some firing off their weapons indiscriminately. The British artillery did what it could with its limited resources and at least discouraged the Sikh cavalry, who seem to have been very feebly handled, from advancing.

To save casualties from the Sikh artillery fire, Gough withdrew his troops to the line of the entrenchments to await the Sikh assault, which would have to be repulsed mainly with bayonets. Then two things happened, one on either flank. On the left the whole of the cavalry and artillery were seen to be moving off down the Ferozepore road. Captain Lumley had appeared again with the orders he had given Smith in the small hours of the morning and this time he was obeyed. It was subsequently claimed that his somewhat peculiar activities resulted from an attack of sunstroke. To the troops lining the entrenchment it must have seemed that they were being abandoned at a critical moment. Then on the right, where the Sikh cavalry had drawn very close, although halted, there was a flurry of horses' hooves as once again the 3rd Light Dragoons launched a charge on the enemy, led by Brigadier White himself. As they passed Gilbert's Division, Sir Walter, incidentally a notable amateur rider, joined in. The Sikh cavalry did not wait for the 'Moodkee Wallahs', but turned and galloped off. Fully justified was Lord Hardinge when, after the battle, he rode up to White and said, 'Your Regiment is an honour to the British Army'. Some of the 4th Light Cavalry supported the 3rd Light Dragoons in their charge, but others turned and rode to the rear, being fired at by the 31st as they passed.

Meanwhile the Sikh fire had slackened and then, to the amazement of the British infantry, the whole force moved off and was soon in full retreat. Tej Singh has been accused of deliberate treachery in breaking off the action, but his own explanation is that he saw little hope of driving the British from the strong position from which they had themselves just driven Lall Singh's army. He was not to know how desperately short of ammunition, nor how exhausted, they were. This is a reasonable explanation, bearing in mind that the Sikhs preferred to fight defensively and, while certainly not lacking in courage, never actually launched a full scale attack on a British force. Another factor was that he seems to have mistaken the movement of cavalry and artillery towards Ferozepore as the start of an attempt to turn his flank and the Sikh army seemed reluctant to manoeuvre in the open field.

So ended what was perhaps the most narrowly won victory in the history of the British Army in India. The Sikhs had been driven from the field and had left seventy-three guns out of a total of little over 100 in British hands, but the British themselves had been fought to a standstill. The men who had marched from Moodkee had been on the go, except perhaps for a snatched doze during the night, for thirty-six hours, during which time they had had very little water, probably none since the afternoon before. Fortunately there was plenty in the Sikh camp, although, as already mentioned, some of the wells were polluted and numbers of men who quenched their raging thirst from them must have suffered for it afterwards. The 29th was lucky enough to find a stock of beer and many a man who had shivered the night before was able to pick up some form of warm covering.

The battle had been won by the stamina, morale and discipline of the Europeans. It is significant that Gough, in his despatch, specifically thanked all the European regiments, and the only other troops he mentioned were the native batteries of artillery whom he coupled with their British comrades. The cost had been high, the total British casualties being given as 694 killed and 1,721 wounded—a total of 2,415, of which just over two-thirds were European, although there were only about 6,000 Europeans engaged as against some 10,000 native troops. The Regiment to lose most heavily was the 62nd, whose casualties have already been mentioned, while the 9th lost 270 and the 29th about 250. Some 30% of the 3rd Light Dragoons had also fallen. There are no reliable estimates of the Sikh losses, but they must have been considerable.

Elements of native regiments did all that could be expected of them, but in general their performance was very poor and they showed a marked reluctance to close with the enemy. Something has already been said of the potential weakness of the Bengal Army, but the main cause of their failure on this occasion was without doubt the fact that, as at Moodkee, they were already exhausted before going into action and they lacked the stamina of their European comrades. It is noteworthy that in the subsequent battles, when properly launched with full stomachs, many of the sepoys fought extremely well.

Most of the British casualties came from artillery fire, mainly from grape shot. The records of those wounded in the 29th show that 137 were hit by artillery fire, forty-three by musketry, four injured by explosions and one had a sword cut. The Sikh infantry normally fired kneeling or lying down and had a tendency to shoot high. The treatment of the wounded presented a serious problem in the absence of field hospitals and the overworked regimental surgeons had a desperate time trying to deal with their casualties as they were gathered in. As soon as transport was available they were despatched to Ferozepore. Once more it was found that the Sikhs had butchered most of the wounded who fell into their hands, although there were exceptions to the rule. Lieutenant Sievewright of the 9th, for example, was approached by a Sikh soldier who appeared friendly and after some conversation agreed to take him to succour. The Sikh carried the wounded officer on his back until he could be placed in a doolie and then accompanied him to Ferozepore and remained with him until he died of his wounds.

It was another untidy battle, the atacks being largely un-coordinated. For this Gough must bear the major part of the blame, for it was mainly due to a lack of clear and concise orders, and some of the dispositions were faulty, particularly in respect of the placing of the two brigades of the reserve division. There were however extenuating circumstances in that the jungle made it extremely difficult to know what was happening and the failure of many of the native troops to 'come on' created ugly gaps in the line of battle. In fairness to Gough it must be remembered that he made a plan, was overruled and was per-force fighting the battle in a way other than that he himself intended—not psychologically the best form of preparation for a man with a very Irish temperament.

Finally, was Hardinge correct to overrule the Commander-in-Chief in the vital question of the timing of the attack? Even if he was serving as second-in-command he was still the Governor-General and, whereas Gough was responsible for the Army, he was responsible for the whole of India. He dared not take risks; yet the proof of the pudding is in the eating. The Sikh position was carried entirely by the troops from Moodkee, whom Gough had available when he wished to attack at 1200 hours on the 21st. Littler's Division was repulsed, and retired shattered from the field, before Gilbert and Wallace even advanced, and the main effect of its efforts had been to boost

Sikh morale. Had the attack gone in as Gough intended his troops would have been far fresher than they were four hours later and there would have been ample daylight to finish the job. There would have been none of the confusion in the darkness and no night bivouac. Moreover as Littler came up he could have been directed against the rear of the defeated Sikh Army. Indeed it is possible that the battle might have had decisive results instead of being something of a pyrrhic victory. The lesson surely is that if you give a man full responsibility you should not then interfere with him. You either accept his judgement or, if you feel you cannot do so, remove him and find someone else or take over yourself, as General Auchinleck was to do in Egypt in 1942.

CHAPTER 5
Aliwal

A<small>FTER</small> the battle the British troops moved on about four miles to Sultan Khan Walla. The Sikhs had meanwhile withdrawn across the Sutlej, except for a small bridgehead covering a ford at Sobraon about twenty miles away. Littler's force garrisoned Ferozepore, where all the wounded had been sent. The Army was in need of a considerable amount of reorganization and was still deficient of some of its requirements. On Christmas day the officers of the 80th were bemoaning the fact that all their baggage had gone to Ferozepore and were consequently very grateful to the officers of the 29th, who invited them to share their Christmas dinner. The morale of the European troops, despite their casualties, was high, but that of the native units was still pretty shaky. The British soldiers had every faith that Gough would lead them to victory, but this view was not held by some of the senior officers. In fact Hardinge (although relations between the two appeared to be very amicable) wrote home to Sir Robert Peel suggesting that Gough should be replaced.

The Commander-in-Chief did not intend to engage the Sikhs again until the reinforcements on their way from Meerut arrived, and until he had his heavy guns, which were coming by a different route. Additional reinforcements had also been ordered in the form of a force from Sind, being organized by Sir Charles Napier; but this would take a long time to arrive on the scene, and it did not in fact reach the theatre of operations until after the fighting was over.

On the 27th the British moved up closer to the river, but still

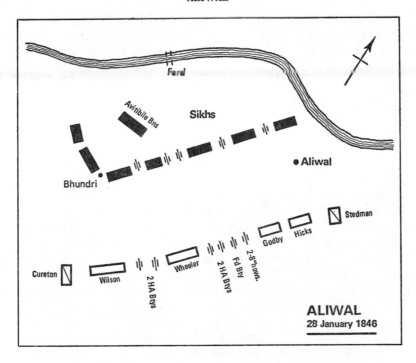

Ford

Avitibile Bns   Sikhs

Bhundri

● Aliwal

Stedman

Godby Hicks

Cureton   Wilson   2 HA Btys   Wheeler   2 HA Btys   Fd Bty   2-8th N.I.

ALIWAL
28 January 1846

about five miles from the Sikh bridgehead, which was well
covered by guns on the higher ground on the far bank. On
5 January there was news that a force of Sikh irregulars had
crossed the Sutlej not far from Ludhiana, sacking the cantonment there. They had not attacked the fort, where there was a
small garrison and which sheltered the European women and
children of the station. They were seen off before they could
do further damage by the timely arrival of the Sirmoor Battalion
of Gurkhas. They had, however, burnt most of the bungalows
and the 50th lost nearly all their kit. It appeared that this incursion was only a raid and was mainly intended to obtain
supplies and also to extract some of the Sikh supporters from
Malwa. Only one of the rulers of the British protected states, the
Rajah of Ladwa, had in fact joined the Sikhs. All the others,
and notably the Maharajah of Patiala, were proving very loyal.
The Sikhs did succeed in putting a garrison of irregulars into

73

the fort at Dharmkote on the road from Ferozepore to Ludhiana. They also occupied the small fort at Fategarh.

On 6 January Sir John Grey arrived from Meerut with the 9th and 16th Lancers, each over 500 strong, the 3rd Bengal Light Cavalry, the 4th Bengal Irregular Cavalry and two batteries of artillery, giving twelve extra guns, together with the 10th Foot, three Regiments of native infantry and a company of Sappers and Miners. These reinforcements made good the losses of Ferozeshah and in particular increased the strength of the cavalry. Meanwhile the Nasiri Battalion of Gurhkas, as well as the Sirmoor Battalion, had arrived at Ludhiana, together with the 38th Bengal Native Infantry and another regiment of native cavalry. Brigadier Godby, an officer of the Bengal Fusiliers, had assumed command there. One incident following the arrival of the troops from Meerut deserves a mention. The 10th and the 80th Regiments had served together in the Ionian Islands some years before and had established a very close relationship. The nights were bitterly cold and when the 10th discovered that the men of the 80th had only got their thin tropical trousers, whereas they themselves had spares of thick flannel trousers, they arranged to hand over 600 pairs of these to the 80th, each company of the 10th bearing its share. Gestures like these count for a lot in the difficult times of war.

Having got his reinforcements, Gough moved up close to the enemy position at Sobraon, but it was soon apparent that the Sikhs had reinforced their bridgehead considerably and intended to make it their main position. They were constructing a bridge of boats in addition to the ford. There had already been a good deal of cavalry skirmishing, but otherwise there had been no contact. On the 14th Gough bombarded the Sikh position and drew fire from the hostile batteries, which thus disclosed their positions. It was apparent that he would be unwise to attack until his heavy guns came up.

On the evening of the 16th Gough ordered Sir Harry Smith to send part of his Division to evict the Sikhs from Fategarh and Dharmkote and thus to prevent them from drawing supplies from south of the river. Sir Harry, who was given some irregular cavalry, decided to go himself and take Hicks' Brigade to do the job. He told the Commander-in-Chief that he would have cleared up both places by the following evening. He was also instructed to find out the attitude of the inhabitants in the area. Dharmkote was twenty-six miles away and Sir Harry marched two hours before dawn on the morning of the 17th. His mission was easily accomplished. Fategarh was found to be abandoned and Dharmkote surrendered on the approach of the irregular cavalry, after a few rounds had been fired at it by the guns of a horse artillery battery which also accompanied Smith's force. The inhabitants in this area were Mohammedan and well disposed towards the British. In the meantime Gough had received news that a large body of Sikhs under Runjoor Singh had crossed the Sutlej near the fort of Phillour, which lay on the Sikh side of the river about ten miles from Ludhiana. It was apparent that this force was no raiding party and Gough feared that it might not only attack Ludhiana but move against his lines of communication. He was particularly concerned about the siege train, which was extremely vulnerable as it occupied about eight miles of road. He ordered Smith to go on to Ludhiana and sent forward the 16th Lancers, the rest of the irregular cavalry regiment Smith had with him and two more batteries of horse artillery to support him. He also sent orders for the 53rd Regiment, which was on the way up and had reached Busseean, to join him. Smith himself had meanwhile received an appeal from Godby at Ludhiana to hasten to his assistance.

Rather than take the direct road, which would have brought him into contact with Runjoor Singh, Smith decided to make a detour by way of Jugraon about twenty miles away, and about half that distance from Busseean, ordering the 53rd to join him there. The Commanding Officer of this Regiment begged to be allowed a twenty-four-hour halt on the grounds that his transport animals in particular were exhausted, but Smith ordered him to move at once, and the 53rd, which had with it detachments of reinforcements for a number of other European regiments, including the 50th, 62nd and 80th and a dismounted party of the 3rd Light Dragoons, duly marched and joined up with Smith at Jugraon on the 20th.

On the morning of the 21st Smith set out from Jugraon, leaving all his wheeled transport behind. When he had covered about seventeen miles he received a message from Godby to the effect

75

that Runjoor Singh's main force was across his route at Bhudowal, about three miles ahead. Smith's object was to form a junction with Godby and secure Ludhiana, so he did not wish to meet a superior force of the enemy head on. His troops were tired and of his European regiments, the 31st had had three hundred casualties at Moodkee and Ferozeshah, and the 53rd, which he describes as a 'young battalion', was as yet untried, although it looked in very good shape. He therefore decided to make a detour about two miles south of Bhudowal and sent a message to Godby telling him of his intention and asking him to co-operate in the coming operations. As the column came abreast of Bhudowal the Sikhs appeared on its left flank, having the advantage of moving along the main track, whereas Smith's troops were marching through thick sand. The Sikhs moved forward their guns and opened fire and the British horse artillery unlimbered and replied. Large bodies of Sikh cavalry advanced as if to attack the column and the 53rd, which was in rear, formed square to receive them; but they showed no inclination to advance further or to engage the British cavalry, which had also moved out to cover the flank. Then Runjoor Singh brought forward some of his infantry and formed line as if to attack the rear of the column. Smith halted and formed up to meet the threat, using the 31st as a firm base. Indeed he himself contemplated attacking at this stage, but the thickness of the sand through which his men would have to move and the exhaustion of his troops decided him against doing so. As the Sikhs did not show any signs of advancing, he resumed his march, the cavalry still screening his flank and the horse artillery batteries unlimbering at intervals and replying to the Sikh fire. The main column was soon clear of the enemy, parties of infantry helping to push the guns through the sand.

The enemy cavalry now made a dash at the baggage train, which was streaming along behind, and which was in some confusion as, owing to the artillery fire, a number of the camels had panicked, broken loose and were rushing all over the countryside. The Sikhs got among the baggage, but they met with a very determined resistance from a party under Quartermaster Cornes of the 53rd, who had with him a sergeant and thirty men of his own Regiment with a few of the 16th Lancers and some sepoys. He found himself attacked by about 1,000 Sikhs who had the support of a gun, but he beat them off, and, realizing he could not get through to his main body, organized a withdrawal to Jugraon, taking with him the rear part of the baggage train. A good deal of the baggage had been lost and much of it was looted by local villagers, who in this area were Sikh and hostile. Unfortunately the doolies containing most of the sick fell into Sikh hands and the unfortunate men in them were all murdered, although it is not clear whether this was done by the Ghorchurras or the local villagers. A number of stragglers were also made prisoners, but they were not badly treated and were eventually returned after the battle of Sobraon.

Meanwhile Smith had made good his junction with Godby near Ludhiana. The latter had not moved forward to his assistance and one can infer that Sir Harry Smith had some pretty hard things to say to him for his inaction; he is certainly very critical of him in his memoirs. But Smith had achieved his object; Ludhiana was secure, and, although he had lost a good deal of his baggage, his total casualties were not unduly heavy —probably about one hundred and fifty. The 53rd had thirty-six killed and fourteen wounded, but a number of the dead must have been among the sick in the doolies. The 31st reported twenty-one men killed and wounded, in addition to nineteen stragglers missing, some of whom were prisoners and rejoined later. It had been a gruelling day and the infantry arrived at its destination completely exhausted, many being helped along by hanging on to the stirrups of the 16th Lancers. The men were all extremely thirsty, for the heat and the sand had combined to make them desperate for water and drinking from muddy cattle pools made a number of them ill. They could, however, feel reasonably pleased with themselves. Both the 31st and the 53rd had shown excellent discipline in trying conditions. What was perhaps more satisfying was that the native troops benefited from their example and had all shown great steadiness. A number of the camp followers had unfortunately run off.

On the 22nd Gough ordered Smith's other brigade, now commanded by Brigadier Wheeler again, to join him. Wheeler reached Dharmkote that night and the next day pushed on by the direct road to Ludhiana. On reaching Sidham he learned

that there was a large Sikh force across his path. He therefore
decided to return to Dharmkote and to make for Ludhiana by
the alternative route through Jugraon the following day. He
preferred to keep to the roads, or rather tracks, and not to make
his way across country, as his troops were already tired. On the
24th he moved to Jugraon, where he met up with the Shekhawati
Brigade, consisting of a regiment of native cavalry and one of
native infantry, which Gough had also ordered thither. Meanwhile Runjoor Singh, hearing of Wheeler's advance and fearing
that he was about to be attacked from two directions, decided
to evacuate his position at Bhudowal. Harry Smith, by his
junction with Godby, had cut Runjoor off from his original
crossing place near Phillour, so he made for a point on the
Sutlej some miles farther west, where there was a ford near the
village of Aliwal. He marched there on the night of the 23rd.

On the 26th, leaving a garrison which included a number of
Patiala troops in Ludhiana, Smith moved to Bhudowal, and was
joined there by Wheeler and the Shekhawati Brigade. He now
had a force of about 10,000 men, roughly 3,000 cavalry and
7,000 infantry, together with twenty-two horse artillery guns and
six field guns. There were also two 8-inch howitzers. He
organized his cavalry into two brigades, one under Brigadier
McDowell with 16th Lancers, the 3rd Light Cavalry and the
4th Irregular Cavalry, and the other under Brigadier Stedman
with the Governor-General's Bodyguard, the 1st and 5th Light
Cavalry and the cavalry of the Shekhawati Brigade, the whole
of the cavalry being under Cureton of the 16th Lancers. As
infantry he had Hicks' and Wheeler's Brigades of his own
Division, the Sirmoor Gurkhas replacing one of the Bengal
native regiments with Wheeler. Brigadier Wilson commanded
a brigade consisting of the 53rd, the 30th Bengal Native Infantry
and the Shekhawati Battalion, while Godby had the 47th Bengal
Infantry and the Nasiri Battalion of Gurkhas. This reorganization was completed on the 26th, but as the troops, particularly
those of Wheeler's Brigade, were very tired after their long
marches, Smith decided to give his force a day's rest on the
27th and move to meet the enemy on the 28th.

Meanwhile Runjoor Singh, whose force at Bhudowal had
been composed almost entirely with irregulars, had been

reinforced by some regular Avitibile battalions of infantry. Thus he felt strong enough to take offensive action and he decided to move on Jugraon. If Smith did not move to attack him here, he would be in an excellent position to sever the British lines of communication and with luck to intercept the siege train.

On the early morning of the 28th, as Smith advanced to engage them, the Sikhs had actually started to move towards Jugraon, but as soon as he realized that Smith himself was advancing Runjoor Singh moved back to receive him at Aliwal. His left rested on the river and the general line of his defences lay along the crest of some rising ground running south eastwards. In front of his left lay the village of Aliwal and to his right he held the village of Bhundri, where his main line curled back somewhat towards the river. In front of him was open plain, with no jungle to interfere with the deployment of the attacking troops or to obscure their objectives.

The British column advanced from the south across the Sikh front, but out of range, with the 4th Irregular Cavalry sweeping wide to cover a dry nullah on the right flank. At a given signal it wheeled into line to face the Sikh positions. Realizing that he had not moved quite far enough to cover their whole front, Smith, to use the phrase of the day, 'took ground to the right' with his Division moving once more across the Sikh front as if it was carrying out manoeuvres in front of the Governor-General outside Delhi. This stately procession by the scarlet columns with their Colours flying and bayonets glistening seems to have had quite an effect on the waiting Sikhs. The cavalry meanwhile had taken up their position on the flanks.

When Smith's deployment was complete he had Stedman's native cavalry on his right flank, then Hicks' Brigade, and then Godby's. Next came some massed artillery consisting of two horse and one field battery, 18 guns in all, and the two 8-inch howitzers. The latter were escorted by detachments of the 62nd and 80th, which earned praise from the gunners for the way in which they helped to manhandle the guns through the soft ground. Next to these guns came Wheeler's Brigade, then two more horse batteries totalling twelve guns, and finally Wilson's Brigade, while the left flank was covered by the 16th Lancers and the 3rd Light Cavalry. The troops did not face anything

79

like so formidable a position as at Ferozeshah, since the Sikhs had not had time to prepare proper defences, and their guns were not dug in.

As usual the battle opened with the British guns being pushed forward to engage the enemy in a preliminary bombardment. Apart from the 18-pounders and 8-inch howitzers they were of lighter metal than those of the Sikhs, but they seem to have held their own fairly well and to have done a good deal to shake the Sikh defence. Smith aimed to take the village of Aliwal, lying slightly in front of the Sikh position, and then roll up the Sikh left towards the ford, which meanwhile would have been threatened by an attack on the left through Bhundri.

Hicks' Brigade carried Aliwal with little difficulty. The troops defending it were Dogra irregulars, who did not seem to have much heart for the fight. With Godby's Brigade on their left, Hicks' men pushed on and soon broke through the Sikh line, then wheeled left towards the ford. Meanwhile Stedman led his cavalry against the Sikh horse and forced them back to the river behind the line of their infantry. On the other side of the gun concentration Wheeler's Brigade, in which, contrary to normal practice, he had placed his own old Regiment, the 48th Bengal Native Infantry in the centre, advanced steadily, halting once or twice to let Wilson's Brigade on the left get on, since Runjoor Singh had, at the beginning of the action, pulled back his right flank, pivoting on Bhundri. Wheeler's men fired one volley as they got close to the Sikh positions and then charged. The Sikh Infantry did not wait for them, although the gunners came forward in many cases to meet the advancing troops. There were a number of hand-to-hand combats and the 50th, which came up against the biggest Sikh battery, had a pretty tough fight. The 48th Native Infantry fully justified Wheeler's faith in it.

Wilson's Brigade was originally deployed in dead ground, and the Sikh positions came into view as it advanced. It then moved forward in a series of short rushes, doubling for some distance, then lying down, then doubling forward again, the 53rd being directed on the village of Bhundri. The Brigade received excellent support from Turton's and Alexander's troops of horse artillery, which kept well forward on its flank. The

8 Lall Singh

9 The battle of Aliwal, 28 January, 1846

10 Sir Harry Smith

53rd, which attributed its slight losses to its method of advance, stormed into Bhundri and had soon cleared the village. Between it and the river were drawn up the Avitibile Battalions. These were now threatened by the British cavalry, who had brushed aside the Sikh horse opposing them. The leading squadron, of the 3rd Light Cavalry, sheared off at the sight of the Sikh regular units, which had thrown themselves into square, but a squadron of the 16th Lancers charged and went right through the Sikhs. The Avitibile troops had barely had time to recover when another squadron of the 16th Lancers thundered through, and then both squadrons, turning round, charged through the square again. Meanwhile the remainder of the 16th Lancers had charged a battery which was still firing and ridden over the guns. While this was going on the 30th Bengal Native Infantry, which had been on the left of the 53rd, had driven through to the river, and it was now ordered to wheel and attack the Avitibile units. It carried out its task perfectly, striking the Sikh battalions in the flank, and forcing them to give way. On the defeat of these troops who, apart as usual from the Sikh gunners, seem to have been the only units which were prepared to fight to the last, the whole defence collapsed and there was a wild stampede for the ford, only the Avitibile troops holding together in some form of order. The 53rd pressed after the Avitibile units in strong support of the 30th Native Infantry and the British cavalry from both flanks streamed in among the fugitives. Few of those who failed to escape across the ford survived and victory was complete.

Fifty-four guns had been captured, eleven sunk in the river in attempts to get them back across the ford and two, which got stuck on the far bank, were spiked by parties which crossed for the purpose. The total British casualties were 580, no less than 142 being suffered by the 16th Lancers. The only other unit to lose at all heavily was the 50th, which had suffered in its attack on the main battery. The most gratifying thing was the excellent performance of the sepoys. The 30th Bengal Native Infantry has already been mentioned, but almost without exception all the native units fought well, and, after the initial hesitation of its leading squadron, the 3rd Light Cavalry had given the 16th Lancers excellent support. The two Gurkha units

81

had both distinguished themselves. The main factor in the greatly improved morale of the sepoys was undoubtedly that they had been launched into battle well fed and with a clear understanding of what was going on and what was required of them. Another factor was the effect of what has been called the stately approach of the British Army and the feeling of superiority and confidence which this instilled in them, just as it had the reverse effect on the Sikhs. The arrangements for the wounded were far better than after the two preceding battles and they were all back in Ludhiana by that evening and being looked after as well as possible. However, it is a sad comment on the medical skill of those days to have to record that out of fourteen men wounded in the 31st, eleven were to die of their wounds.

Among the few prisoners taken was a deserter from John Company's army named Potter, who held the rank of Colonel in the Khalsa. He had deserted from the Bengal Artillery about twenty years before and had been in Sikh service since. Many people expected him to be hanged, but in fact he was able to show that he had interceded on behalf of the Bhudowal prisoners and may well have been responsible for their lives being spared. He was consequently allowed to go free.

Immediately after the battle there was some fear that parties of the defeated Sikhs would make a dash at Ludhiana. Wheeler's Brigade was sent back to that area to watch the fords. It was, however, withdrawn after twenty-four hours, although Wheeler and his regiment remained, and Smith's Division then marched to rejoin the main army. Meanwhile Taylor's Brigade, which had been on its way to join him, had got as far as Dharmkote, where it heard the guns of Aliwal in the distance and realized it was too late to be of use.

The immediate and most important result of Aliwal was that the Sikhs abandoned all their posts south of the Sutlej, except for the bridgehead of the main army at Sobraon. Sir Harry Smith was able to report that the Mohammedans of Malwa were delighted and were proving co-operative. The Sikh villagers were correspondingly sulky. Another less direct result was that, on the news of the battle spreading further north, a number of the Mohammedan hill tribes started to become restive in the hope that an opportunity of throwing off Sikh rule might be approaching.

On receiving news of the battle the Governor-General ordered a Royal Salute to be fired in honour of the victory. Not to be outdone, the Sikhs reciprocated and the bands in both camps were to be heard playing 'God Save The Queen'.

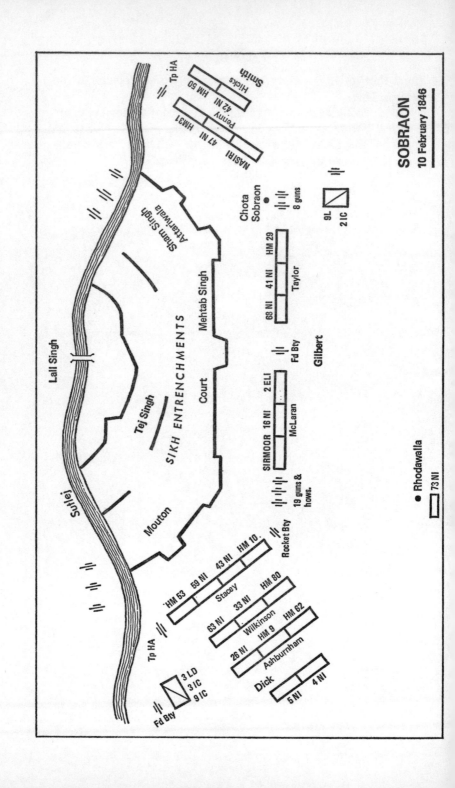

SOBRAON
10 February 1846

Sikh forces: Lall Singh, Tej Singh, Mouton, Court, Mehtab Singh, Sham Singh Attariwala

SIKH ENTRENCHMENTS

Sutlej

Chota Sobraon

British forces:

Smith — Hicks, 42 NI, HM 50, Tp HA; Penny, 47 NI, HM 31, NASIRI

9 L / 2 IC, 8 guns

Gilbert — Taylor: 68 NI, 41 NI, HM 29; Fd Bty; McLaran: SIRMOOR, 16 NI, 2 ELI; 19 guns & hows.

Dick — Stacey: HM 53, 59 NI, 43 NI, HM 10; Rocket Bty; Wilkinson: 63 NI, 33 NI, HM 80; Ashburnham: 26 NI, HM 9, HM 62; 5 NI, 4 NI; Tp HA

3 LD / 3 IC / 9 IC, Fd Bty

Rhodawalla

73 NI

CHAPTER 6

Sobraon

Smith's Division rejoined the main force on 8 February and now, apart from detachments under Littler at Ferozepore and Wheeler at Ludhiana and a native brigade and regiment of cavalry under Sir John Grey watching the fords at Attaree, which lay between Sobraon and Ferozepore, Gough's army was concentrated and ready to fight a decisive battle against the Sikhs. He at last had sufficient heavy guns, for the siege train had joined the day before Smith's Division marched in, bringing with it five 18-pounders and fourteen 9-inch howitzers. The artillery commander tried to improve things further by converting the bore of some of the existing 9-pounder guns to take 12-pound shot.

Major-General Joseph Thackwell, like Gough and Hardinge a Peninsular War veteran, who had lost an arm at Waterloo, now commanded the cavalry. He had served in the 16th Lancers and more recently in the 3rd Light Dragoons, and had led the British cavalry in the early part of the Afghan War. The Division which had been Wallace's was commanded by Major-General Sir Robert Dick, formerly of the 42nd Highlanders and another Waterloo veteran. The morale of the army was good and it is noteworthy that, despite Sikh attempts to tamper with their loyalty, there had only been three desertions from among the native regiments during the period since Ferozeshah.

There was some discussion as to the best plan to adopt. One proposal was to cross the Sutlej in the Ferozepore area and thus turn the Sikh position, forcing them to abandon the strong defences that they had constructed at Sobraon. Hardinge seems to have favoured this idea as an alternative to risking the casualties from a frontal assault. He may also have been influenced by his knowledge of the political situation in Lahore, where Gholab Singh, who was now the Vizier, was in touch with the British authorities. He may have felt that once the British crossed into the Punjab proper the Lahore Government would sue for terms. Gough, however, appreciated that if he were to cross the river lower down he would still have to face the Sikh army in the field in the Punjab, where it would be operating in friendly country and with further reinforcements available. His main object was to inflict a decisive defeat upon the Khalsa and he saw an opportunity of doing so now by attacking it while it stood in a position with a river at its back. This was the plan which was adopted.

All this time there had been a certain amount of cavalry skirmishing between the two armies, but there had been a lighter side to this too. There had been plenty of wild pig about and on more than one occasion that keen horseman Sir Walter Gilbert went pig-sticking between the British and Sikh lines. On these occasions the Sikhs sportingly refrained from firing on him. Now active preparations were pushed forward for the coming battle and redoubts were constructed for the British guns and to cover the encampment. As has already been said, the Bengal sepoys were not very good with the spade and Bunbury relates that a working party of the 80th completed in one day a task similar to one which had previously taken an equivalent number of Bengal Sappers ten days to finish.

The Sikhs of course fired on the working parties and on officers making a reconnaissance. There is an amusing story of Gough in this connection. In the 80th sector was an old tower which provided a splendid observation post and where visiting officers nearly always drew fire. The sentries were instructed to warn visitors of the danger and to try and keep them away. On one occasion Gough appeared there and after the 80th sentry had remonstrated with him several times, turned to the man and said 'Sure my good man, aren't I the Commander-in-Chief, and can't I do what I like?'

A little incident which occurred elsewhere a short time previously is worth recording. A group of invalids was being

sent up the Sutlej from Sind escorted by a party of twenty-six
of the 4th Bengal Native Infantry under a subedar. They were
attacked by a vastly superior number of Sikh irregulars, but they
fought them off and got their invalids safely through, the subedar
being killed in the process.

The Sikh position lay across a bend of the River Sutlej and
was shaped rather like a bow, with both flanks 'refused' towards
the river, more particularly on the right, where the line of entrenchments reached the bank very nearly at a right angle to
the front. There were three lines of defences, the front line on
the left and centre being based upon a ditch and a bank about
ten feet hight, well revetted with wood. To the right, however,
where the ground was much sandier, the defences were less
formidable, and the bank only reached a height of about six
feet. In addition to the ford, the position had been linked with
the far bank by a bridge of boats. On the far side of the river,
where the banks were much higher, the Sikhs had massed artillery to cover both flanks of their position and enfilade any attack
upon them. In view of the fact that their right was obviously
the most vulnerable part of their defences, it is somewhat surprising that they concentrated their irregular troops on that flank
and held the centre and left with regular units, massing also the
main part of their artillery in the centre, where Generals Court
and Mehtab Singh were in command. The left flank was in
charge of Sham Singh Attariwala, while the senior officer on
the right appears to have been the Frenchman, Mouton, who
commanded their irregular cavalry. Tej Singh was in overall
command of the army within the entrenchments, while Lall
Singh had the major part of the cavalry on the far bank. The
defences had actually been designed and laid out by the Spanish
engineer officer Huebra.

Gough decided to launch his attack on February 10. His plan
was to make his main effort against the Sikh right flank, while
the rest of his force delivered holding attacks against the Sikh
left and centre. Reveille was about midnight and at 0100 hours
the troops were given breakfast and a rum ration. They then
moved off to take up their positions for the attack. The deployment plan was affected by the existence of the hamlet of Rhodawala, which lay on rising ground about 2,500 yards in front of

the Sikh right, and was normally held by them as an outpost. Two companies of the 62nd were sent ahead to clear this post, first having removed their white cap covers the better to achieve surprise in the darkness. In fact they found Rhodawala unoccupied. Throughout the war the Sikhs tended to withdraw their picquets at night and on this, as on other occasions, they were in for a rude shock when daylight came.

The British deployed Smith's Division on the right, Gilbert's in the centre, and Dick's on the left to make the main attack. Within Smith's Division Brigadier Penny had taken over Godby's Brigade and Hicks had assumed command of the Brigade which originally had been Wheeler's. In Penny's Brigade, the Nasiri Battalion of Gurkhas had been brought in to replace one of the Bengal native regiments, while Hicks had only two battalions, one of his native regiments having been left at Ludhiana. Penny's Brigade was first in line, Hicks in support. Gilbert had Taylor's Brigade on the right and McLaran's, in which the Sirmoor Battalion of Gurkhas had replaced one of the Bengal native regiments, on the left. Dick's Division was led by Stacey's Brigade of four battalions which had HM's 10th, the 43rd and 59th Bengal Native Infantry and HM's 53rd in line from right to left in that order. With the exception of the 53rd, the troops of this brigade had not yet been in action against the Sikhs. Wilkinson's Brigade, with HM's 80th and two Bengal native infantry regiments, was in support, while further back in reserve was Ashburnham with HM's 9th and 62nd and the 26th Bengal Native Infantry. This brigade was used in the initial stage to cover the deployment of the guns. Two other native infantry regiments were also in reserve on this flank, while the 73rd Bengal Native Infantry was left to hold Rhodawala. On Stacey's left, ready to exploit success, was Scott's Cavalry Brigade with HM's 3rd Light Dragoons and the 3rd and 9th Irregular Cavalry.

The 9th Lancers, whose officers had substituted chain bridles for leather ones on learning that the 3rd Light Dragoons had had a number of their bridles cut by tulwars in the previous battles, together with the 2nd Irregular Cavalry, were positioned behind the hamlet of Chota Sobraon, which lay about five hundred yards in front of the Sikh left, ready to support Smith or Gilbert.

The remainder of the cavalry under Cureton was despatched to watch the Hurrekee fords behind the British right flank, over which it would have been possible for Lall Singh to lead his Sikh cavalry against the British rear, once the troops were committed to the attack.

Just behind Chota Sobraon, between Smith and Gilbert, were eight heavy guns or howitzers, while a field battery was in the centre. The main attack was supported by eight 8-inch howitzers, six 10-inch howitzers and five 18-pounders, while away to the left there was a rocket battery. There were not enough men to man the heavier guns and in consequence gunners were drawn from the horse batteries and their men also manned the rocket battery. This decreased the number of horse artillery guns available to go forward with the advancing infantry, although the horse gunners were to revert to their proper role at a later stage of the battle.

The river had risen considerably during the night and the ford behind the Sikhs was virtually impassable. The British were deployed by first light, but there was a thick mist over the battle field, and this delayed things. When the mist lifted the Sikhs were astounded to see the British formed up ready to attack and both sides opened fire. The bombardment continued for two hours, but the British guns appeared to have little effect on the Sikh defences. The 18-pounders had been sited too far back and were only reaching the entrenchments at extreme range, while the projectiles fired by the howitzers had been fused to burst too early and were doing little damage. Yet another error soon became apparent; adequate reserves of ammunition for the heavy guns had not been brought forward and by the end of two hours they were running out.

When this fact was reported to the Commander-in-Chief he is alleged to have made the celebrated remark 'Thank God, then we'll be at them with the bayonet'. The story is probably apocryphal, but it was a good one and went the rounds of the Army fairly quickly. If Gough did say anything of this nature, it was probably because his Irish temperament was upset by the lack of success of the bombardment. In any case he gave the order to advance.

Stacey's Brigade with its four regiments in line advanced

steadily, halting every now and then to correct distances. It had about 2,000 yards to go. Fordyce's Horse Artillery Battery moved on its left flank and opened fire at about 800 yards, thereafter limbering up and galloping forward by bounds to support the infantry. When the line was about 300 yards from the Sikh entrenchments a body of irregular cavalry came out as if to attack its flank. The Flank Company of the 53rd engaged them with musketry and Fordyce's Battery gave them some rounds of grape, which soon sent them scuttling back. Apart from this not a shot was fired by the regiments of Stacey's Brigade and the account of one of the Sikh gunners, Hukham Singh, speaks of the considerable moral affect which this steady silent advance had on the waiting artillerymen. Fortunately for the advancing troops the Sikh guns were firing consistently high and, although they changed to grape at about 500 yards, there were comparatively few casualties. Stacey's Brigade crossed the first line of the Sikh defences and started to exploit into the position, their line of advance carrying them, owing to the configuration of the entrenchments, across the rear of the Sikh troops holding their centre. However, progress proved difficult, for the 53rd on the left flank, which seems to have been the first unit to break through, came under heavy fire from Sikh guns on the far bank of the river, the staves of both the Colours being broken; while on the right the 10th were enfiladed by Sikh guns in the batteries further along the entrenchment which were swung round by their gunners. At this stage they were reinforced by Wilkinson's Brigade, which had moved about 400 yards behind them. Colonel Bunbury of the 80th swung three of his companies to the right and, together with some of the 10th, swept up along the entrenchments, capturing a couple of Sikh batteries; but they were held up by point blank fire from a further one. Sir Robert Dick, who was urging the Regiment on, was killed at this point. The Sikh infantry had dug a number of what are described in most accounts as deep pits, in which they had massed men intended to wait until the British troops had passed and then attack them in the rear. However the 80th had suffered from this tactic at Ferozeshah and were prepared for it. Few of the Sikhs in these so-called pits survived and following the battle some were found with thirty to forty bodies in them.

Meanwhile the infantry of the Sikh centre had launched a counter-attack on Dick's Division. His men were hard put to it to hold on. Indeed some ground was lost and some of the guns captured by Stacey's men were retaken by the Sikhs. Realising what was happening, Gough decided to convert his feint attacks against the Sikh left and centre into real ones and ordered Smith and Gilbert to assault the defences opposite them.

Gilbert's Division had been sheltering in a deep nullah, which ran parallel to the Sikh entrenchments, and had suffered very little from the Sikh artillery fire, the 29th for example having only had one man hit during the waiting period. This Division appears to have advanced before Smith's, for the regimental account of the 50th refers to sitting with piled arms, watching the attack of Gilbert's men go in, and seeing the repulse of their first attempt. The men of the 29th on the extreme right of the Division advanced at a rapid pace, leaving the native units of the brigade behind. Pausing briefly at another nullah about seventy yards from the entrenchments, they charged, but they were met with a storm of fire and the bank of the entrenchment was too high for them to get up. Brigadier Taylor was killed and the Regiment fell back to the nullah again. From this shelter they saw Sikhs jump down from the top of the entrenchment and despatch some of their men who lay wounded at its foot. Forward they went again, this time with the native regiments in line, but once more they were repulsed and fell back to the nullah. A third time they went forward and on this occasion, with the men standing on the shoulders of their comrades, they broke into the Sikh defences. On their left the 1st European Light Infantry and the other regiments of its brigade had a similar experience. Twice they assaulted unsuccessfully and twice fell back. They had veered to the left for their second assault and for the third they again moved further leftwards, and this time they succeeded in breaking in.

Meanwhile Smith's Division, which had been covered while waiting by skirmishers of the Nasiri Battalion, had also advanced. At the first attempt the 31st was halted about thirty yards away from the entrenchment and fell back to some broken ground to recover. Then it went forward again, but like the troops on their left the men could not get over the entrenchment,

loose sand making it very difficult for them to climb up. Once
more they fell back and passed through the 50th moving up in
support. As had been the case elsewhere the Sikhs swooped
down to despatch the wounded they had left behind. The 50th,
infuriated by what it had seen, rushed forward and succeeded
in scaling the obstacle and, overrunning the guns, advanced
towards the second line of entrenchments. It was unable to put
the guns out of action as it had no spikes and, as soon as it had
passed, the Sikh gunners contrived to man their weapons again
and turned them around to fire on the 50th's rear. The Regiment
turned about and recaptured the guns, this time making sure
that it despatched all the gunners. Meanwhile the 31st had come
forward again, apparently veering a bit to the left, and now
succeeded in breaking into the entrenchment. The ensign carrying the Regimental Colour was killed and the first man to
mount the obstacle was Colour Sergeant McCabe, who had
seized the Colour and planted it firmly on top of the parapet.

As the pressure from Smith's and Gilbert's Divisions increased,
the Sikhs who had been drawn towards their right began to
move back to their original positions and Dick's troops were
able to press forward. The British cavalry now came into the
picture. Personally led by General Thackwell, a squadron of
3rd Light Dragoons found a ramp over the Sikh entrenchments
and, crossing in single file, formed up and charged the enemy.
Another squadron soon followed them. By then the British
sappers had made other gaps rather more to the left, and the
rest of the Regiment filed through, followed by the 3rd and 9th
Irregular Cavalry, and charged. After the battle Gough referred
to the 3rd Light Dragoons as 'that Regiment which no obstacle
usually held formidable by horse appears to check'. Some horse
artillery also got across the entrenchment and poured grape into
the Sikh masses, which, now under concentric pressure from the
British, were being forced towards the bridge. At this stage the
discipline of the regular troops still held and Bunbury relates
that a column of Sikh infantry marched across the front of the
80th making for the bridge in perfect order.

The Sikhs were now being pressed on all sides, and, although
many of them were still fighting valiantly, there was a general
movement towards the bridge. Tej Singh had already left the

field and unfortunately for his army part of the floating bridge broke away and numbers of his men were drowned in the river trying to swim across or to make their way over the ford, which was now too deep for normal use. On the British left the remnants of the Sikh cavalry were being shepherded towards the bridge and elsewhere it was a matter of hand-to-hand fighting, with the bayonet as usual proving superior to the Sikh tulwars. Sham Singh organized a last stand around the bridgehead with the regular battalions, but gallantly as they fought they were overwhelmed. The British infantry was irresistible and when in later years Lord Napier of Magdala said of the 10th 'the deeds of gallantry that this Regiment performed ought to be recorded in letters of gold and engraved in the memory of all British soldiers', he could well have been referring to other regiments present. Sergeant Murphy of the 10th was commissioned in the field for capturing two Sikh Colours. He was to be the Regimental Paymaster for thirty years.

The Bengal Native Infantry vied with its British comrades and restored much of the faith in it which had been shaken by Moodkee and Ferozeshah, while the two Gurkha units showed that their performance at Aliwal had been no flash in the pan. The British, infuriated by the murder of their wounded, gave no quarter and before long there were few if any Sikhs on the south bank. The victory was complete. The Sikh losses were estimated at 10,000 and they also lost all their 67 guns. The total British casualties were 320 killed and 2,063 wounded.

Writing after the battle, Sir Harry Smith described it as the hardest fight in his life except Badajoz, Waterloo and New Orleans. Gough later paid tribute to the gallantry of the Sikhs in these words, 'Policy prevented my publicly recording my sentiments of the splendid gallantry of the fallen foe—I could have wept to have witnessed the fearful slaughter of so devoted a body'.

As usual the British medical arrangements after the battle were very inadequate and the sufferings of the wounded, who were moved as soon as possible into a so-called hospital at Ferozepore, were considerable. By modern standards too the proportion who died of wounds was far higher than it should have been; many of the more severely wounded were evacuated

93

down river towards Sind and Karachi, most of the amputees who survived being shipped home to England.

On the night of the battle Wilkinson's Brigade was despatched on a twenty-five mile march to cross the river at the fords of Hurrekee where, it will be remembered, a force of cavalry had been observing the Sikh horse on the opposite bank. Some of the army crossed by the repaired bridge at Sobraon, while others took the main road from Ferozepore to Lahore and on the 13th they were at Kussoor about sixteen miles into the Punjab. Here on the 15th they were met by a deputation from the Durbar headed by Gholab Singh, who arrived to discuss terms, while the Governor-General issued a proclamation declaring that the British objectives had been achieved.

Another result of the successful conclusion of the campaign was to put an end to the attempts to remove General Gough as Commander-in-Chief. It has been mentioned that, after Ferozeshah, Hardinge had written a critical letter to Sir Robert Peel suggesting his removal, and it was noteworthy that in speeches in Parliament describing the events at Moodkee and Ferozeshah, Gough's name was not mentioned, although Hardinge was referred to. In February Hardinge was privately warned by the authorities at home that he must be prepared to take over both political and military control of the Punjab and the frontier areas, and he was told that official authority for him to do this would be given by what was known as a Letter of Service. The Duke of Wellington, who was Commander-in-Chief of the Army, approved of this proposal and suggested that Gough might continue as Hardinge's second-in-command. Gough came to know of these proposals and intimated that if they were put into effect he would resign. Then before further action could be taken news reached London of the victories of Aliwal and Sobraon and the whole atmosphere changed. The Letter of Service was never sent and the matter was allowed to drop. Gough and Hardinge were both raised to the Peerage, each being created a Viscount.

CHAPTER 7

The First Sikh War in Retrospect

T HE first Sikh War had started when the Khalsa, its soldiers supremely confident of victory, had crossed the Sutlej to invade India. It ended two months later with the decisive defeat of the invading army. The Sikh nation had been brought to its knees and its government was suing for the best terms it could get. There had been no actual fighting in the Punjab itself and it is conceivable that the Sikhs might have continued the struggle, but the result could not have been in doubt. The campaign had led to perhaps the hardest fighting the British had ever had in India. Their opponents had proved as formidable as any they had ever met and they had to put into the field a larger army than they had done since the siege of Bhurtpore twenty years before. There had been four major battles considered worth the award of a Battle Honour to the units concerned, at Moodkee, Ferozeshah, Aliwal and Sobraon and a fairly large scale action at Bhudowal. At Ferozeshah, as the Viceroy remarked, 'the fate of India trembled in the balance' and indeed, had Tej Singh chosen to launch an attack with any determination on the second morning, the hard-won victory might well have ended in defeat.

There is no doubt that the British owed their success to the fighting qualities of their European troops, both those of the Queen's Regiments and of the Honourable East India Company's service. It was indeed the British Infantrymen who bore the heat and burden of the day. Their discipline, sheer determination against odds, and their esprit de corps based on their regimental spirit and helped by their strong superiority complex when facing native enemies, carried them through time and again. All the battles were ultimately decided by the steady advance of the British regiments and the superiority of their bayonets over the tulwar when they came to close quarters. There was only one instance during the campaign when a British regiment appeared to fail, but the repulse of the 62nd at Ferozeshah was the result of bad handling and no reflection upon the gallantry and determination of the Regiment itself. While the main tribute must be paid to the British Infantry for it was, so to speak, the cutting edge of the bayonet, this is no reflection upon the British cavalry. Indeed, if the palm had to be awarded to any regiment for its performance in the campaign, it would undoubtedly go to the 3rd Light Dragoons. It is doubtful if ever in the history of cavalry one regiment carried out such a succession of magnificent charges as they did at Moodkee, Ferozeshah and Sobraon over such a short period of time. No wonder that to the Sikhs they were *Shaitan Ke Bacchi*. The 16th Lancers at Aliwal emulated their example. The value of a high standard of discipline under peacetime conditions is sometimes denigrated. People have been known to argue that units well disciplined in peace are not necessarily the most effective in war. If anything is needed to refute that argument, it is the story of the 3rd Light Dragoons in this campaign. They had created what was almost an Indian record by going for six months without a court-martial shortly before the war started and no regiment could have proved itself more thoroughly in action. The artillery, which all belonged to the Bengal Army, although most of the batteries were European-manned, set a splendid example of devotion to duty. They were heavily outgunned by the Sikhs and yet in all the battles the horse gunners pushed forward their 6-pounders to engage the Sikh guns of heavier calibre at ever closer range.

The British infantry cheerfully faced hardships from heat, cold, lack of food and lack of water. The march of the main force up to Moodkee, and that of the 29th and the 1st European Light Infantry down from the hills, were performances of which any infantry could be proud. The men suffered from very bad

11 The battle of Sobraon

12 The British Army crossing the Sutlej

13 Sir Colin Campbell, Lord Clyde

14 The Storming of Multan, 2 January, 1849

administrative arrangements and were called on to fight on empty bellies, parched with thirst, but they never gave up.

It cannot be said that the native troops of the Bengal army covered themselves with glory at either Moodkee or Ferozeshah, although they did a lot to redeem their reputation in the later battles of the campaign and few regiments could have done better than the 30th Bengal Native Infantry at Aliwal. The inherent weaknesses of the Bengal Army have been touched upon already and it is hardly surprising that these weaknesses showed up on the battlefield under adverse circumstances. It is perfectly true to say that the men had not the stamina of their European comrades and that when thrown into battle, as they were at Moodkee and Ferozeshah, already exhausted and without a proper meal, and on top of this not really knowing what was going on, they could hardly be expected to give of their best. At Aliwal and Sobraon they went into action fresh, well fed and knowing what was expected of them. The blame for their early failures must rest largely upon their officers, and the gap which had so often been allowed to occur between officers and men in the native regiments had an unfortunate effect. The European troops had complete confidence in their officers and would follow where they led. The Bengal sepoys would no doubt have done the same if they had always known and trusted their leaders; but they could not be expected to do so in the conditions which existed in some units. Mention has been made of the lack of discipline in the regiment in which Hodson was serving at the beginning of the campaign and of the apparent lack of interest which the officers took in their men. It is hardly surprising that that regiment failed to 'come on' at Ferozeshah and in the crisis of the night very few of its men were left with the Colours. At Ferozeshah it seems that none of the native regiments of Littler's Division made any serious effort to get into the fighting; yet here there was at least one exception, for a party from one regiment joined in to help the attack of the 9th. It was noteworthy that at Aliwal and Sobraon the two Gurkha battalions showed themselves to be of very much higher calibre than the average run of the Bengal native infantry. The cavalry do not appear to have been particularly effective until inspired by their British comrades. One unfortunate result of the

97

poor performance of the Bengal sepoys in the earlier battles was to lower the confidence of the officers and men of the British regiments in their native comrades. Contemporary reports from these sources nearly always infer that they were not to be trusted and disparaging references to 'the nigger troops' are common.

The central and most controversial figure of the campaign was the British Commander-in-Chief, Sir Hugh Gough. This was a period in which officers did not hesitate to write to influential friends at home criticizing their superiors or to communicate their views to the press. The following years too were a time when authors seemed to find it extremely difficult to write objectively and nearly everyone tended to be partisan. Those critical of Lord Gough included Lord Hardinge and Sir Harry Smith, both men of considerable influence and forceful views. Their friends and supporters tended to denigrate Gough. This became the popular view, particularly after Ferozeshah, when undue optimism gave way to pessimism and people were looking for a scapegoat. Gough then narrowly escaped the fate of the member of his family who suffered that way after March, 1918. The popular view has grown up that Gough was a stupid officer, pig-headed and quite callous about the number of casualties his men suffered. He was a fighting Irishman by temperament and would go bull-headed at any opposition regardless of the consequences and his usual solution to any problem was 'Let's get at them with the bayonet'. This is a very false picture. He was certainly not a great general, but he was by no means a bad one, and he compares favourably with some of those who were to lead British troops in the Crimean War and the Indian Mutiny.

His initial plan for dealing with the Sikh invasion, allowing for the political restrictions placed on his preparations and his deployment, was perfectly sound and he did succeed, as intended, in bringing Lall Singh's army to battle at Ferozeshah before Tej Singh could join up with him. He appreciated Runjoor Singh's threat to his communications and took adequate steps to deal with it. He realized that his main task was to destroy the Sikh army in the field and he waited until he had sufficient strength to smash it at Sobraon; and he declined to be tempted to manoeuvre it out of its position, thus winning a cheap victory at the expense of prolonging the war by carrying it into the Punjab. His tactics are more open to criticism. He certainly should not have allowed himself to be so nearly surprised at Moodkee but once he had he probably would have been wiser to have remained on the defensive and waited for the Sikhs to attack him; but he did know of their superiority in artillery and from the intelligence at his disposal he tended to underrate the capabilities of the Sikh army. He learnt from his experience at Moodkee and it was no fault of his that he was overruled by Hardinge at Ferozeshah and was unable to fight the battle as he wished to. Had he attacked at the time and place which he intended, there is every reason to suppose that he would have carried the Sikh entrenchments, as in fact he did, with the same troops later in the day. With ample daylight and with Littler's fresh division available to strike the Sikhs in the rear or to take up the pursuit, he could well have smashed Lall Singh's army completely. It is unfair to criticize a general who is overruled and forced to adopt a plan in which he does not believe on the eve of a battle, because he does not gain a decisive victory. At Sobraon he appreciated the weak spot in the Sikh defences and made his main attack there. He used the rest of his troops only when his main attack was threatened by Sikh counter-action. It is indeed possible that had he made simultaneous efforts on his left and right, as has been suggested, the men of Smith's and Gilbert's Divisions might never have broken into the Sikh position, as their opponents would not have been weakened by withdrawals to deal with Dick's Division on the left. Gough's main weakness seems to have been that he was essentially a 'fighting general', did not realize the importance of good staff work and could not really appreciate the need for first-class administrative arrangements. Neither at Moodkee nor at Ferozeshah did he ensure that all his subordinate commanders really knew what was required of them. He did not seem to realize the vital importance of everyone being well briefed before they went into battle. It can be argued that at Moodkee, with the knowledge that darkness was coming on, there was little time, but this excuse does not apply at Ferozeshah. It was not impossible that he was upset by Hardinge's interference with his plan. He may have relied too much on incompetent or inexperienced staff officers to see that his intentions were well known. That there were so many examples of bad staff work during the campaign must reflect upon him, for a commander has the responsibility of seeing that he has a good staff. At Sobraon, where he had time to plan what was a set piece battle, he does seem to have ensured that everybody was in the picture.

The administrative weaknesses from which the army suffered were by no means all Gough's fault. He had done all he could to persuade the Governor-General to allow him to prepare sufficient transport and other services before the campaign started. For political and financial reasons Hardinge had refused to allow him to take the necessary steps. He had to fight without adequate logistic and medical resources but he could hardly be blamed for the fact that the Governor-General had turned a deaf ear to his recommendations. He must take the blame for the fact that the guns had insufficient ammunition at Sobraon, although no doubt he left it to his Commander Royal Artillery. A Commander-in-Chief is responsible for the acts of his subordinates and he should not keep them unless he is sure they will not let him down. There was plenty of time for planning before Sobraon and as Gough intended to have a thorough artillery preparation before he attacked this is certainly one of the points which he should have checked. One thing about Gough is quite certain—whatever some of his senior officers may have thought and said about him his men had faith in him and trusted him. They would do anything for the old man who rode out on a flank in his white coat at Ferozeshah to draw the enemy fire away from them. One does not find British troops showing devotion to a bad general. Apart from his undoubted physical bravery Gough also possessed the moral courage so important in a commander. Faced with the problem he had on the night of Ferozeshah, when he had to withdraw his troops from the positions they had captured and the Sikhs had manned their batteries and opened fire again, when he know that the morale of half his men had cracked and that he could only rely on his European units, when he had no idea where some of his men were, a lesser general might well have given up the struggle and withdrawn. Gough realized he must hang on.

Seldom has a Commander-in-Chief had to take the field with

his political master breathing down his neck, and however well Hardinge played his part as second-in-command, it can never have been a comfortable situation, and it is much to his credit that he never complained and never made public statements about his invidious position. Instinctive loyalty both to his superiors and his subordinates was part of Gough's make up.

Hardinge was a very different type of man—a soldier who had become involved in politics, and the two roles do not usually mix well. In the military sphere he was Gough's contemporary, although just junior. He may well have been a better all-round soldier. Certainly there were many people who thought so. Whether he would have been better if in actual command during the campaign is doubtful, for he lacked Gough's Indian experience and one feels that he would have been more at home as a staff officer than as a commander. As Governor-General, determined to follow his brief from London and avoid war with the Sikhs if possible, he had been responsible for the lack of preparation to meet the invasion and in particular for the shortages on the administrative side which his Commander-in-Chief had wished to make good in the weeks before the war. A Governor-General's place is not with the army in the field and he should have left his Commander-in-Chief to carry on, or replaced him if he had no confidence in him. He was hardly in a position to control events all over India while leading the advance against the entrenchments of Ferozeshah. His 'noble gesture' in offering himself as Gough's second-in-command may have appealed to a Victorian sense of the romantic, but he would have been better able to exercise his overall powers elsewhere. Once he had taken up his subordinate position he should at least have stuck to his guns and not interfered with his Commander-in-Chief's plans. It was also unfortunate that, while keeping up a façade of loyalty to the Commander-in-Chief, he was writing home to criticize him and suggest his removal. He was in fact 'wearing two hats' and while, with his Governor-General's hat on, he was justified in appealing to the authorities to replace Gough, he should never have done so while wearing that of his second-in-command. It is unfortunate that partisan accounts of the campaign in the years which followed tend to laud Hardinge as a means of denigrating Gough, which results in a rather distorted picture of the man. One is left with an idea that he was at heart a soldier, did not enjoy being Governor-General and could not resist the chance to get back to his old trade.

By far the most prominent of the other British leaders involved was Sir Harry Smith. It fell to him to conduct the only independent operations of the campaign and he carried out his role perfectly, in that he protected the lines of communication and relieved Ludhiana, preventing Runjoor Singh from doing any harm, and his decisive victory at Aliwal was well planned and well executed. His conduct of the action at Bhudowal can be criticized, since a general who loses more than half his baggage in moving his division from A to B can hardly be given full marks. Actually Smith was probably as competent a general as either Gough or Hardinge and although he was very much given to criticism he does not seem at least to have tolerated any covert intrigues against his Commander-in-Chief. He certainly had no doubts about his own capabilities and he made quite sure that the doings of his own Division were given every prominence. One is left with the impression that he was one of those people all of whose geese are swans and some writers, having studied his own account of events, have tended to assume that Smith's men exercised a more decisive influence on events at Ferozeshah and Sobraon than perhaps they did.

All the British generals were of course by modern standards very old men, but whatever their failings they did not lack powers of leadership nor personal bravery. McCaskill and Dick were both killed at the head of their divisions, and Wallace fell at Ferozeshah. Gilbert, perhaps the best of the other divisional commanders, could not resist joining in a cavalry charge in the final phase of Ferozeshah, which may have been a very gallant gesture but could well have had the effect of depriving his Division of its commander. Thackwell personally led the cavalry into the entrenchments at Sobraon. The one general who did not enhance his reputation was Littler. He mishandled his division at Ferozeshah and, accepting his reverse, took little further part in the proceedings. The casualty rate among infantry brigade commanders was on the same level as the divisional commanders. Possibly Wheeler was as good as any of them and it is only right that his efforts in the Sikh wars should be remembered. He should not just go down in history as the gallant but ineffective man who surrendered Cawnpore to the Mutineers in 1857.

The Sikh army proved itself as a first class fighting machine, but it was not well led. The personal bravery of the regimental officers and of the men was beyond question, but it had suffered from the purges of the years of confusion in the Punjab which had preceded the war. The efficiency of the artillery came as a complete surprise to the British. The infantry, and particularly the Avitibile battalions, were well disciplined and well trained and, unlike the Bengal sepoys, were prepared to get down to it with the spade. Their musketry was not of the same standard as their opponents and when it came to close combat they could not stand up to the bayonets of the British infantry. It is a surprising fact that, although the Sikhs were traditional horsemen, their cavalry appears to have been comparatively ineffective and indeed that arm comes out badly in comparison with both the artillery and the infantry. Tactically the Sikhs showed a predeliction for fighting on the defensive and, although to some degree at Moodkee and at Bhudowal they went through the motions of making an attack, they in fact never launched themselves at the British. Their great faith in their superior artillery and its ability to shatter the advancing British columns largely explains this attitude. With their masses of Ghorchurras one would have expected their reconnaissance to be excellent, but in this they were particularly weak. It is certainly difficult to see how, with active cavalry patrolling, Littler could have been allowed to slip away from Ferozepore. Likewise Runjoor Singh seems to have been quite unaware of Harry Smith's movements before the battle of Aliwal. The Sikh habit of murdering the enemy wounded on the battlefield cannot be condoned, but can be explained by their own attitude for, as they showed a number of times, they were prepared to go on fighting even when mortally wounded. It is noteworthy that prisoners who fell into their hands other than in the heat of battle were often quite well treated.

Both the principal Sikh generals, Lall Singh and Tej Singh, have been accused of treachery, but this accusation can at least

be said to be not proven. Indeed, as has been remarked elsewhere, it does seem a little unlikely that they would have been
allowed to remain in one piece if their men had suspected them
of such dealings. Lall Singh was more a courtier than a soldier.
Both of them were more in sympathy with the Durbar than
with the Khalsa. They can have had little real enthusiasm for the
cause in which they were fighting. It is not unfair to say that
neither of them were very competent and indeed they were not
really worthy of the men they led. The reason for their employment, apart from Lall Singh's involvement with the Rani, was
presumably that there was no one else, after the anarchy which
had gone on in the country, who was capable of doing the job.

The main accusation against Tej Singh is based on his somewhat inept proceedings at Ferozeshah. He certainly should not
have let Littler get away so easily or apparently to have taken
so long to realise that he had moved. His own explanation of
his failure to attack the following morning, that he saw no
chance of driving the British out of the entrenchments from
which they had driven the Sikhs and that he feared that the
cavalry disappearing towards Ferozepore were in fact engaged
in a turning movement, may have disclosed errors of judgment,
but not necessarily sinister motives. Lall Singh's lack of drive in
the early stages can be accounted for by his determination to
fight a defensive battle, as he did on ground of his own choosing
at Ferozeshah.

The Sikhs certainly missed an opportunity of using their
cavalry to raid towards the British supply bases in those early
days. There could be something in the suggestion that their
leaders' actions at this period were conditioned by their desire
not to compromise themselves too much with those whom they
thought would ultimately be the victors. Runjoor Singh, the
only Sikh general to operate independently, does seem to have
had more drive than his superiors, but even he showed undue
hesitancy at Bhudowal. This may have been due to the fact that
his men were largely irregulars and he was awaiting the arrival
of the Avitibile battalions. When they joined him, he appeared
to be about to adopt the offensive, but on Harry Smith's appearance again went on the defensive. Why the Sikhs twice deliberately chose to fight with a river at their backs must remain a

mystery. The tragedy for the ordinary fighting soldier of the Khalsa was to have to go into battle with a government which more than half hoped for his defeat and with ineffective leaders who did not believe in the cause they were fighting.

As a result of the war British India was saved and the legacy left by Ranjit Singh shattered. Inevitably British influence would have to be established on the far side of the Sutlej. The soldier had done his job and it was now up to the politician to find a solution for the future.

CHAPTER 8

Between the Wars

T HE Governor-General made it clear that he would not deal with the Sikh emissaries until the young Maharajah himself had submitted as head of the Sikh state. In consequence on 18 February, 1846, Dhuleep Singh arrived at Kussoor with a large retinue. He was received coldly and no salutes were fired, but once he had made his formal submission he was treated with all the dignity due to the soverign ruler of a state and full compliments were paid to him. The British force moved on to Lahore, accompanied by the Maharajah, and occupied the military cantonment at Meean Meer, also putting a garrison into the citadel in the capital itself. The Sikh inhabitants were resentful of the arrival of the British and obviously in a surly mood, but the Mohammedan element of the population appeared to welcome the new arrivals.

There were three possible courses open to the British. Firstly they could annex the Punjab outright but, although a number of prominent people favoured this course, it was against the policy of the East India Company to accumulate more territory. Moreover there were practical difficulties. There were about 25,000 members of the Khalsa still at large in the Lahore and Amritsar areas and there were another 8,000, who had not been engaged in the fighting, around Peshawar, quite apart from a number of isolated garrisons. These troops could be expected to resist the annexation of their country and the British forces available were hardly strong enough to cover the whole province, while they lacked the heavy guns necessary to besiege the cities which the Sikhs would be holding. These reasons outweighed the views of the minority that the Sikhs were bound to wish to revenge their defeat and another contest would almost certainly occur in the future if the Punjab remained independent.

The second course was to establish what was known as a subsidiary alliance with the government in Lahore. This idea dated from the time of Warren Hastings when, faced with the reluctance of the East India Company to absorb more territory, the system was developed of raising a force under British officers for service in a native state, but at the cost of the ruler concerned. The Company did not interfere with the internal affairs of the state, but it was in a position to ensure that its ruler was friendly and there was an efficient force ready to meet any external aggression and co-operate with the Company troops if necessary. The system had been adopted in Oudh and Gwalior among other places. There would have been many difficulties in applying it to the Punjab, not the least being that it would be necessary to build on the Khalsa, which would have provided a far from firm foundation in the circumstances. Moreover, government policy was opposed to extending the number of these alliances and Lord Hardinge had explicit instructions from London that the system was not to be employed in this case.

The third course was to try and establish a friendly government in Lahore, such as had existed in the days of Ranjit Singh, and this was the solution it was decided to adopt. It would, however, be necessary to exact reparation for the war which had been fought and to provide tangible proof to the people of the Punjab that their army had been defeated. It would also be essential to clip the wings of the Khalsa and to have a mission in Lahore which could keep a careful eye on developments in the situation.

Lord Hardinge had these objects in mind when he laid down his terms to the Sikh Durbar, in discussions which resulted in the signature on 11 March of the Treaty of Lahore. By its terms the British annexed the Jullundur Doab, the territory which lay between the Sutlej and the Beas, and the Durbar relinquished all claim to lands in Malwa which had been the property of the Sikh state. British troops were to have freedom of movement across the Punjab on demand and the British were to have control of all movement on the rivers Sutlej and Beas, including the charge of all ferries. The Khalsa was to be reduced to 20,000 infantry, comprising 25 battalions, and 12,000 cavalry, organized and paid as in the days of Ranjit Singh. All the remaining guns which had been in action against the British, thirty-six in number, were to be handed over. No European nor American advisers were to be employed. An indemnity of $1\frac{1}{2}$ crores of rupees, equivalent to about £$1\frac{1}{2}$ million sterling, was to be paid as reparations for the expenses of the war.

The Durbar was unable to find the required sum and could only produce $\frac{1}{2}$ a crore, so the cession of Kashmir was obtained instead. The occupation and government of this mountainous province would have been a difficult and expensive business, which the British had no wish to undertake, and when the wily Gholab Singh offered to make up the balance of the indemnity, Kashmir was sold to him for this sum, to be joined to his existing fief of Jammu. In recognition of the attitude he had adopted during the conflict he was to become independent of the Lahore government and his new position was regularized in the treaty.

A Council of Regency, to be headed by Lall Singh, was set up to govern the Punjab on behalf of the boy Maharajah, and Henry Lawrence, the eldest of three remarkable brothers, who were all to leave their mark on the history of northern India, was appointed as British Agent in Lahore. His younger brother John had meanwhile been entrusted with the administration of the newly annexed Jullundur Doab.

Lord Hardinge, the treaty having been duly signed, was anxious to remove all British troops from the Punjab, but the Council of Regency felt far from sure of its security if the British left and requested that a British garrison should remain in Lahore at least until the end of the year. This was agreed, but Hardinge stated publicly that there was no question of troops remaining after that date.

The first sign of trouble after the Treaty had been signed occurred in Lahore when a European sentry, faced with a herd of inquisitive cattle, slashed at some of them with his sword. This led to what was to become known as the 'cow row'. The whole city was soon in an uproar and some British officers were mobbed. However, a combination of firmness and good humour calmed down what had looked like developing into a serious situation and things soon returned to normal.

What threatened to be a much more serious situation developed when the Governor of the fort at Kangra, in the hills some 150 miles north-east of Lahore, declined to recognize the new government. Kangra was considered virtually impregnable, for it was built on a knife-edge ridge and it was impossible to elevate siege guns to bombard it. A British force was sent against it and the sappers constructed approaches which enabled the heavy guns to be brought into action, whereupon the fort surrendered.

The next problem arose when the Mohammedan governor of Kashmir, Imam-ud-Din, refused to hand over the province to Gholab Singh. This time no British troops were employed, as it was considered that it was up to the Lahore government in the first place to enforce the treaty it had signed. Henry Lawrence set out to bring the recalcitrant governor to heel at the head of 10,000 Sikh troops. Odd as it may have seemed to despatch a British officer in command of recent enemies to enforce obedience to an agreement which had been forced upon them by the British, on behalf of a Dogra most of them distrusted, the result was entirely satisfactory and Imam-ud-Din surrendered without firing a shot. The whole episode was a tribute to Henry Lawrence's strength of character.

Imam-ud-Din had in his possession correspondence which definitely implicated Lall Singh. When Lawrence got back to Lahore, the case against the head of the Council of Regency was heard by a court of five British officers, sitting in the presence of the principal Sikh sirdars. Lall's guilt was proved beyond doubt and he was sent into exile in British India. Few people in Lahore shed any tears on the departure of the Rani's boy friend, except perhaps the lady herself. The Viziership was placed in the hands of a commission consisting of Tej Singh, Shere Singh, of whom much more will be heard, Dewan Nath and Fakir-ud-Din.

Meanwhile, in May there had been a tragic occurrence at Ludhiana. A sudden hurricane struck the cantonment and the barracks of the 50th Foot collapsed, fifty men and forty-eight women and children being killed and many more injured.

The Sikh sirdars were by no means happy about the future of

the country, and continued to fear that when the British withdrew it would again revert to anarchy. All fifty-two of those
present in the Lahore area therefore unanimously requested the
establishment of a British protectorate until Dhuleep Singh came
of age. Their request resulted in the Treaty of Bhyrowal, under
which it was agreed that the British presence should remain for
the required period. The Regency was to continue, but with
certain additional members, namely Runjoor Singh, Shumsher
Singh and Bhai Nidhan, and it was to operate under the control
and guidance of the British Resident. It was stated that 'the power
of the Resident extends over every department and to any extent'.
British forces might be stationed wherever the Governor-General
wished 'within the territories of Lahore'. The Sikh treasury was
to find twenty-two lakhs of rupees annually towards the cost of
the protectorate. The Treaty was signed on 4 September. Under
the new arrangements the British deployed three brigades, one
at Lahore, one at Jullundur and one at Ferozepore.

Hardinge appears to have been unduly optimistic about the
future. He was always being pressed to reduce expenditure and
he now, against the advice of his Commander-in-Chief, felt
justified in ordering reductions in the Bengal Army. Units were
not disbanded, but the authorized establishment of a cavalry
regiment was reduced from 500 to 400 and that of an infantry
battalion from 1,000 to 800. Moreover, the transport organization, which had been built up for the war, was broken up and
the transport dispersed. Gough was not so sanguine as his
political chief and he did persuade the latter to allow the
strength of the garrisons between Meerut and the Punjab Frontier to be increased to about 50,000 men with 60 guns over the
next few months.

Lawrence soon found that he faced a major task in establishing an efficient civil administration in the Punjab. During the
period of anarchy following the death of Ranjit Singh corrup-
tion had become rife. Few districts seemed to have remitted
more than half their assessed revenue to Lahore and in at least
one case nothing at all had been sent in for the last two years.
Apart from straightening out this financial chaos, he initiated
extensive measures of land reform, following a pattern which
had already been introduced by his brother John in the recently

110

annexed Jullundur Doab, and which brought the Punjab into line with the more equitable system in force in British India. These measures were very unpopular with the Sikh landlords, although most welcome to the Mohammedan peasantry. He also followed British Indian practice in making suttee, the burning of widows on their husbands' funeral pyre, illegal and abolished cruel punishments such as mutilation, which had been permitted under Sikh law. At the same time he initiated an extensive irrigation scheme in the Bari Doab between the Beas and the Ravi.

Henry Lawrence, who had to a marked degree the fortunate knack of choosing good subordinates and inspiring them with his own ideals, had the assistance in his task of settling the Punjab of a remarkable band of men, mainly young Indian Army officers, some of whose names were to become almost household words in the years ahead and who were, with their chief, to be largely responsible for the loyalty of the Punjab when the Indian Mutiny broke out in 1857. Apart from Sir Henry's other brother James, the group included such men as John Nicholson, George Abbott and Herbert Edwardes. Lawrence's initial instructions to them were 'settle the country, make the people happy and take care there are no rows'. They were employed mainly in the turbulent Pathan-inhabited districts between the plains and the Afghan frontier, which in later years were to form the North West Frontier Province. Intended initially to act as advisers to the Sikh governors, they soon found that they had to take the reins into their own hands, since most of the local rulers proved to be either ineffective or disaffected and sometimes both. Moreover it was essential to protect the interests of the hitherto exploited Mohammedan minority.

The experience of Edwardes, then only a subaltern in the Bengal Europeans, was typical. He took over the district of Bannu, where he found that every village was a walled fortress and that the Sikh method of collecting revenue had been virtually to conduct a series of armed raids in each area. Edwardes soon won the confidence of the tribesmen and convinced them that in future they would receive fair treatment from the authorities, but that in return he would expect the headmen to ensure that discipline was maintained. He had the advantage of appearing to the Pathans as their deliverer from the unpopular Sikh yoke,

111

but the fact remains that within a year not only was the revenue coming in on time, but the villagers had been persuaded to knock down their walls and Edwardes had constructed a central government fort, from which it was understood the garrison was ready to sally out and protect the local inhabitants against any outside intruders. All this showed how well Edwardes had succeeded in impressing his personality on the tribesmen. It was not all achieved without risk, for on one occasion he had to shoot an intended assassin in his tent.

In December, 1846, Lumsden raised in the frontier districts a Regiment, the Guides, which was to become possibly the best known in the Indian Army. Hodson became his second-in-command. At first intended, as the name implies, for use as scouts rather than as a regular unit, it had a squadron of cavalry and two companies of infantry. The men were originally drawn largely from Hindustanis who had served in the Khalsa, but with a proportion of Pathans and Mazhbi (low caste) Sikhs. They were followed shortly by a Frontier Brigade of three regiments, which were to form with the Guides in the future the nucleus of the famous Punjab Irregular Force. Meanwhile two other Regiments, which were to play an honourable part in the story of the Indian Army, the Regiments of Ferozepore and Ludhiana, were being raised mainly from the Sikhs of Malwa.

Throughout 1847 the Punjab remained calm and there was little trouble in the frontier districts. In February Lumsden did a successful drive through Hazara with a force of 1,000 Sikhs, including two regiments which had fought Gilbert's Division at Sobraon, leaving a peaceful district behind him. There was, however, a great deal of restiveness below the surface. This was particularly so in Lahore and Brigadier Colin Campbell, alarmed by rumours from Mohammedan sources that the Sikhs intended to rise, was worried about the vulnerability of the 10th Regiment stationed in the citadel and took steps to strengthen its position. Actually the only outbreak during the year was in the Jullundur Doab, where a local chief rebelled and the Jullundur Brigade, including the 61st (South Gloucestershire) Regiment took the field against him. His fort at Rungur Nunglo, together with a smaller one at Horab, was captured without much difficulty and peace was restored.

Before this there had been, in August, a more serious development. A plot to poison Henry Lawrence and Tej Singh was unearthed at Lahore and the Rani Jindan was clearly implicated. She was also found to be conducting a clandestine correspondence with Mulraj, the Governor of the southernmost district of Multan, and this seemed somewhat suspicious, although its deeper significance was not realised at the time. It was decided that the Rani must be separated from her son and she was packed off to Sheikapore about twenty miles from Lahore, virtually under house arrest.

In December Lord Hardinge was relieved as Governor-General by Lord Dalhousie, a young peer of liberal views, who, at thirty-six, was the youngest man ever to be appointed to the post. At the same time Henry Lawrence, whose health had suffered from the pressure of work to which he had been subjected, went home on sick leave and was succeeded at Lahore by Sir Frederick Currie. It was an unfortunate time for a double change. Despite the apparently peaceful atmosphere there was plenty of inflammable material about if someone chose to strike a match. The garrison of Lahore was strengthened by another European regiment, the 53rd, and Major-General Whish, an officer of the Bengal Artillery with a distinguished career behind him but, like most of the senior officers, on the wrong side of sixty, came up to command.

The main danger appeared to come from the ambitions of the Attarawala family whose head, Chuttur Singh, was in command at Peshawar and who had set his heart on his daughter marrying Dhuleep Singh and so becoming Maharani. The British authorities appear to have discouraged the idea and there was some fear that Chuttur might call in aid from Sultan Mohammed, brother of the Amir of Afghanistan, who was anxious to recover Peshawar, which the Afghans had lost to the Sikhs in Ranjit Singh's time, and of which he had been the last Afghan Governor. George Lawrence, however, seemed to be establishing considerable influence over the hill tribes in that area and although Chuttur's loyalty might be suspect, his son, Shere Singh, was a member of the Council of Regency and appeared to be thoroughly dependable.

CHAPTER 9

The Revolt of Mulraj

SERIOUS trouble was not long in coming. It came not in one of the predominantly Sikh areas near Lahore nor from the troops of the Khalsa, but in the southernmost district of Multan, and the leader of the rising was not a Sikh but a Hindu. Mulraj had taken over the governership of Multan, which had only been annexed to the Punjab some twenty years before, from his father and soon found himself at odds with the new régime. He had failed to pay the traditional accession fee and his assessment for tribute to the central government had been raised. Moreover an adjustment of boundaries had removed the town of Jhang from his rule. He therefore offered to resign his appointment and in due course his resignation was accepted by the Durbar. A new Sikh governor was sent to replace him, accompanied by Mr Vans Agnew of the Bengal Civil Service and Lieutenant Anderson, with an appropriate escort including a regiment of Gurkhas in Sikh service. The fact that British officers were being sent seems to have caused resentment.

The party was received civilly enough and taken into the fort by Mulraj; but as they left it later to go to a building outside the walls, where they were to lodge, one of Mulraj's retainers attacked Vans Agnew with a sword and in the resulting scrimmage both Britons were wounded. They reached the comparative safety of their lodgings and Vans Agnew managed to send off two letters saying what had happened, one to Lahore and another addressed both to Lieutenant Edwardes, who had recently taken over in Derajat, the district across the Indus opposite Mulraj's territory, and to General Van Cortlandt, who had returned to serve with the Sikh army after the late war and was now commanding the troops in the Bannu area. Whether Mulraj himself was involved in any way in the original attack seems doubtful, but he rode off when it happened, and later sent a message saying his own people would not let him resign. The excitement increased rapidly and the extremists were soon in control. The escort went over to the Multanis, a mob attacked the building which housed the two wounded Britons and they were murdered. The Sikh governor designate was imprisoned by Mulraj, who was by now in open rebellion against the Durbar.

When Vans Agnew's messenger reached him on 22 April, 1848, Edwardes' instinct was to take immediate steps to save the British officers at Multan, but he was hardly in a position to do so single-handed. He had with him the equivalent of twelve companies of infantry and 330 irregular cavalry, with 2 guns and 20 zamburaks. His men were partly Sikhs, partly Poorbeahs and partly Pathans and it was only upon the latter that he could rely. He was lucky in that the principal Pathan chief with him, Foujdar Khan, was an able and thoroughly loyal man on whom he could depend for sound advice. Edwardes would often express an opinion and Foujdar Khan would say it was an excellent idea 'but . . .' and then proceed to point out the flaws and suggest a better course.

Edwardes' first action was to send the letter from Multan on to Van Cortlandt in Bannu, with the urgent request that he should come to his aid with a Mohammedan regiment. Then, learning that Mulraj had despatched agents to secure the boats on the Indus, he ordered Foujdar Khan to send horsemen to frustrate this design and seize what boats they could to enable him to cross the river himself into Multani territory. His immediate object was to seize the market town of Leia on the left bank as a bridgehead. He also started urgently to recruit more Pathans. The crossing of the Indus itself was quite a problem, as the river was several miles wide, and at first he only had one boat which he used to ferry his men to an island in mid-stream. But Foujdar Khan's efforts brought the total up to thirteen and he was able to land near Leia, which surrendered without resistance.

He had now heard that Vans Agnew and Anderson had been

115

murdered, but he still felt that energetic steps should be taken to suppress the rebellion and he assumed that troops would soon be on the move from Lahore. He wrote in this strain to Currie, describing his own situation as being akin to that of 'a Scotch terrier barking at a tiger'. However, early in May, knowing that a greatly superior force with eight guns and sixty zamburaks had crossed the Chenab to move against him, and having been warned by a Poorbeah officer that his Sikh companies were proposing to go over to the enemy, Edwardes withdrew his main body to the west bank of the river, leaving only a detachment of about 100 newly raised Pathans at Leia, and placing all his boats under the guard of his Poorbeah troops. Shortly after this Van Cortlandt arrived by boat with the Soorbhan Khan Regiment and six horse artillery guns.

There was then a pause, as the Multani forces withdrew to the Chenab and a certain Mustapha Khan arrived, obstensibly to treat with Edwardes, but obviously at the same time to try and 'buy' Foujdar Khan. He was told Edwardes would guarantee Mulraj a fair trial and was given a promise of a pardon and employment for any Pathans who came over. After this the Multanis again advanced towards the Indus, and part of the force with some guns went to occupy Leia. Edwardes had sent over a further 200 Pathans and his garrison, of whose presence the Multanis do not seem to have been aware, gave the intruders a 'bloody nose' and they retired in disorder with the loss of their guns. This action did a lot to boost the morale of Edwardes' men.

Meanwhile in Lahore Sir Frederick Currie's initial reaction on receiving news of the outbreak had been not dissimilar to that of Edwardes and a warning order had been issued to the available British troops to prepare to move to Multan; but when news of the death of the two British officers was received, Currie thought again. His military advisers pointed out that Multan had very strong defences—a siege would be necessary and that meant heavy guns. None was available and there would be a considerable delay before a siege train could arrive. Moreover, he himself was becoming increasingly concerned at the restiveness in Lahore and he was loath to decrease the British garrison. He therefore referred the matter to the Commander-in-Chief.

Lord Gough decided firmly against taking any immediate action. He estimated that to undertake another campaign in the Punjab he would need 24,000 men with 50 siege guns and 78 field guns, and in addition the help of a column from Sind. He only had 10,000 men, including units in the hill stations, and 48 guns immediately available and there would be considerable delay before the necessary strength could be built up. A fresh transport organization would have to be created. The manpower difficulties were accentuated by the fact that the leave season had started and up to 25% of many of the native regiments were on furlough. Furthermore the southern Punjab in mid-summer is possibly the hottest place in India and Gough was most unwilling to commit European troops to a campaign there in the hot weather. Finally he felt that the effect of British troops reappearing in force in the Punjab would be to antagonize the Sikhs and bring them into the field in support of the rebellion itself. It might even be localized and die away from lack of general support. He was supported in these views by the Governor-General, who took the line that the rebellion was against the Lahore government and that it was therefore the responsibility of the Durbar to suppress it. Gough stressed that even if no offensive action was taken at the moment, the British must be prepared for a campaign in the cold weather if things went wrong. He asked for the Bengal native infantry regiments to be brought back to the strength of 1,000, but this step Lord Dalhousie refused to take.

It was thus decided that the responsibility for suppressing the outbreak should rest with the Durbar without assistance from British troops. The plan was for three columns of the Durbar forces to move on Multan. The main one, 5,000 strong under Shere Singh, who had Shumser Singh and Uttar Singh with him, was to advance along the Ravi from Lahore, while to the west of it a force under Jewahir Mull moved through the Sindh Sagur Doab beyond the Chenab, and to the east another under Imam-ud-Din, the governor who had refused to surrender Kashmir, advanced along the Sutlej. A fourth column was to come from the Mohammedan state of Bahawalpur, which lay south-east across the Sutlej, to the Nawab of which the British had appealed for assistance. His troops, known as Daudpatras,

117

would operate against Multan from the opposite direction to the main columns. Another young 'political', Lieutenant Edward Lake, was ordered to join the Daudpatras as military adviser. Edwardes was meanwhile to make Derajat secure and ensure that no assistance came to the rebels from across the Indus.

Edwardes was far from pleased when he heard this plan of campaign, for he considered then, and always maintained, that the rebellion was still a purely local affair and that it would have been possible to 'rush' Multan and stamp it out. Had prompt action been taken, the trouble would not have spread to the rest of the Punjab and no war would have broken out later in the year. In later life, however, he did admit that a second clash with the Khalsa was inevitable and that in the long term it was a good thing it occurred when it did, nearly a decade before the Indian Mutiny. It is interesting that some Sikh authorities maintain that the main reason for the lack of British intervention was political and that the trouble was deliberately allowed to spread, so that it would involve the Khalsa and provide an opportunity finally to smash it. This theory is hardly tenable, for the British had learnt a healthy respect for the Sikhs as opponents in the late war and would hardly have reduced the strength of their army, and been in such a hurry to put everything on a peace footing, had they anticipated war again in the near future.

Early in May there was a serious development in Lahore. One of Lumsden's Guides, who had made friends with the retainers of a certain Sikh General called Kahan Singh, reported that the General appeared to be involved in a plot against the régime and to be responsible for attempts to seduce the Company's sepoys from their allegiance, which had been causing the authorities worry for some time. Lumsden and his men surrounded the General's house one night and arrested him with some of his accomplices. He was subsequently tried and hanged and this appeared to have a good effect locally.

Lumsden had, however, discovered irrefutable evidence that the Rani Jindan was mixed up in the business and in consequence Currie decided that she must be removed from the Punjab. The Guides went down to Sheikapore as escort to the Sikh sirdars who were to conduct her to the frontier. They had anticipated resistance and two squadrons of the 14th Light Dragoons were saddled up in Lahore ready to come to their help. In fact everything went smoothly and the Rani, who apparently thought that she was merely being moved elsewhere in the Punjab, was extremely polite until she arrived at Ferozepore and realized that she was being sent into exile in British India. She then treated the Sikh sirdars to a flow of invective which would have done credit to any Khalsa barrack room; but it did not prevent her from being sent on to Benares. Although the Rani had been the centre of intrigue and it was for that reason a good thing to get her out of the way, her removal from her own country did elevate her into something of a martyr in the eyes of the Sikh people. She was after all a widow of Ranjit Singh and allegedly the mother of his son. The British were only ruling the country until the young Maharajah came of age and the removal of his mother from the Punjab gave plenty of ammunition to those who were throwing doubt on British intentions and saying that they could not be trusted.

Following these events the garrison at Lahore was strengthened by a regiment of irregular cavalry and two regiments of native infantry. The only actual outbreak of trouble occurred when a Sikh Guru, Bhai Maharaj Singh, raised a body of horse and foot near Lahore with the object of joining up with Mulraj; but his force was easily dispersed by the Durbar forces with the assistance of a regiment of Irregular Cavalry and the wing of the 14th Light Dragoons, who did quite a lot of chasing around the countryside without actually having to do any fighting. Maharaj Singh made his way individually to Multan. But there was still much restiveness in the Lahore area and at least one case of a European sentry being murdered on his beat.

Down in Derajat Edwardes' first problem was to deal with a chief named Cheytun Mull, a Baluchi who had been promised the governorship of Dera Ghazi Khan in the south of the area and who had established himself in the fort at Mangrota, which was the key to the north. Edwardes consequently moved against Mangrota, but Cheytun Mull abandoned it and went south to make sure of his new fief, where his nephew, Louza Mull, was acting as governor. Edwardes followed him, having put in his Sikh regiment to garrison Mangrota, being confident that the local Pathan tribes, on whom he felt he could rely, could keep it quiet. He was expecting further reinforcements from Bannu, and a force part Dogra, part Mohammedan and part Sikh was on its way when trouble threatened in the Bannu area and Lieutenant Taylor, who was in charge there, called for its return. Only the Dogras obeyed the order and it was quite clear that the Sikhs at least were only looking for an opportunity to join Mulraj. However they had not reckoned with Mrs Van Cortlandt, who was accompanying the force. She had the guns accompanying them turned on the recalcitrant Sikhs and Mohammedans, who thereupon obeyed orders and went back to Bannu. Meanwhile Edwardes' work had been done for him. The Khosuh tribe of Baluchis, who were hereditary enemies of the Lugharees, to whom Cheytun Mull belonged, attacked and captured Dera Ghazi Khan. Cheytun Mull was killed and Louza Mull made captive; 400 Khosuh horsemen subsequently joined Edwardes. The strong fort at Hurrund further south was also held for Mulraj, but Edwardes felt, rightly as it proved, that the Pathans in the garrison, which was surrounded by friendly tribes, could be won over and this isolated force had no effect on the main issue.

Edwardes now faced the main Multani forces across the River Indus, but he had taken the precaution of securing all the boats on his own side. There was as yet no sign of the Durbar columns which were moving very slowly. The only column to be showing any offensive spirit was that from Bahawalpur. The Daudpatras had crossed the Sutlej and moved into the southern part of the Multan district, where they had met and dispersed a revenue-collecting party sent out by Mulraj.

Early in June Edwardes received discretionary powers to cross into Multani territory and to co-operate with the Daudpatras if he wished. The Multani forces had withdrawn to the Chenab in order to concentrate against the Daudpatras and Edwardes was worried because the latter were advancing on both sides of the river and he feared they might be defeated in detail. On 15 June,1848, Edwardes got his force across the Indus, none too easy an operation as it was thirteen miles wide, and marched straight away to the Chenab, where he occupied the fort at Khangpur, which he found unoccupied. The Daudpatras had meanwhile called in their detachment on the west bank and were concentrated near Kineyree.

The situation on 17 June was that 8,000 to 10,000 Multanis and 10 guns under Rung Ram were on the left bank about fifteen miles from the Daudpatras who were 8,500 strong and had 11 bad guns and about 30 zamburaks. Edwardes was on the right bank at Khangpur with about 1,500 regulars under Van Cortlandt and about 5,000 irregular Pathans with 30 zamburaks. Edwardes moved south to the ferry at Kineyree to join up with the Daudpatras. He succeeded in getting about 3,000 of his irregulars across the river under Foujdar Khan, but the men were all on foot and only the officers were mounted. Meanwhile Rung Ram, who had waited to see what Edwardes would do, moved too late to engage that day. Edwardes himself got over early next morning, the river here being three miles wide, just as the battle opened. It was very jungly country and the Multani forces had established themselves on a ridge facing the Daudpatras' position. The latter advanced to the attack and were repulsed and when Edwardes reached them he found them in a state of considerable confusion, with their eighty-year-old Commander, Futteh Mohammed Khan, sitting under a tree telling his beads. His Second-in-Command, Pir Mohammed Khan, who had been responsible for the Daudpatras moving to cover Edwardes' crossing, was made of different stuff and some organization was re-established. Lake had not yet arrived. Edwardes impressed upon the Daudpatras that they simply must hold on until he could get Van Cortlandt's regulars and especially the guns across to join the force. He estimated that they could not arrive for about seven hours. Meanwhile the Multani guns, which outclassed the Daudpatras artillery, inflicted a number of casualties. Edwardes' Pathans on the left flank had some losses, but he made them lie quiet and reserve their fire, although they took a good deal of restraining. For some reason the Multanis do not seem to have realized they were there. By 1400 hours, after the firing had been going on for six and a half hours, Futteh Mohammed ordered the Daudpatras to retire and the Multanis followed up. The Pathans then opened up with their zamburaks, whereupon the Multanis turned their attention on them. The situation was critical and Foujdar Khan collected his mounted officers and led a gallant cavalry charge, which caused the advancing Multanis to halt, just in time to save the situation. In the nick of time Van Cortlandt's leading troops arrived with the guns and one of his Mohammedan regiments promptly launched a counter-attack and captured a Multani gun. This was the signal for the Pathans, who had been straining at the leash, to surge forward and they carried all before them. The Daudpatras returned to the fray and the Multani force was completely defeated and withdrew in confusion. Eight of their ten guns were captured and it is estimated that they left a thousand dead on the field. Edwardes' men lost 58 killed and 89 wounded. It was all over by 1630 hours. Just as the fall of Dera Ghazi Khan had secured the Derajat, the victory of Kineyree removed any danger of Mulraj re-asserting his authority over the Sindh Sagur Doab between the Chenab and the Indus. The initiative had now passed to Edwardes and the road to Multan lay open.

He decided to push on northwards to the enemy stronghold, which lay some fifty miles away. There was a short pause while he reorganized his force and got the remainder of his troops across the river. Lake had arrived shortly after the battle and took over virtual command of the Daudpatras. Edwardes now had at his disposal about 18,000 men, the large majority of them Mohammedans, and some thirty guns. He moved forward towards his objective and on 30 June he was joined by the Durbar column under Imam-ud-Din, who had sent all his Sikh troops away and had only Mohammedans with him.

On 2 July, when he was about four miles from the city, Edwardes' scouts reported that Mulraj's troops had moved out and taken up a position to oppose his advance where a canal crossed the main road near the village of Suddoosam. Their front was covered with low jungle and there were a number of mud villages and palm groves, in which they had positioned their guns. It transpired later that the local Gurus had assured Mulraj, who was present in person, that the day was an auspicious one and that he was assured of victory. The heat was intense and Edwardes relates that before the battle he put his head into a bucket of cold water and then wrapped it in a well-soaked turban.

He deployed his force with the Daudpatras on the right, then Van Cortlandt's two regular regiments in the centre and then his own Pathans. On his extreme left were Imam-ud-Din's troops, of whose loyalty he was somewhat suspicious. His line seems to have outflanked the Multani's. Before the fighting actually began he sidestepped his whole force to his right in order to avoid the main obstacle and to bring him nearer to Multan and better placed to threaten Mulraj's line of withdrawal. The battle was opened by the guns of both sides and it was soon apparent that Edwardes, who had twenty-two guns against ten, was having much the better of the exchange. He thereupon ordered his infantry to advance. The Daudpatras rushed forward and carried some high ground on the Multani's left and then Van Cortlandt's regiments and Edwardes' Pathans both broke into the enemy position. To do so they had to cross a deep nullah and this nullah prevented the guns moving forward to give further support. However, about this time it became known that Mulraj, having fallen off his elephant which had probably been frightened by a cannon shot, had left the field, though before doing so he appears to have posted a couple of guns to fire on a bridge over another nullah in rear to prevent his troops following his example. From then on his men showed little fight and began to stream towards the rear; some guns which were covering their retreat were gallantly carried by a charge of the Suraj Mukhi Regiment, led by a young civilian volunteer, Mr Quin, who had made his way to Edwardes' force and offered his services. Edwardes was left in possession of the field, having taken most of Mulraj's guns.

The morale of the Multani troops sank to a very low level after the battle and there were a number of desertions to Edwardes' force, including several of the Gurkha regiment which had been the escort to the unlucky Agnew and Anderson. Needless to say the morale of Edwardes' men soared even higher. The news of his successes spread throughout the Punjab and it seems very likely that they were instrumental in postponing the main outbreak. Had it come in June it would have entailed committing British troops before they were ready for a campaign in the very hottest part of the year, just what Gough wished to avoid.

The city of Multan, which Edwardes now faced, had a reputation for strength and had, as an Afghan outpost, for many years proved too difficult a nut for even Ranjit Singh to crack. Its walls were some three miles in circumference. Immediately to the north of the town was a strong fort erected on a large mound. To the south-east and south-west suburbs extended for half a mile beyond the walls and these the enemy were already preparing to defend. East of the city ran the Wali Mohammed Canal, which looped to within a quarter of a mile of the walls. On this side there were extensive inundations, which precluded an attack from that direction. Although the countryside in that part of the Punjab was in general barren, a flat plain often covered with scrub jungle, there were in the vicinity of the city a number of groves of trees and scattered tombs and houses with gardens as well as small villages. There were also several mounds to break the general flatness of the ground.

Edwardes was still quite sure that he could storm the city, especially in view of the morale of its defenders, but he realized that he could not hope to take the fort without heavy guns. He sent a message to Lahore asking for Major Napier with a company of Sappers and a few large guns to be sent urgently, emphasizing that every week's delay meant a strengthening of the defences. Currie, who had been much heartened by the news of Suddoosam, having consulted General Whish, now decided to intervene and took upon himself the responsibility of exercising his authority to act in an emergency. He issued a warning order for troops to move from Lahore and Ferozepore to Multan. They could not, however, mobilize and reach Multan for at least a month, while Edwardes had hoped for speedier assistance to enable his own men to carry the place before the Multanis recovered from their reverses. On hearing of Currie's decision Gough rather reluctantly felt he must back him up, a decision supported by Lord Dalhousie.

The force finally despatched actually comprised a native cavalry brigade and an infantry brigade including the 10th from Lahore and the Ferozepore Brigade with the 32nd (Cornwall) Regiment. There were also two troops of horse artillery and the siege train was put under orders to join up.

Gough was still unhappy about committing European troops

at that time of year. He felt that Multan was too strong to be captured by the force that could be made immediately available, and was inclined to regard Edwardes as an over-enthusiastic young optimist. He still thought that a full scale rising might be avoided and that the presence of British troops could well be the signal for an outbreak.

Currie proclaimed his intentions on 22 July, twelve days after he had made the decision. The troops from Lahore were to move down the Ravi, the Europeans going by boat and the native troops marching by night. The Ferozepore Brigade would move in the same way along the Sutlej. The Lahore troops left in two columns on 24 and 26 July. When the native cavalry left Lahore the rest of the 14th Light Dragoons moved up from Ferozepore. The fact that 13 men died on the march and that on their arrival in Lahore they had 220 sick add force to Gough's reluctance to use European troops in the hot weather; and these were mounted men, not footsoldiers.

Meanwhile Edwardes' force was sitting before Multan, skirmishing with the enemy and watching their efforts to make the defences stronger. Edwardes had been given a gold medal by the East India Company in recognition of his successes and promoted to the rank of Major 'within the territories of Lahore' and he was shortly to learn that he had also been made a Companion of the Bath, not a bad achievement for a subaltern. He now met with a most unfortunate accident. He was briefing his subordinates in his tent when there was a sudden alarm of an enemy attack. He accidentally discharged his pistol while putting it into his belt and shot himself in the hand. His wound incapacitated him and for some time he had to exercise command from his bed. He had been joined by Lumsden and his Guides from Lahore and also by some individual European volunteers, including some officers of the Company's river boats who would be a help to him as leaders. He had, incidentally, all along had a small detachment of the Guides with him as his personal escort and five of them had succeeded in getting into Mulraj's camp as spies. One of them actually succeeded in being appointed as Mulraj's orderly and had the misfortune to be wounded by a round shot at Suddoosam. Edwardes was getting good intelligence, the morale of the force was high and more Pathans were joining him. One of his main worries was the condition of his wounded, for he had no European doctor with him and their sufferings were considerable until eventually a doctor arrived with the troops from Lahore. He had another difficulty in that some of his followers were hereditary enemies and he had to keep them at opposite ends of the camp, while when he held a 'durbar', which he did regularly, they were always placed on opposite sides of the carpet. Families and clans tended to form groups and he encouraged this by allowing each to have its own standard, which helped to form something of a 'regimental spirit'. The one thing on which discipline was strictly enforced was plundering. Anyone caught was punished and dismissed. Edwardes claimed that he had no desertions during the campaign.

His problems were made no easier by the arrival of Shere Singh's troops about five miles from Multan. The Sikh general had a regular infantry regiment of Poorbeahs, with about 500 irregular infantry and 3,000 Sikh Cavalry with two mortars. He and his chief subordinates appeared loyal but his troops, and especially his Poorbeah regiment, could not be trusted. Shumsher Singh told Edwardes that but for the news of Suddoosam his men would have gone over to the enemy. The situation improved a bit when news was received that British troops were on the move from Lahore. Indeed when a conspiracy to go over to Mulraj was discovered in Shere Singh's force, led by a Ghorchurra named Soodan Singh, the leader was arrested and handed over to Lake for trial. He was found guilty and with the concurrence of the Sikh Sirdars was blown from a gun. Shere Singh himself had several long conversatons with Edwardes and the latter always maintained that at this time he was loyal and was trying to influence his father Chuttur Singh, up in Hazara, against rebellion. He was under a good deal of paternal pressure himself and it was clear that the Attarawala clan had set their hearts on the marriage of his sister to the Maharajah and if this was not to take place it would be difficult for Shere Singh to stand out against them.

Meanwhile in the frontier area there had been, as Taylor had feared, trouble in Bannu, but it had been easily suppressed. In Derajat the troops whom Edwardes had left to blockade Hurund had been showing signs of disaffection, but they were neutralized by the local tribesmen, who were loyal. The real danger was further north. At first it seemed that the influence of George Lawrence and his colleagues was sufficient to hold the Sikh garrisons in check and early in August an emissary of Mulraj's was handed over by a Yusufsai chief and executed. Then on 6 August, just as Abbott reported to Lahore that the Pakli Brigade was preparing to move on the capital, Chuttur Singh threw off the mask and raised the standard of revolt at Haripur. His guns were in charge of an American officer, Colonel Canora, who refused to hand them over without orders from Abbott and was killed endeavouring to prevent Chuttur getting hold of them. Abbott and Nicholson both started raising Mohammedan levies and soon had a number of men under their command. This seems to have held the rebels in check for a while, but the levies were not yet capable of standing up to Sikh regular troops in the field. Nicholson managed to seize the fort at Attock with a body of Pathan horse. This fort covered the crossing of the Indus on the main route from Peshawar to Lahore and as long as it was held the Sikh troops in the Peshawar area could not pass to unite with Chuttur Singh's troops in Hazara and march on the capital. Lieutenant Herbert took over the responsibility for the defence and Nicholson made his way to Lahore.

CHAPTER 10

The First Siege of Multan

T HE leading troops from Lahore, including the 10th Foot, some 800 strong, had arrived at Sirdapur on the Ravi on 12 August. Here General Whish established a depot to hold fifteen days' supplies for the force. Communications up the Ravi were maintained by the Company's steamer *Conqueror*. He also despatched a party of labourers with an escort to dam up the headwaters of the canals which were feeding the inundations near Multan. He then set off for the city. Mulraj of course was aware of his approach and sent out a force of cavalry, with the intention of carrying off his guns, when he was about a day's march away.

At the same time Edwardes arranged to change camps with Shere Singh, so that the latter's troops were no longer between him and the Lahore Column as they had been. When the change was completed both forces fired a feu de joie. This was heard by Whish's men, who stood to and in consequence were fully prepared to receive Mulraj's cavalry. The latter thus got a pretty hot reception and were seen off in a smart little action, in which the Light and Grenadier Companies of the 10th were involved, with the loss of about forty men and some prisoners. The British casualties were six.

The Lahore troops reached Multan on 18 and 19 August and the leading elements of the Ferozepore Brigade came in next day. There was, however, a shortage of boats on the Sutlej and the 32nd did not actually leave Ferozepore until 11 August and arrived at Multan on 25 August. Even then two of its companies had to follow later. It suffered badly from the heat on its march from the Sutlej, no less than fourteen men dying of heatstroke. There were 175 sick when it got into camp.

Initially Whish's and Edwardes' camps were six miles apart and it was decided that Edwardes should sidestep to his right in order to close the gap. This involved clearing the enemy from two large walled gardens. The task was successfully accomplished, both Edwardes' Pathans and Lake's Daudpatras distinguishing themselves. The main incident was the attack by Lumsden's Guides on a battery with guns and zamburaks which covered the area. The Guides carried this successfully and spiked the guns, but were unable to bring them away. Shere Singh co-operated with this attack and his artillery gave Edwardes' men good covering fire. A part of his force also carried out a diversionary attack. It was noticeable, however, that the troops he employed were Mohammedans and that his Sikhs seemed unwilling to fight. The enemy, who consisted mainly of Akali Sikhs and Rohillas, put up a stout resistance, but Edwardes' men were not to be denied. Unfortunately in their new position they were under constant artillery fire and this was a little trying for the nerves of irregular troops.

The time had now come to decide how the city was to be taken. Three plans were considered, namely to seize the city by coup de main, to attack the fort direct by regular approaches or to clear the suburbs to the south-west of the city and work through them into an assaulting position close to the walls. The idea of a direct all-out assault was rejected on the grounds that the casualties would be very heavy and the urgency of the political situation was not such as to demand the immediate capture of the city. The idea of assaulting the fort was rejected because it would involve a move from the present positions which could be construed as a retreat, since Whish's men and Shere Singh's contingent would initially be moving in the direction whence they had arrived. This would be bad for morale, especially among the irregulars, and could swing Shere Singh's Sikhs over to the enemy. There was also a lack of water in that area and the move would uncover the line of communication with Bahawalpur and the Sutlej. It was therefore decided to adopt the third alternative and to start by digging a first parallel (trench) from a place named Ramtirat about 1,600 yards from

129

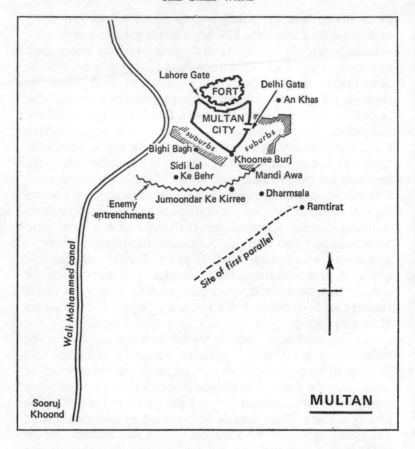

MULTAN

the walls facing the Delhi Gate to a point opposite the Khoonee Burj, a bastion which lay at the southern extremity of the city.

The siege train had arrived near Bahawalpur on 28 August and set out for Multan next day. There were twenty-four 18-pounders or 12-pounders, ten 8-inch howitzers and ten 8- or 5½-inch mortars. They made a long and unwieldly column, for there were altogether 4,000 camels, many elephants and masses of hackeries carrying the ammunition. The train arrived at Multan on 4 September. Whish then issued a formal demand for the surrender of the city. There was little likelihood that it would be acceded to and what slight chance it had of acceptance was nullified by tactless wording, which implied surrender to the forces of the Queen rather than to the Lahore Durbar.

Work on the first parallel actually started on 7 September. As has already been said the Bengal Sepoys were not very good with the spade and such work did not suit Edwardes' irregulars, as it did not conform with their ideas of fighting. The Pathans and the Daudpatras had proved themselves to be brave men and battleworthy, but they were not much use in a regular siege and the business of preparing the approaches for the attack fell largely on Whish's men and, within his force, mainly upon the Europeans. Owing to the heat it was decided that the European troops should dig by night and rest by day. Two 8-inch howitzers and three 8-inch mortars were soon established near Ramtirat, four 18-pounders a little to their left, and a rocket battery was added to these shortly afterwards. It was found, however, that the range from the first parallel was too great for the 18-pounders to do any effective damage. On 8 September the 52nd Bengal Native Infantry was involved in a skirmish with the enemy, probing towards the parallel, and suffered a few casualties. That night there was a more determined effort by the Multanis, when the digging party from the 32nd behaved extremely well and drove back the attackers for the loss of six men. Part of the 72nd Bengal Native Infantry was also involved. Its men had been digging surprisingly well for Bengal Sepoys, but when the attack occurred that night they lost their heads and started firing wildly, their shots hitting some of their own picquets.

By 9 September Major Napier, in his capacity of Chief Engineer, was expressing doubts as to the possibility of Multan being captured by the forces which Whish had available, but it was nevertheless decided to go on with the operations. The site of the next parallel was dominated by some buildings and it was decided that these must be occupied. On the night of 9 September. Lt. Col. Pattoun of the 32nd, who was field officer of the trenches, was detailed to carry out this task and he was given two companies of the 10th and of the 49th Bengal Native Infantry and the rifle company of the 72nd Bengal Native Infantry. He was also to be supported by two of Van Cortlandt's horse artillery guns. Little opposition was expected as it had been reported that the buildings were not occupied at night. In

131

fact this intelligence proved to be wrong and they were strongly held. Pattoun's men met with a sharp repulse, he himself being wounded. The brunt of the fighting seems to have fallen on the 10th. The men afterwards complained bitterly that they had not been well supported by the native troops. This is rather borne out by the fact that they suffered more than half of the seventy-six casualties incurred. Everyone agreed that Van Cortlandt's two guns had given them all the support they could. The whole affair had been badly laid on, there had been no proper reconnaissance, information was faulty and the troops were not used to night fighting.

Preparations were made to resume the attack on 12 September and a force was assembled consisting of a wing each of HM's 10th and 32nd and the 8th and 49th Bengal Native Infantry. It was supported by a troop of horse artillery and by one squadron each of the 11th Bengal Light Cavalry and the 7th and 11th Bengal Irregular Cavalry. Meanwhile Edwardes' men were to make a holding attack on the left to distract attention from the main effort. However, before the British were ready to launch their assault the Multanis, who had been making strenuous efforts to improve their defences in the area, forestalled them and launched a counter-attack against Edwardes. This was repulsed and the Daudpatras, who were in the centre of Edwardes' line, rushed forward to pursue their enemy, soon to be followed by the Pathans, who were on the left. They were held up, but Van Cortlandt, whose regular troops were on the right flank and had been kept well in hand, now moved forward and succeeded in capturing the hamlet called Jumoondar ke Kirree which was only about 800 yards from the Khoonee Burj.

The main attack was then launched, led by the European troops. The men of the 32nd were surprised to find a nullah in front of the first enclosure, the existence of which they should surely have known about after the fiasco on the 9th. However, they had scaling ladders and were soon across and over the wall. The Multanis within the compound fought fiercely and both the Commanding Officer and the Quartermaster, who may have been a brave officer but who was hardly in his place taking part in an actual assault, were killed. The compound was successfully cleared and the troops went on to the next one which

132

contained a large temple. There were a number of fruit trees around the wall and Edwardes, who was watching from the flank, records seeing 'the Irishmen of the 10th' swinging over the wall on the branches of the trees. Whether he assumed they must be Irish because of the number of that nationality in the Regiment or whether he simply thought that only Irishmen would swing on trees like that is not made clear. In any event there was again fierce fighting for the temple. Private Waterman of the 32nd relates that those defending the top floor of the temple were thrown to the ground below. The troops then moved on to the next group of buildings, but here they came under heavy fire and the attack bogged down. It was therefore decided to consolidate the objectives already gained and the British were recalled. As they retired the Sikhs attempted to follow up. They were counter-attacked by some of Edwardes' men and by a troop of cavalry and forced back to their positions. Unfortunately the British troops around the temple, which was known as the Dharmsala, were unable to distinguish friend from foe and some of Van Cortlandt's men were certainly hit by British fire. It had been a successful day, but owing to the tenacity of the Multanis it had been costly. The British casualties were 5 British officers, 5 native officers and 32 other ranks killed; 12 British officers, 1 native officer and 203 other ranks wounded. The enemy left 500 dead behind them. The British line had been advanced about 800 yards.

Up to this point it was considered that Shere Singh and his generals were still loyal, but no trust could be placed in his troops and many of his Sikhs had deserted to the enemy. On 12 September General Whish, through Edwardes, ordered Shere Singh to move his troops to Tolumba on the Ravi and other places on the lines of communication, where they would not be so subject to the temptation of desertion. This order could have brought things to a head, but it seems probable that Shere Singh had already decided to go over to Mulraj. He had, as has already been stated, been under considerable family pressure, although there is evidence that he had tried to dissuade his father, Chuttur Singh, from resorting to arms. Now that Chuttur Singh had taken the decisive step it was even more difficult for his son to hold back. He was being taunted by some of his own

133

Sikhs with being a Mohammedan. It is certain from subsequent investigations that the first letter he sent to Mulraj disclosing his intention was on 12 September, although he may have been in touch with his intermediaries previously. In this letter he referred to his duty as a son and a Sikh, and after the war he told Edwardes, for whom he always had a high regard, that he reached his decision on that day.

It was Edwardes' habit always to dine with his officers and it had become customary for Shere Singh and some of his senior officers to visit Edwardes every evening after dinner. That night Shere Singh arrived as usual, but with an exceptionally large number of retainers, and took his seat next to Edwardes at the head of the table. Van Cortlandt, who was sitting at the foot of the table and had had long experience of handling the Sikhs, immediately smelled a rat, slipped out and collected a number of loyal Pathans, with whom he surrounded the tent. He then came back and contrived to convey to Shere Singh exactly what he had done. The latter looked rather embarrassed and shortly afterwards took his departure. Edwardes and Van Cortlandt felt that there had been a plot to seize Edwardes and his officers and carry them off, presumably as hostages, before Shere Singh deserted. In any event the following morning he and his army went over to Mulraj. The latter was suspicious of his motives, refused to admit his troops to the city and made them camp outside just north of the fort. Neither of Shere Singh's main subordinates supported him in his action, although their own troops, who were almost entirely Sikh, went with him. Uttar Singh slipped away and joined Edwardes and although Shumser Singh was carried off with Shere Singh's army, he got away and reported to Edwardes at the first opportunity.

With the desertion of Shere Singh, General Whish decided that the siege must be abandoned until the arrival of the Bombay Army column, which was expected from Sind. Although his forward trenches were only six hundred yards from the walls, he was now markedly inferior in numbers and he could not take the risk of Shere Singh's army operating against his rear while his troops were deployed in front of the city. He therefore withdrew, first about a mile and a half further back across the canal and then to the area near Sooruj Khoond which Edwardes

134

had occupied initially, where he was in a position to cover the roads south to Bahawalpur and westwards to the Raj Ghat ferry across the Chenab, which was the direct route to Dera Ghazi Khan and the Derajat. Edwardes' men withdrew first and were harassed in their retirement by Shere Singh's cavalry, but these were effectively kept off by the Pathan horse. Whish's own troops followed and again Shere Singh made to follow up, but with the 10th as rearguard putting up a bold front his efforts were not very effective. The retirement seems to have been carried out with somewhat undue haste and apparently the artillery left a certain number of cannon balls behind, although Edwardes' irregular horse assisted by carrying shot back on their mounts. The new area was in scrub jungle and once again there was difficulty in getting the Bengal Sepoys to undertake the manual labour of clearing the ground and an undue amount of work fell on the Europeans.

For the next three weeks nothing much happened, although Shere Singh and his troops did demonstrate towards the British camp in a half-hearted manner. He also sent emissaries to try and seduce Edwardes' men from their loyalty. He directed his efforts particularly at Van Cortlandt's regulars. He made much of the point that, if the Khalsa was defeated and finally disbanded, they would be without jobs. Edwardes countered this propaganda by giving an assurance that those who remained faithful would be guaranteed employment in the Company's service if the British took over the country. It is good to relate that his undertaking was subsequently honoured by the authorities. Mulraj would still not admit Shere Singh to the city and kept the guns of the fort trained on his men. His suspicions were kept alive by means of correspondence addressed to Shere Singh by Edwardes, which was allowed to fall into his hands and which inferred that Shere Singh was in league with the British.

Then on 9 October Shere Singh suddenly struck camp and marched north along the Chenab. Whish does not seem to have been aware of what was happening until Shere Singh was well on his way. It has been argued that he should have tried to intercept him, but his task was the capture of Multan and, if he had endeavoured to follow Shere Singh in any strength,

Mulraj could have operated against his rear and certainly have raided his camps and depots. His lack of action was resented by many of those under his command and one contemporary diary speaks of their 'disgust' with his leadership. Shere Singh has been criticized by some Sikh sources for failing to act more offensively against Whish. He was, however, now playing for higher stakes. He had issued a proclamation calling upon the Khalsa to rise, drive out the British and avenge the insult to the Maharani. His eyes were on Lahore and the Sikh heartland; Multan had now become a sideshow. Edwardes gives his total casualties during this first siege as forty-four killed and 238 wounded, eighteen of those killed and ninety-eight of the wounded belonging to Sheik Imam-ud-Din's contingent, which thus obviously had borne its fair share of the fighting.

Although more important events were happening elsewhere it will be as well to finish the account of the happenings in Multan before the arrival of the Bombay Army column made it possible to renew the siege.

After Shere Singh's departure, Mulraj sent out numbers of emissaries, including some to the Afghans, to gain further support, but they did not meet with much success. A number of groups of dissidents did, however, make their way into Multan and these made up for Mulraj's men who had gone off with Shere Singh. Meanwhile the British worked on preparations for a renewed siege, constructing altogether some 15,000 gabions and 12,000 fascines. Whish's troops were camped on the eastern side of the Wali Mohammed Canal, which was now dry since the British had dammed the inflow of water from the Chenab, while Edwardes' men were on the western side.

At the end of October the Multanis began to work their way along some water courses towards the British camps and established two batteries, which opened fire on them at an uncomfortably close range. The British started to construct two batteries to cope with them, the European troops providing most of the working parties at night to dig emplacements for the guns. These opened fire on 3 November, but by then the Multanis had inflicted a number of casualties, particularly upon Edwardes' men. In the early morning of 6 November the Multanis launched an attack on the British guns, which were guarded by two companies of the 32nd. These two companies went forward to meet the attackers and drove them back with the bayonet, rallying back on the batteries they were guarding as soon as it was clear that the Multanis were on the run. A later attempt was also easily repulsed.

General Whish decided that the Multanis must be dislodged and an attack was planned for 7 November. Both Whish's and Edwardes' troops were to go forward simultaneously, each keeping on their own side of the canal. On the evening of 6 November, a number of Edwardes' men, including Van Cortlandt's Kuthar Mookhee Regiment of Poorbeahs, relieved the British troops guarding the batteries to free them for the assault and during the night a good half of the Poorbeah Regiment went over to the enemy. Edwardes therefore opted out of the attack, as he felt Van Cortlandt's regulars were not to be trusted, and it was agreed that Whish's men would go in alone. However, just before the attack was due to be launched the Multanis advanced on Edwardes' side of the canal. Van Cortlandt called on his two remaining regiments to prove their loyalty, which they did splendidly, repulsing the attackers and following them up. The irregulars followed their example and so the whole of Edwardes' force attacked after all, forcing back its opponents.

Meanwhile the British attack had gone in. Moving off in a wide arc, the assaulting column struck the Multanis in the flank, and although they must have seen the British advancing, the defenders made no effort to change front to meet the threat. Led by the 10th and 32nd Regiments, supported by the 8th, 49th, and 52nd Bengal Native Infantry, the British burst into the position, meeting very little resistance and carrying all before them. Private Waterman of the 32nd records that the only man he saw to show any fight was one old grey-bearded Sikh. There was one unfortunate incident. Some of Sheik Imam-ud-Din's Rohillas crossed to the wrong side of the canal in pursuit of their enemies and came under fire from the 32nd, to whom they were indistinguishable from their foes. The Rohillas' shouts to try and identify themselves were unintelligible to most of the Europeans, but fortunately Private Howell of the 32nd knew some Urdu and, realizing the position, dashed forward

137

and stood in front of the Rohillas waving his shako. It is good to relate that his gallantry was recognized and next day he was presented with fifty rupees, donated by Edwardes, in front of the whole Regiment. The British cavalry, consisting of two squadrons each of the 11th Bengal Light Cavalry and the 7th and 11th Bengal Irregular Cavalry under Major Wheeler, had in the meantime charged the Multani horse, which had moved up in support, driven it back towards Multan, and then swept along the rear of the Multani batteries, preventing their guns from engaging the British infantry.

The whole action was a resounding success, for the Multanis lost all but three of their guns and abandoned their positions, being much harassed by the British cavalry as they retreated in disorder to the city. Their losses were considerable and those of the British comparatively light, the 10th for example only having eleven men wounded.

There was one noteworthy incident a little later. A report was received in Edwardes' camp that a body of Sikh horse was driving away a number of General Whish's camels. It so happened that all the British officers were out on reconnaissance, and Risaldar Futteh Khan of the Guides collected a party of seventy men and rode at once to the scene. He found himself faced with no less than 1,200 Sikh cavalry but without hesitation he charged, went right through them, charged back again and then returned once more and charged through them yet again. The Sikh horse rode back to Multan and the camels were saved. Futteh Khan only had two men killed.

On 10 December Colonel Cheape, the Chief Engineer of the Army, arrived to join Whish's force. There was again considerable discussion as to the method by which the siege should be renewed, with Napier still advocating a direct attack upon the fort. After considering the various courses open Colonel Cheape recommended that the previous plan should be followed and that when the Bombay troops arrived the force should work forward through the suburbs to assault the Khoonee Burj and the Delhi Gate.

CHAPTER 11

Across the Chenab

FROM the time the news of Shere Singh's desertion to Mulraj had become known in Lahore there had been a marked increase in tension in the city and the surrounding country-side. The temper of the Durbar troops in the area became more than ever uncertain. The British authorities took steps to meet the situation and the 53rd took over the palace guard and also the custody of some of the state treasure, including the Koh-i-Noor diamond. They also took charge of the Sikh state prisoners. There were soon indications that plotting was going on in high places and Currie arrested Runjoor Singh and a brother of Shere Singh's who was in the capital.

One source of worry was the strong fort of Govindgarh, which dominated the sacred Sikh city of Amritsar and had a Durbar garrison. It was decided that this must be secured. The task was achieved by a piece of bold strategem. A party of the Guides under Rasul Khan, who was a brother of the Futteh Khan who was distinguishing himself before Multan, arrived at the gate of the fort one evening, escorting some treasure and a party of bogus prisoners. They managed to obtain admittance after some fast talking by Rasul Khan and at dawn the following morning overpowered the guards and admitted two regiments of Bengal sepoys, which had approached by a night march from Lahore. Thus the fort, which might have played an important part in the events to come if in the wrong hands, was secured without bloodshed. Officially it only mounted two guns, but in practice it was found that there were no less than eighteen in position. A

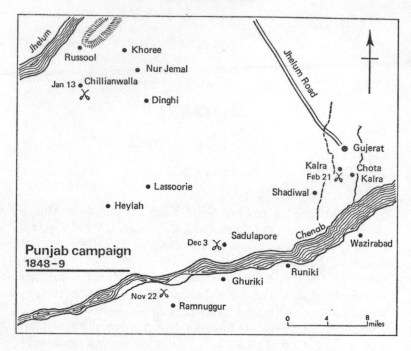

Punjab campaign
1848-9

large number of additional ones, which should have been surrendered, were found buried, the total coming to fifty-two.

There was also trouble in the Jullundur Doab, while Ram
Singh headed a rebellion in the Bari Doab across the Beas,
which threatened the security of the newly annexed British
territory. Brigadier Wheeler moved out with a column, including
the 61st, to cope with the situation. A detachment of the 15th
Bengal Irregular Cavalry and 29th Bengal Native Infantry dealt
with forts at Pathankot and Shahpur. Wheeler then crossed the
Beas. He was preceded by a party of the Guides under Hodson,
who arrived before the main enemy stronghold, a fort at Rangar
Nagal, which he successfully blockaded with only fifty cavalry
and 100 infantry, for two days before Wheeler came up. The
latter bombarded the fort, intending to assault it next day, but
the garrison fled during the night. Another fort at Morari on the
Ravi was abandoned at Wheeler's approach. He then crossed
the Ravi to deal with a recalcitrant sirdar at Kallanwala. Here

again Hodson and his Guides distinguished themselves, working ahead of the main column. He secured one small fort, which blocked the road, largely by bluff and then, as he neared Kallanwala, he found himself with 100 men facing about 3,000 Sikhs. For a time the situation looked serious, but fortunately Wheeler was close behind and the Sikhs retired when they realized the fact. Hodson was given two regiments of irregular cavalry and sent in pursuit, a task he carried out with complete success, while Wheeler occupied Kallanwala with little trouble. Lahore itself had meanwhile remained quiet, although at one stage a party of rebels raided a post across the Ravi from the city, held by Durbar troops, and got away with a number of zamburaks.

Meanwhile the Government in Calcutta had gradually realized that things were coming to a crisis and by the end of August Lord Gough was allowed to start making the serious preparations for war which he had been seeking to do since May and which so far had been held up on the grounds of financial stringency. By a letter dated 30 September Lord Dalhousie at last acceded to his Commander-in-Chief's request to bring the Bengal infantry regiments back to a strength of 1,000 each and the cavalry regiments to 500. During the previous two or three months George Lawrence had been urging the despatch of a British Brigade to the Peshawar area, but Gough had refused to agree to this as he did not wish further to disperse his forces. He was at this time more than a little concerned with the possible attitude of Gholab Singh in Kashmir. Few people really trusted the Dogra chief and Gough feared that, if there was an early British repulse, Gholab Singh might easily switch sides and come out in support of the Khalsa.

By the end of September Lord Dalhousie was perfectly aware that war was inevitable and on 10 October, the day after Shere Singh left Multan, he set out from Calcutta for the Punjab. Before leaving he made a speech at a public banquet in which he said, 'Unwarned by precedents, uninfluenced by example, the Sikh Nation has called for War and on my word, sirs, they will have it with a vengeance.' Indeed from that moment it seemed that the British were once again at war with the Sikhs, although Lord Dalhousie never formally conveyed the fact to the Durbar. His Commander-in-Chief appears to have been in some doubt as to whether he was carrying out operations to suppress a rebellion on behalf of the Durbar or whether the Durbar in Lahore was itself to be regarded as an enemy.

The Army of the Punjab, which was now formed under Lord Gough's personal command to undertake the campaign, was organized into one cavalry and three infantry divisions. The Cavalry Division under Brigadier Cureton was divided into two brigades, the first under Brigadier White of the 3rd Light Dragoons, consisted of the 3rd and 14th Light Dragoons and the 5th and 8th Bengal Light Cavalry. The second brigade, commanded by Brigadier Pope, had the 9th Lancers and the 1st and 6th Bengal Light Cavalry.

Cureton was a British service officer who, having been involved in a scandal over debts, had resigned his commission in the Militia, faked death by drowning, and then enlisted as a trooper in the 14th Light Dragoons under an assumed name. He had risen to the rank of sergeant in the Peninsular War, in which he had been wounded three times. His true identity then became known and he was given a commission in the Infantry, later transferring to the 16th Lancers. He had commanded a cavalry brigade in the Gwalior Campaign, and was widely regarded as the best cavalry leader in India. At the time of his appointment he was Adjutant-General and there was no one really suitable to take his place. This is another example of Gough's lack of appreciation of the importance of having a competent staff and good as no doubt Cureton was, Thackwell was available, and there were other officers who could have taken over his infantry division.

Brigadier Pope was an officer of the Bengal Army long past his prime and indeed he had to be helped on to his horse. The 1st Infantry Division was that already serving before Multan. The 2nd was commanded by Sir Walter Gilbert and consisted of a brigade under Brigadier Mountain, with HM's 29th Regiment and the 30th and 56th Native Bengal Infantry and another under Brigadier Godby which had the 2nd Bengal Europeans and the 31st and 70th Bengal Native Infantry. Mountain had recently been transferred to the 29th from the 26th, with which he had served in the China War. He was an intensely religious officer, who made a practice of reading the bible for an hour a day. The 3rd Division was commanded by Sir Joseph Thackwell and had three brigades. The first under Brigadier Pennycuick consisted of HM's 24th and the 25th and 45th Bengal Native Infantry. The 24th, although very strong, was a young regiment which had not been long in India. It had a new commanding officer and a number of other officers had only recently joined. Judging from names, it seems to have had a lower percentage of Irishmen than most other regiments. The second brigade under Brigadier Hoggan had HM's 61st and the 36th and 46th Bengal Native Infantry. The third, under Brigadier Penny, had no European unit and consisted of the 15th, 20th and 69th Bengal Native Infantry. The Irregular Cavalry formed a separate brigade under Brigadier Hearsay, who was an officer of the Bengal Cavalry, as his father had also been. The artillery, under the command of Brigadier Tennant, consisted of six troops of horse artillery, three field batteries and two heavy batteries. The morale of the Bengal Sepoys was very much higher than at the beginning of the first war. Then they had been rather afraid of the Sikhs; now they knew that they could beat them. There is incidentally some evidence that a number of the sepoys reduced as a result of the cuts insisted upon by Lord Hardinge had found their way to the Punjab and joined the Khalsa.

Shere Singh has been criticized for not moving direct upon Lahore. It seems that his main concern at this time was to ensure that he was joined by the troops who had risen in the frontier area and particularly those from Bannu. Unfortunately for him that part of the Rechna Doab which he had first to traverse was inhabited largely by Mohammedans, who were hostile to him, and indeed he did not particularly help his cause in the eyes of that community by leaving a trail of burned Mohammedan villages behind him as he moved eastwards, his troops behaving particularly badly at the town of Jhang. Some of his irregular cavalry got within a few miles of Lahore, but the main force halted at Gujeranwala, about thirty-five miles north of the city.

To counter the threat to Lahore, Cureton was sent towards Gujeranwala with the 3rd Light Dragoons, the 8th Bengal Light Cavalry, the 12th Bengal Irregular Cavalry and three horse artillery batteries, passing through Brigadier Godby's Brigade,

143

which had already established a bridgehead over the Ravi. Godby soon moved forward to support Cureton, who was reinforced by a field artillery battery, the 14th Light Dragoons and two more native infantry regiments. Brigadier Colin Campbell was then ordered forward from Lahore, but partly owing to transport difficulties and partly owing to the situation in the city, he was only able to take with him his two native regiments, leaving HM's 53rd behind.

The British had expected the Sikhs at least to make a stand at Gujeranwala, even if they did not act offensively, but Shere Singh, intent upon securing his junction with the troops from Bannu, withdrew his force to the Chenab at Ramnuggar, where there was a ford over the river. Here he was joined by the troops from Bannu and then had rather over 6,000 men and thirty guns. Much of the country in the Rechna Doab is scrub jungle, but nearer to Ramnuggar it was more open with some cultivation. There was little contact between the two forces, apart from a few cavalry skirmishes with the Ghorchurras. A party of Sikhs had seized the fort at Wadni and Colin Campbell was ordered to capture it on his way forward, being supported by some cavalry, including the 9th Lancers. It proved to be a bloodless operation, as the fort surrendered without resisting. Campbell then joined Cureton, leaving two companies of native infantry to hold the fort. He and Cureton were under orders not to attack the enemy until the main force came up. Gough hoped that Shere Singh would re-cross the Chenab and he would then be able to defeat him with the river at his back. He was, after the experience of the first war, particularly anxious to capture as many Sikh guns as possible.

By the first week in November the main army was moving up. The Commander-in-Chief himself crossed the Sutlej on 9 November and was in Lahore on the 13th. He crossed the Ravi on 16 November and on 21 November the Army of the Punjab was concentrated some eight miles from Shere Singh's army. On the way up most units had trouble with robbers and quite strong numbers of 'badmashes' hovered in the neighbourhood of smaller detachments. A party of the 24th Bengal Native Infantry escorting treasure was attacked by 150 men, mostly mounted, when they were one march short of Moodkee. Another

Sikh party got away with fifty camels belonging to the 2nd Bengal Europeans just after they had crossed the Ravi, but most of these were subsequently recovered by the cavalry. The troops noted the restless state of Lahore as they passed through and it was because of Currie's nervousness about the situation there that a number of heavy guns, which would have been useful with the army, were left behind with the garrison of the city. One minor operation was carried out by Brigadier Penny's Brigade. The fort at Jubbur had been occupied by dissidents and Penny was sent to eject them, as they might well have raided the lines of communication. The place was captured after only a slight resistance.

By 21 November the Sikhs had nearly completed their withdrawal across the Chenab, but still had some outposts on the southern bank. Gough decided to close up to his opponents the next day, sending his cavalry ahead to make a reconnaissance in force to discover their exact disposition and to find out in particular if there was any hope of cutting off any considerable body on the near side of the river. He had no intention of being involved in a general engagement.

The village of Ramnuggar lay about two miles from the river, which was here very wide, but mainly dry with a sandy bottom, the actual channel being quite narrow. At one point in the river bed there was a patch of greenery which formed a sort of island in the sand. Both banks of the river were high and the ground leading up to the south bank was intersected by a number of dry nullahs. The Sikhs had evacuated Ramnuggar itself, but still held the green island and had a number of men lying up in the nullahs, while they had massed their artillery, with only the muzzles of their guns showing, on the high north bank which dominated the river bed. They hoped, and as it turned out not without justification, that the British cavalry would become involved in the broken ground along the bank of the river, and in the soft sand and in places quicksands of the river bed, and would suffer heavily from their artillery fire and from the sharpshooters lying up in the nullahs.

When the British cavalry advanced, Captain Ouvry's squadron of the 3rd Light Dragoons was first sent forward alone. Seeing a body of Sikhs near the river bank he charged, crossed a

145

nullah and drove straight through them, overrunning their tents and dispersing them. Ouvry then led his squadron in loose order right round the island, coming under heavy fire from the Sikh guns on the far bank. He had few casualties from this fire, but he lost no less than seventeen horses in the quicksands along the river bed. By this time the rest of his Regiment had come up and had been joined by the 8th Light Cavalry. It was apparent from his experience that there was no future for cavalry operating in the river bed and that to attempt to do so was to invite disaster from the artillery on the far bank. The order was therefore given to withdraw. As soon as it was apparent that the British cavalry were retiring, numbers of Sikhs emerged and started to follow them up. Twice the British turned and faced their enemy, who would not accept the challenge. Finally Brigadier White, considering that he had drawn the Sikh force far enough away from the river, ordered his Brigade to charge, supporting it by two batteries of horse artillery. The 3rd Light Dragoons and the 8th Light Cavalry obeyed his orders with alacrity and the Sikhs were driven back to the river, the cavalry again being halted on the near bank. Unfortunately one of the horse artillery batteries was pushed too far forward and a gun and a couple of limbers sank in the sand. Every effort was made to recover the gun, but after an hour's futile effort, which drew heavy fire from the Sikh artillery on the far bank, it had to be spiked and abandoned.

Meanwhile a large body of Ghorchurras had crossed the river by a ford further to the British right. The 14th Light Dragoons supported by the 5th Light Cavalry were ordered to charge them. This they did successfully. Unfortunately Colonel Havelock, their commander, who had a reputation as a brave and some-what impetuous cavalry leader, then saw another body of Sikhs along the river bank and decided to dispose of them. They were in fact Sikh infantry and any charge against them would carry the cavalry down into the river bed. Brigadier Cureton, seeing Havelock forming his men for a charge, realized this fact and galloped forward to stop them. Unfortunately he was killed before he could reach Havelock. Havelock led the bulk of his regiment in a gallant charge against the Sikhs, and rode over them, but then went careering down into the river bed, where his

146

horses were soon floundering in the deep sand and suffered heavy losses from the Sikhs on the far bank. Havelock himself was killed and the Regiment suffered fifty casualties before it could be withdrawn. Its withdrawal was in fact threatened by another body of Ghorchurras, who were engaged by its reserve squadron and by the 5th Light Cavalry and driven off.

This ended the action at Ramnuggar, in which the British cavalry had shown considerable gallantry, but, as a result of Havelock's ill-judged charge, had suffered a number of unnecessary casualties. Brigadier Campbell asked for permission to bring forward some infantry, but the Commander-in-Chief declined to commit any further troops that day. He had found out what he wanted to know and he was now in a position to plan his crossing of the Chenab. One of the lessons noted by some observers of the action was the reluctance of the Bengal Light Cavalry to rely on their regulation swords when meeting the Sikh Ghorchurras. They preferred to use their pistols. It was remarked that to this extent they were inferior to the irregular cavalry, who were themselves armed with tulwars and who used them with complete confidence.

The British had now established their camp near Ramnuggar. The Sikhs had withdrawn their permanent posts on the south side of the river, but parties of their Ghorchurras were still about and the British, who always stood to an hour before dawn, were kept very much on the alert. One raiding party of Sikhs did get away with quite a number of camels. They also picked up the occasional straggler and it is recorded that one soldier of the 2nd Bengal Europeans, who fell into their hands, was returned unharmed, having been well treated in his short period of captivity. The inhabitants of the area were friendly to the British, being mainly Mohammedan, and the force orders of this period show that there was a good deal of concern to prevent the native troops, and particularly the followers, looting and mistreating the local people. As usual the administrative arrangements do not appear to have been particularly good and the records of the 61st show that on their first night at Ramnuggar, which was extremely cold, the men had no blankets nor greatcoats, while the 3rd Light Dragoons had no food nor fodder for their horses. On the other hand the British troops as usual made the best of

147

things as the time went on and an account from the 2nd Bengal Europeans refers to several cricket matches. General Thackwell was appointed to command the Cavalry Division in place of Cureton and Colin Campbell was given his infantry division. Thackwell appears to have been regarded by Gough as his Second in Command.

Gough was determined to cross the Chenab and defeat the Sikhs before they could be further reinforced. A direct assault upon their position across the wide river with its shifting sands, and with their artillery strongly emplaced as it was, was out of the question except at an unacceptable casualty rate. It was therefore decided to make a turning movement and cross higher up the river with part of the force, while the remainder kept the Sikhs' attention fixed on the Ramnuggar crossings. There was a ford at Ghuriki about eight miles from Ramnuggar, but this was known to be strongly held by the Sikhs. There was another at Runiki about five miles further on, and close to that another at Ali Sher Ke Chuck. Failing these it would be necessary to go on to Wazirabad, which lay about 22 miles from Ramnuggar.

General Thackwell was placed in charge of the turning movement and he was given White's Cavalry Brigade, but with the 3rd and 12th Bengal Irregular Cavalry replacing the 14th Light Dragoons, and Campbell's Division. He also had the three horse artillery batteries of Christie, Huish and Warner and two native light field batteries, commanded by Austin and Kinleside. The force was to be accompanied by the pontoon train and to take with it two days' provisions.

The column was due to move off at midnight on 30 November. Unfortunately the start was delayed for about two hours as it was a very dark night and Campbell's troops were unable to find the rendezvous. This was probably due to the inexperience of his very young AQMG, who had failed to issue proper orders. As a result the column, which made a tremendous noise on the move, particularly owing to the creaking of the pontoons, the jabbering of the followers and the loud grunts of the camels as they were urged along, did not reach the Runiki ford until 1100 hours. There was then a delay of about three hours while the feasibility of getting across at that ford, and also at Ali Sher Ke

Chuck, a little farther up, was examined. It was finally decided that neither was practicable for wheeled vehicles. There were also at Runiki some Sikhs on the far bank, who were out of range of Thackwell's guns and, although they did not appear to be in great strength, that meant an opposed crossing without artillery support. So much time had been lost that Colin Campbell advocated returning to Ramnuggar, but Thackwell decided to push on to Wazirabad and John Nicholson, who had recently so distinguished himself at Attock, was sent ahead with some irregular cavalry to secure the ford there and seize any boats available. It is not clear why it had not been possible to carry out a thorough reconnaissance of the fords beforehand. Lack of proper information about them reflects very little credit upon the British intelligence services. The Sikh intelligence also appears to have been remarkably lax. In spite of the noise of the move they do not at this time seem to have realized what Thackwell was trying to do, nor that such a large detachment had been made from the main force.

By the time the column arrived in Wazirabad it was dark. Nicholson had done his work well and secured about twenty boats. Thackwell was able to get over the 24th and two regiments of native infantry in the boats. However, the current was fairly strong and the 24th lost three men in the crossing. One regiment of native infantry started to cross by the ford and reached an island near the far bank, where it halted and bivouacked, as it was impossible to find the continuation of the ford in the darkness. Thackwell therefore decided to bring the rest of his troops across as soon as it was light next day, although he managed to ferry some of his guns over to join the troops already on the far bank.

Next morning the remainder of his troops crossed, but it was a slowish business. By the time he was ready to move it was 1400 hours. The men had to be fed and those on the far bank had had nothing the night before, as it had been impossible to take supplies over to them. He found it very difficult to transport his 18-pounders across the river and he consequently decided to rely entirely on his horse artillery and to send the field guns back to Ramnuggar under escort with the pontoon train, which had proved completely useless and had indeed been nothing but an encumbrance. Thackwell's instructions from Gough were that he was not to hurry unduly, not to take chances and above all not to risk attacking the Sikhs too late in the day, so that he would have to fight in darkness. The memory of Moodkee and Ferozeshah was still fresh in the Commander-in-Chief's mind. Thackwell therefore advanced to a point about nine miles from the Sikh position and there halted. He met no opposition and as he advanced the Sikh detachments covering the fords withdrew to their main army and he was able to establish communication with Gough at Ramnuggar.

Thackwell's intention for the next morning was to advance against the Sikhs, anticipating that Gough would be supporting his attack by a thrust across the river from the main position. As he started to move he received two messages from Gough, telling him that Godby's Brigade would join him by the Ghuriki ford and that he was not to attack until it had done so. He therefore despatched two squadrons of the 3rd Bengal Irregular Cavalry and a wing of the 25th Bengal Native Infantry to secure the ford, which appeared to be still threatened by a force of the Sikh Irregular cavalry. He himself advanced to Sadulapore, which lay about a mile beyond Ghuriki. Here the countryside, as it had been the whole way from Wazirabad, was open and well cultivated. To his front were three small villages, surrounded by fields of tall sugar cane. Campbell sent forward some of his infantry to occupy these villages. Quite suddenly Sikh guns opened up and the British realised that they were in the presence of a considerable hostile force. Shere Singh had at last realized his danger and had detached 10,000 men to deal with the threat from Thackwell. The sepoys who had occupied the three villages were ordered back, as the sugar cane gave no field of fire, and the whole British force withdrew about 200 yards to prevent the Sikhs getting any closer under cover. Why the latter had been allowed to approach so close in force without being discovered remains a mystery, but it is another black mark against the skill in reconnaissance of the British cavalry. As it was, seeing the British infantry retire, the Sikhs came on as if to launch an attack, but realizing there had only been a short tactical withdrawal, they halted and made no further effort to press forward. Then a large body of Sikh cavalry appeared on each flank and made as if to start a turning movement. They were engaged by the British horse artillery, which as usual was used very offensively, Christie's battery on the right and Warner's on the left particularly distinguishing themselves. The British cavalry had also moved out and on the right flank the 3rd Light Dragoons and the 8th Light Cavalry had some skirmishing with the enemy, but the Sikhs showed no inclination to close and held off, while on the other flank the 5th Light Cavalry and the 3rd Irregular Cavalry showed an equally bold front and kept the Sikhs well in check. All this time the cannonade continued, the British infantry lying down with piled arms and fortunately not suffering very severely.

Meanwhile there had been no sign of Godby's Brigade, which in fact had found the ford at Ghuriki impracticable for wading and had to get hold of some boats before any troops could get across. It was not until 1700 hours that the leading unit, the 2nd Bengal Europeans, was over. The remainder of the Brigade did not cross until the following morning. About 1530 hours a further message was received from Gough giving Thackwell permission to use his own discretion about attacking the Sikhs.

There is a distinct conflict of evidence as to what happened then. Thackwell claims that he consulted all his leading commanders and only Pennycuick was in favour of launching an attack. Colin Campbell claimed that he twice urged Thackwell to attack, but the latter denied this. Thackwell reasoned that it was not within the spirit of Gough's original instructions to launch his troops against a position screened by sugar cane with the darkness coming on and he preferred to wait until the following day. The battle then just petered out, after lasting perhaps three hours.

Thackwell has been much criticized for failing to act offensively and it seems fair comment to say that, once he knew Godby's Brigade was unable to cross the river to join him, as it had been expected to do, he might have appreciated that Gough's instructions to wait for it no longer applied, if he thereby missed an opportunity for bringing about a successful engagement. Gough himself took this view, although he was careful not to criticize his subordinate openly.

151

One factor which could have influenced Thackwell in his
decision not to push on that afternoon may well have been
the exhaustion of his troops. It must be remembered that they
had left Ramnuggar with only two days' rations on the night of
30 November. It was now the evening of 3 December. They had
had no breakfast and no grog and had thus been fighting on
empty stomachs, except for what had been picked up in the
fields. The only food available appears to have been what were
known as elephant chapattis, made up of bhoosa, the local hay
normally used as fodder for horses, and a certain amount of
raw carrots and turnips which they found. In at least one regiment of Bengal Native Infantry the sepoys seem to have existed
largely on some sweetmeats they had with them. Officers and
men of the 24th made a hearty meal of their major's charger,
which had been killed.

It does not seem to have occurred to anyone that the Sikhs
might not be there in the morning, but in fact when dawn broke
it was found that they had gone. Indeed Shere Singh's whole
army was in retreat to the Jhelum. It is difficult to explain why
no effort was made to keep in touch, as it is also difficult to
account for the fact that Gough's main force, beyond engaging
the Sikhs in the Ramnuggar position with artillery fire, did
remarkably little to keep them occupied. Gough appears to have
been for some time the following morning quite unaware that
the Sikhs had departed. In fact Captain Chamberlain, later a
most distinguished officer, swam the river to find out if they
were still there. None of this speaks very highly of the alertness
of the British commanders.

As soon as he realized that the enemy had gone, Thackwell
sent his cavalry in pursuit and these were shortly reinforced by
more cavalry which came across from the main force. Thackwell's infantry followed up, but they found the going through
jungly country pretty difficult. The Sikh withdrawal seems to
have been made rather hurriedly, for there was a good deal of
abandoned equipment lying about and they had even left behind
some of their wounded. The pursuing cavalry came up with no
rearguards until they had got past Heylah, which lay about eight
miles from the Ramnuggar fords, but they then began meeting
opposition, and not knowing what lay ahead, decided not to

push on further. Thackwell halted his main force at Heylah to wait until the Commander-in-Chief could join him.

Gough was in no great hurry to move. It would take a few days to organize his lines of communication to ensure that his army would be supplied when it reached Heylah, and in any event he did not want to attack Shere Singh, who had received more reinforcements when he reached the Jhelum, before the troops from Multan arrived. Moreover he had received instructions from Lord Dalhousie not to cross the Chenab with the main army 'except for the purpose of attacking Shere Singh in his present position', without prior reference to the Governor-General. Taken literally this meant that if a war of movement developed after he crossed the river the Commander-in-Chief could not attack before referring to his civilian master, who was miles away at Ambala. It placed him in an impossible position. Lord Dalhousie had doubtless listened to criticism of Gough's methods during the first war, considered him unduly rash and wished to curb any tending to impetuosity; but another factor which probably influenced him was that Gough had been stressing his logistical difficulties. On 11 December Gough wrote that these were being overcome. Then on the 17th Dalhousie sent fresh instructions which at least gave his Commander-in-Chief more or less a free hand and on the 18th, having meanwhile constructed a bridge of boats at Ramnuggar, Gough crossed the Chenab and advanced to Heylah.

That same day Shere Singh, who had initially retired to the banks of the Jhelum near the village of Russool, about sixteen miles north of Heylah, advanced to Dinghi, which was some ten miles north west of Heylah and on the road towards Wazirabad, the direct route to Lahore. He made no further move, and shortly fell back again to his position at Russool. He has been criticized by Sikh authorities for doing so. It is certainly possible that, had he pushed on to try and force the Chenab at Wazirabad and make straight for Lahore, he might have placed the British in a very awkward predicament, as it is more than likely that the city would have risen on his approach. It would, however, have involved him in serious risks, as Gough would have been able to strike at his flank. No doubt he felt it safer to wait until he had received reinforcements from Chuttur Singh and

153

probably from the Afghans. Gough realised the danger of leaving the crossing at Wazirabad inadequately guarded and sent Brigadier Pope with two regiments of irregular cavalry to that spot.

There was now a pause for a month. Lord Gough still had no intention of attacking Shere Singh until he was joined by the troops from Multan, and it was quite clear from his instructions that Lord Dalhousie did not wish him to do so. Shere Singh was in a very strong position along the Jhelum, he outnumbered Gough, and he had a marked superiority in artillery. He had, however, been forced away from the fertile valley of the Chenab, and he was now in an area in which his army could not support itself. As long as he did not actively threaten Lahore, or until there were signs that he would be strongly reinforced, Gough could afford to wait.

Herbert still held out at Attock. As long as he did there was little chance of Chuttur Singh moving to join his son or of Afghan reinforcements coming into the field. Abbott was holding out at the fort of Srikote and keeping Hazara in check. George Lawrence from Peshawar had been forced to seek sanctuary with a Pathan chief who had then handed him over to Chuttur Singh. Away to the south in the Derajat a force of rebels who had seized the fort at Lukki had been ousted by Reynell Taylor, who was now in charge of that area. One uncertain factor still was the attitude of Gholab Singh's troops from Kashmir. They were under the command of a mercenary named Steinbach and had moved down the Jhelum to Meerpur. It was felt that they might be waiting for the result of the next battle.

While Gough was at Heylah there were further operations nearer to Lahore. The Guides under Lumsden, who were on their way back from Multan, helped to reduce a fort at Fulda about thirty miles from the capital, which had been seized by rebels. Another fort in the same area surrendered without resistance to a force which included two companies of the 53rd. There was a good deal of skirmishing and in one case a body of fifteen sowars of the Guides met, charged and dispersed a body of 150 Sikh horse near a place called Baddi Dand. Early in January a party of Sikhs under Gunda Singh crossed the Chenab with the aim of causing trouble in the Jullundur area. They were

154

intercepted by the Guides and after a four day pursuit completely dispersed. Meanwhile a column under Brigadier Wheeler had set out finally to deal with Ram Singh, who was again threatening to make trouble in the Jullundur Doab, drove him across the Beas and finally defeated him on 8 January at Bassu near Nurpur, completely dispersing his force. Detachments of the 7th Bengal Light Cavalry, the 15th and 16th Bengal Irregular Cavalry, the 4th and 71st Bengal Native Infantry and the 1st and 2nd Sikh Local Infantry were engaged in these operations. It was the first time that the newly raised Local Infantry, the ancestors of the Punjab Frontier Force, had been in action and it fully justified its new master's faith in it.

CHAPTER 12

The Second Siege of Multan

THE Bombay Army column was due at Multan in mid-November, but it was delayed owing to difficulties over command. The Bombay authorities appointed General Auchmuty to the post, but he was senior to General Whish, whose appointment had been approved by the supreme government. When the news of Auchmuty's appointment was received in Calcutta it was over-ruled for this reason and Bombay was instructed to find somebody else in his place. They therefore appointed Brigadier Dundas, a British service officer who had been in the 60th Rifles. All this caused rather needless delay and in consequence it was not until 10 December that the leading Bombay troops arrived at Multan and the last did not get there until the 21st. The Bombay column had with it three native cavalry regiments, the 1st Bombay Light Cavalry and the 1st and 2nd Scinde Irregular Horse. These last units had been raised for service in Sind, but were actually composed almost entirely of Hindustanis, who were predominantly Mohammedan. There were two British infantry regiments, the 60th Rifles and the 1st Bombay Fusiliers, together with four native infantry regiments, the 3rd, 4th, 9th and 19th Bombay Native Infantry. Its guns brought the total available up to 67 siege and 30 field guns. The Bombay troops created a distinctly good impression on the members of the besieging force and the British regiments were inclined to compare them very favourably to the Bengal sepoys. Their native officers were younger, their discipline appeared to be better and they were better equipped. As has been remarked earlier, it was noticeable that they were far more prepared to

156

get down to work with the spade than were the Bengal sepoys. To help work the heavy guns they brought with them a number of lascars from the Bombay flotillas of the Indian Navy and these men impressed everybody by their good work. Another advantage which the Bombay gunners had over those of Bengal was that they were using gun cotton as opposed to powder. This seems to have been the first time it had appeared in this campaign, if not in India. With these reinforcements Colonel Cheape had seven and a half companies of sappers at his disposal.

On the arrival of the Bombay troops there was fresh discussion about the plan of attack. Major Scott, Brigadier Dundas's chief engineer, agreed with the proposal, which had originally been put forward by Major Napier, that the main attack should be made on the fort. He was supported in this view by his chief and after a good deal of argument it was decided to adopt this plan after all. However, before General Whish accepted the change, the troops had been deployed to carry on with the operations through the suburbs which had previously been decided upon, and in agreeing to the new plan Whish stipulated that before any units were moved round to invest the fort, the Sikhs should be driven back from the forward positions they had taken up in the suburbs. It appeared likely that they would interfere with his movements if this was not done.

The British force was deployed with Whish's Bengal troops on the right facing the Delhi Gate and the part of the city walls nearest to the fort; the Bombay troops in the centre, reaching to the Wali Mohammed Canal, and Edwardes and the Daudpatras on the left beyond the canal. A large number of the irregulars, including the whole of Sheik Imam-ud-Din's contingent had, on the arrival of the Bombay column, been sent back to guard depots and posts on the lines of communication. The British line was approximately that which had originally been reached in the first siege just before Shere Singh deserted.

For the preliminary attack the force was divided into four columns. On the right five companies of HM's 10th and the 52nd Bengal Native Infantry, supported by four horse artillery guns and a squadron of the 11th Bengal Irregular Cavalry, were to seize some brick kilns about a mile from the south-east angle of the fort. On their left three companies of HM's 32nd and six companies of the 72nd Bengal Native Infantry, also supported by four guns, were to clear the ground towards the Delhi Gate. Then a column consisting of five companies of the 60th, and the 3rd Bombay Native Infantry, supported by the 3rd Bombay Light Field Battery and a squadron of the 1st Bombay Lancers, was to seize a mound called the Mandi Awa, while on the left five companies of the 1st Bombay Fusiliers, with the 4th Bombay Rifles, supported by the 7th Bombay Light Field Battery and a squadron of the Scinde Horse, were directed on to a small conical hill called Sidi Lal Ke Behr, near to which was a white mosque. These two points were not far from the Khoonee Burj, the southern bastion of the city. The orders allowed each column to exploit success. Edwards, beyond the canal, was to create a diversion to distract the Sikhs from the main threat.

The attack was a complete success. On the right the Bengal troops soon secured the brick kilns and pushed on to a building called the Ankhas, only about 500 yards from the south-east angle of the fort. The Sikhs counter-attacked to retake it but were driven back. Meanwhile the left Bengal column drove some of the Sikhs right back through the Delhi Gate. Part of this column seems to have veered to the left to co-operate with the Bombay troops who had assaulted the Mandi Awa. After capturing this, the 60th and the 3rd Bombay Native Infantry had pushed on to seize a mosque near the city walls, while the former unit then worked its way close to the Khoonee Burj. The left column took Sidi Lal Ke Behr without much trouble and, while the Bombay Fusiliers consolidated the position, the 4th Bombay Rifles pushed on towards the walls. They soon found themselves entangled in narrow lanes and, although they seized an enclosure called the Bighi Bagh and a party of them reached one of the city gates, they began to run out of ammunition and had to withdraw. This was said to be due to the fact that they had only recently been converted into a rifle regiment and they had had no previous experience upon which they could calculate the ammunition expenditure of the new weapons. The Sikhs followed up their withdrawal, whereupon the Bombay Fusiliers charged forward to meet them. Once more it was

158

bayonet against tulwar and the bayonet in disciplined hands proved superior. The Bombay Fusiliers forced their opponents back to within 200 yards of the city wall. They then withdrew again to Sidi Lal Ke Behr, while the 4th Bombay Rifles, having replenished their ammunition, went forward again and occupied the Bighi Bagh once more, remaining until relieved by the 19th Bomby Native Infantry in the evening. The latter repulsed some Sikh counter attacks. While this was happening, the British guns had been established on Sidi Lal Ke Behr and were able to bombard the walls at close range.

As a result of the success of the attack on 27 December, it was decided to revert to the original plan of assaulting the city through the suburbs and to abandon the idea of a direct attack upon the fort. On the 28th Edwardes' men were moved to the right and relieved the Bombay troops on Sidi Lal Ke Behr and at the Bighi Bagh to free them for use in the coming assault. Soon after they had moved to their new positions Edwardes' troops were heavily attacked by the Sikhs, the deserters from Van Cortlandt's Regiment being especially prominent. But they were beaten back at all points and the same happened when they made a further attack three days later. Meanwhile the British guns had opened fire on the walls and those about Sidi Lal Ke Behr began making an impression on the Khoonee Burj. On 30 December there was a tremendous explosion when fire from a British battery hit a large magazine just inside the city walls and on the following day there was a big fire in the fort, a range of godowns with stores and grain being set alight. These events can have done nothing to improve the morale of the defenders.

By now the British had brought eleven 8-inch mortars, ten 10-inch mortars, four $5\frac{1}{2}$-inch mortars, six 18-pounders, two 8-inch howitzers, two 10-inch howitzers and ten 24-pounders to bear upon the walls. By 2 January the engineers pronounced two breaches practicable, one near the Delhi Gate and the other at the Khoonee Burj. The Bengal troops were detailed to assault the former and the Bombay troops the latter. Colonel Franks of HM's 10th, whose Regiment was not directly involved in the initial assault, had offered to lead it to escalade the fort, while the assault on the town was going on, but his offer had been rejected. The assault was timed for 1530 hours and Whish has been severely criticised for his decision to attack so late in the day. It was within a fortnight of the shortest day of the year and inevitably his men would be involved in street fighting in the dark, a difficult task for the best of troops in a strange city.

The Bombay column was led by the 1st Bombay Fusiliers, supported by the 19th Native Infantry and followed by the 4th Bombay Rifles. One company of each regiment carried scaling ladders. When the Fusiliers arrived at the Khoonee Burj breach, receiving splendid support from the artillery, which fired over their heads until the very last minute, they discovered that the Sikhs had dug a trench beyond it, which they defended tenaciously and there was some hard hand-to-hand fighting. However, the attackers broke through and soon found themselves enmeshed in the narrow streets of the city. It took the Bombay Fusiliers about fifteen minutes to cover the first fifty yards from the walls, but thereafter progress was rather quicker, although the debris from buildings ruined in the bombardment blocked many of the streets. They forced their way across the city to the Lahore Gate on the western side, having captured two Sikh Colours. The two native regiments had supported them well and the 4th Bombay Rifles established themselves in the grain market in the centre of the town. Having reached the Lahore Gate, the Bombay troops worked along the ramparts between it and the Khoonee Burj and cleared them completely of the enemy.

Meanwhile the Bengal column led by HM's 32nd Regiment found the breach at the Delhi Gate to be impracticable. It consisted only of a small hole which would hardly admit one man. Thereupon the column moved round the walls to the Khoonee Burj breach and followed the Bombay troops through, taking the right hand or eastern side of the city, and working through to secure the ramparts near to the fort. It was now dark and there was a good deal of confusion within the city. It was not helped by the fact that Whish had ordered that all civilians should be concentrated in the central square, presumably to discourage them from taking part in street fighting. Part of the walls round the Delhi Gate remained in Sikh hands and these were not cleared until the following morning. As was so often

15 The Battle of Chillianwalla; Viscount Gough, in his characteristic white coat, is in the centre of the picture seated on a white horse

16 Her Majesty's 24th Regiment at Chillianwalla, 13 January, 1849

17 Dewan Mulraj

18 The battle of Gujerat seen from the rear of Lt-General Sir
Walter Gilbert's division

the case after a storm, a number of the troops got out of hand and there was a good deal of looting and quite a few cases of rape before order was restored the following day. It seems that the native troops were worse offenders in this respect than the Europeans. During the night a large magazine near the Lahore Gate caught fire and blew up, inflicting a number of casualties. However by mid-day next day the city was firmly in British hands.

All efforts were now directed towards the capture of the fort, which was completely invested, and, as soon as the batteries could be got ready, a continuous bombardment was opened, the British effort being directed mainly at the north-east angle, although batteries were also established firing across the esplanade between the fort and the city. On 12 January the Sikhs made a sortie against the British sap-heads, but they were beaten back at all points. The fort was surrounded by a formidable ditch and the sappers mined the forward edge so that the counter-scarp could be blown down to give easy access to it. Hand grenades were used to clear out Sikh posts established in the ditch. By 21 January two breaches were pronounced practicable, access to the ditch had been made possible and a battery had been pushed forward to within about forty yards of one of the breaches. It was intended to assault next day, but at this point Mulraj asked for terms. The fort and the buildings within it had suffered considerable damage, and quite a few of the garrison had slipped away, mainly to join Shere Singh. Mulraj's officers insisted that he must either cut his way out or surrender. He chose the latter course and, when it was clear that no terms would be offered, he did so unconditionally.

So ended the siege of Multan, which in point of ammunition expenditure came second only to that of Bhurtpore in the history of the British in India. The garrison was marched into British territory, where some of them were detained for the duration of hostilities but the majority were allowed to disperse to their homes. Mulraj was sent up to Lahore under escort, where he was accorded the one thing which Edwardes had promised him, namely a fair trial. He was charged with complicity in the murders of Vans Agnew and Anderson and he was found guilty, but with extenuating circumstances. He was

161

condemned to life imprisonment and sent to serve his sentence in British India, but he did not live long afterwards. His property was also declared confiscated to the State. The justice of this last decision is at least questionable. Mulraj had to some extent been the victim of circumstances and it does seem a little hard that his family should have been deprived of any benefit of his considerable personal possessions.

One thing which the British did after the surrender was to ensure a decent burial for Vans Agnew and Anderson. They were reinterred with full military honours and considerable ceremony within the walls of the fort, where a memorial was erected to them. Then, as soon as possible, General Whish set off with his troops to join the main army in the field, leaving the 11th Bengal Light Cavalry, the 7th Bengal Irregular Cavalry, the 1st Bombay Light Cavalry, the 49th Bengal Native Infantry, the 4th Bombay Rifles and the 9th Bombay Native Infantry, with the necessary ancillary troops, behind as a garrison.

CHAPTER 13

Chillianwalla

W HEN Multan fell the main army was still encamped about Heylah and Gough was determined not to move forward against Shere Singh until General Whish's troops could join him. The delay in crossing the Chenab had given the Sikhs ample time to prepare good defensive positions and any further improvements they could make in this respect would be outweighed by the advantages the additional troops and guns from Multan would give him. Circumstances would however soon occur which would cause Gough to change his mind.

On 7 January, 1849, Lord Dalhousie wrote to him, having heard of the fall of Multan, to say that it would give him great pleasure if he were soon able to announce a similar success on the Jhelum. Gough knew that one of the reasons which had persuaded the Governor-General to advocate a more belligerent attitude was that the delay was having an unfortunate effect upon public opinion in India. Then on 10 January Gough received definite news that Attock had fallen eight days before. This meant that Chuttur Singh's troops, and also Afghan reinforcements from the frontier area, would soon be able to join Shere Singh which would neutralize the advantage of waiting for General Whish's arrival. It had been hoped that Attock would hold out longer, but after a most gallant defence Herbert had been obliged to surrender because of the fears of his Mohammedan garrison, whose families were in Sikh hands and received threats that harm would come to them if they continued to hold out. Apart from the news from Attock, and the Governor-General's obvious wishes, another factor which influenced

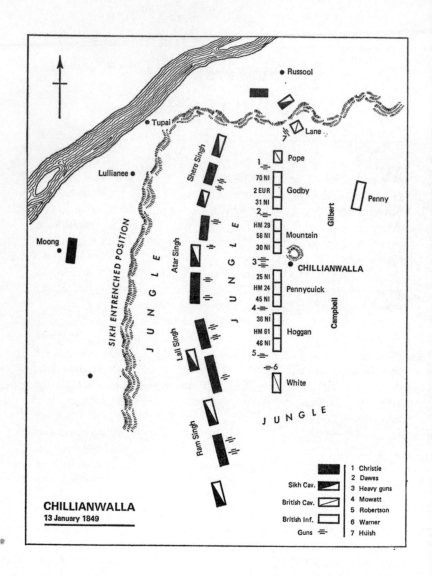

Russool

Tupai

Lullianee

Shere Singh

Moong

SIKH ENTRENCHED POSITION

JUNGLE

Atar Singh

JUNGLE

Lall Singh

Ram Singh

JUNGLE

Lane

Pope
1
70 NI
2 EUR   Godby
31 NI
2
HM 29
56 NI   Mountain
30 NI
3
CHILLIANWALLA
25 NI
HM 24   Pennycuick
45 NI
4
36 NI
HM 61   Hoggan
46 NI
5
6
White

Gilbert   Penny

Campbell

Sikh Cav.
British Cav.
British Inf.
Guns

1 Christie
2 Dawes
3 Heavy guns
4 Mowatt
5 Robertson
6 Warner
7 Huish

CHILLIANWALLA
13 January 1849

Gough was that Sikh agents were busy trying to undermine the loyalty of his sepoys and while he maintained a passive attitude their efforts were more likely to meet with success.

In view of the above considerations Gough decided to take the offensive before General Whish and his troops arrived. On 11 January he notified the Governor-General of his intentions and gave him his outline plan. On the following day he advanced to Dinghi, which was some eight miles to the east of the Sikh position.

Gough was aware that the Sikhs were dug in on a line in the shape of a tulwar with their backs to the River Jhelum. To their left the point of the tulwar was about the village of Russool, which lay at the top of some hills near the river bank. They were reputed to be steep and difficult of access owing to a number of ravines. The line then continued through a string of villages, which lay on a slight ridge near the river, as far as a place called Lucknawalla. Gough aimed to direct his advance on to the village of Chillianwalla, which lay roughly in the centre of this position and about a mile forward of it and where there was known to be water, which did not exist anywhere else on the line of advance. On arrival at Chillianwalla he proposed either to halt, while he made a more thorough reconnaissance, or to attack should circumstances permit. From his briefing of his divisional commanders that evening it would seem that his initial idea was to launch an attack on the high ground at Russool on the Sikh's left flank. It has been suggested that if this were the case he would have been wiser to have aimed his main effort at their more open right flank about Lucknawalla, with the idea of rolling up the Sikh line towards the high ground.

The Army advanced the following morning and the men found the going rather difficult as they were moving through jungle. It was about noon before they approached Chillianwalla, which they found held by a Sikh outpost. This was easily driven in and the 24th seized a mound just beyond the village, the Commanding Officer signalling success by standing on top and waving his sword. Gough as usual was well forward and he himself climbed the mound, where he could see the full extent of the Sikh position from Russool along to Lucknawalla. It

165

was difficult to pick out details owing to the intervening jungle. He decided to halt, camp and carry out a detailed reconnaissance before making his firm plan.

The ground was already being marked out for the camp when suddenly some Sikh guns opened fire, to be followed shortly afterwards by the whole range of their batteries, which had obviously moved forward from the entrenchments into the jungle. Gough at once ordered up his heavy guns to Chillianwalla to reply and gave instructions for his army to deploy. His critics have since painted a picture of a hot-headed Irishman either losing his head on smelling powder or just determined to get into a fight, and flinging his troops upon the Sikh batteries without further consideration. In fact it was Moodkee all over again. Gough had no option but to fight. His only alternative, since the Sikhs were well within range of his camping ground, was to withdraw with the Sikh Army probably in close pursuit and this would have been unthinkable, quite apart from the fact that he needed the water. One can be permitted to wonder how at Chillianwalla it was that the Sikhs were able to open fire without their presence being even suspected and what the large number of cavalry at Gough's disposal had been doing to allow this to happen. Surely the British should have sent out patrols as soon as they arrived in the area.

Actually Gough had very nearly walked into a trap laid for him by Shere Singh. The Sikh general had banked on the fact that the British would make for Chillianwalla with its water supply and that they would camp there while they prepared for an attack on the morrow. He intended to wait until they had settled in, and then open up with his guns achieving, he hoped, complete surprise. He must to some extent have relied on indifferent British reconnaissance. He might have achieved his aim had not some of his guns opened prematurely and disclosed his new position.

The Sikhs were deployed with the Bannu troops under Ram Singh, consisting of one regiment of cavalry and four regiments of infantry with seventeen guns, on the right. Then came the troops commanded by Lall Singh and Atar Singh, consisting of two regiments of cavalry and ten regiments of infantry, of which six were old Khalsa units and four newly formed. This force also had seventeen guns. The left wing of the main line was under the personal command of Shere Singh, who had a regiment of cavalry with four old and five new regiments of infantry and twenty guns, together with the main body of the Ghorchurras. Russool was held by two new infantry regiments and five guns, with more irregular horse. Other irregulars were in rear of the main line around the village of Moong. The total Sikh strength was about 30,000 with 62 guns.

The Sikh front was covered by jungle, with bushes about seven or eight feet high and a number of trees. The Sikhs had posted men in many of the higher trees partly as observers and partly as snipers, their main task being to pick off European officers. In this role they do not seem to have been particularly successful and in general the level of musketry in the Sikh infantry was far from good. It must be noted that nearly half of the Sikh infantry were newly raised troops, not yet battle tested, and not to be compared with the original Khalsa of the first war.

Gough was virtually committed to a frontal attack and he therefore aimed to break through the centre of the Sikh Army. He appreciated that the Sikhs had abandoned their prepared defences and they would hardly have had time to dig in properly. Once again they were fighting with a river at their backs and given sufficient daylight he hoped to drive them into it. He ordered forward his guns and opened up a bombardment, which he decided must be limited to one hour's duration if he was to have sufficient daylight to achieve his object.

On the British left was White's Cavalry Brigade with Warner's horse artillery battery. Then just to the south of Chillianwalla came Campbell's Division, with Hoggan's Brigade on the left and Pennycuick's on the right. It was to be supported by Robertson's field artillery battery, which was on the left of Hoggan, and Mowatt's field battery, which lay between the two brigades. Campbell's third brigade, Penny's, was in force reserve. The heavy guns were in front of Chillianwalla and then came Gilbert's Division with Mountain's Brigade on the left and Godby's on the right. Between them was Dawes field battery and on Godby's right, Christie's horse battery. This battery also had the task of supporting Pope's Cavalry Brigade, which was on the right flank. It now included the 14th Light Dragoons, formerly with White. Pope early on detached a wing from each of the 9th Lancers and the 1st and 6th Bengal Light Cavalry, together with Huish's horse artillery battery, under command of Colonel Lane, an officer of the Bengal Horse Artillery, to watch a number of Sikh Ghorchurras who were on the slopes leading up to Russool. Penny's Brigade was initially placed just north of the mound of Chillianwalla, and was to be used to exploit success. The whole British line was about three miles long, and was overlapped at each end by the Sikhs. Gough had about 12,000 men in the field and was therefore outnumbered by five to two, although this was offset by the fact that most of his troops were better trained and more experienced than the majority of the Sikhs.

Warner's battery on the left flank pushed forward and became heavily engaged with a Sikh battery, well placed to enfilade the advance of Campbell's Division. Some time before the main attack was due to start a staff officer appeared at Robertson's battery, which had been reduced from six to three guns, the other pieces having been sent back in reserve, and ordered him to go to Warner's assistance. Robertson did so, moving some 500 yards to the left, and with the aid of the fire of his heavier weapons the Sikh battery was silenced. This move, however, was to have unfortunate results as far as Campbell's Division was concerned. The whole incident is one of the mysteries of Chillianwalla, for nobody ever succeeded in identifying the anonymous staff officer, although both Robertson and his second-in-command vouched for his appearance. General Thackwell, who was on that flank, denied giving the order. Campbell certainly knew nothing about it and sent an officer to try to find the missing battery after Pennycuick had started his advance. The cavalry on this flank then worked forward, finding the going very difficult in the jungle. They were faced by a considerable number of Ghorchurras. Thackwell ordered the Grey squadron of the 3rd Light Dragoons under Captain Unett, together with the 5th Bengal Light Cavalry, to charge the enemy. The Grey Squadron's charge went home and Unett cut right through his opponents. The 5th Light Cavalry failed to come on. There are very contradictory reports of its behaviour but it seems that afterwards it did rally on the 8th Light Cavalry behind it. Whatever happened, Unett appears to have been left to go it alone. Having charged through his enemy, he charged back again, suffering a number of casualties, particularly as the jungle prevented him from keeping his men together. The British cavalry on this flank appear to have neutralized their opponents more or less successfully but, as will be seen, were unable to prevent some attacks against the flank of Campbell's infantry.

As soon as the bombardment stopped the infantry prepared to go forward. Colin Campbell considered that the jungle was too thick for him to control both his brigades and he therefore decided to accompany Hoggan and to leave Pennycuick to act on his own. This was, to say the least of it, an unfortunate decision, and is difficult to justify in view of the fact that Gilbert controlled his Division throughout the battle. Campbell may have been influenced by the fact that Hoggan was reputedly extremely short-sighted; at least one account refers to him as being 'as blind as a bat'. The fact remains that Campbell fought the battle as a brigadier and not as a divisional commander. He also told the 24th not to fire, but to go in and take its objective with the bayonet. Captain Blachford, who was fated to take command of the Regiment in the later stages of the battle, quotes him as saying, 'Let it be said the 24th stormed the guns without firing a shot.' He relates that afterwards Campbell told him he was very sorry he had said this. Campbell had earlier told members of the Regiment that he remembered the 24th carrying out an attack in just this way in the Peninsular War and said how much he admired them. Several contemporary accounts claim that the 24th did not even load. Others who were present claim that it did so and there is evidence that, although the Regiment did not fire a volley, as was usual before delivering a charge, some individuals did fire in the course of the attack. The explanation for this conflict of evidence is almost certainly that the 24th had loaded in the morning when it arrived at Chillianwalla and was about to seize the mound which was thought to be held by the enemy. Witnesses may well have seen other regiments loading before the attack went in, noticed that the 24th, whose men were by then already loaded, was not doing

169

so and therefore assumed that the men went into the attack with nothing in the barrel.

Pennycuick's Brigade was formed up with the 24th in the centre, the 25th Bengal Native Infantry on the right and the 45th on the left. The 24th, for some reason that has never been explained, but presumably because its Commanding Officer thought it was good for morale, was in full dress, the men wearing their tall Albert Shakos. It also took with it its antelope mascot. The Regiment advanced with great 'elan', moving very fast and soon leaving the native regiments on its flanks behind it. It had nearly half a mile to go before it reached the enemy. The jungle was partly open at first, but it soon grew thicker and broke up the Regiment's formation, while the branches of the trees constantly knocked off the men's shakos—a small point, but one not calculated to help the maintenance of discipline during the advance. Sikh snipers in the trees also caused trouble and, with orders not to fire, there could be no retaliation. To make matters worse the Brigade appears to have veered somewhat to the right and to have lost contact with Mowatt's battery, which was supposed to support it. The blame for this must lie partly with Colin Campbell, who had failed to give any proper orders to his gunners. Eventually the 24th came into a clearing in the jungle with the Sikhs ahead on a little ridge about six feet high. The direct approach was blocked by several ponds with steep sides, round which the men had to make their way, and reports speak of two companies filing to the rear to find an alternative route round the obstacle. A further difficulty was that over the last patch of jungle the Sikh grapeshot had blown all the foliage off the trees, and while the Sikh gunners could see them coming the men of the 24th were still impeded by the low branches which remained. Under a hail of fire from the Sikhs the 24th pressed on.

The Grenadier Company on the right had found a clearer patch of jungle and penetrated the Sikh position first on its own, was driven out, but quickly came back again and captured and spiked two or three guns. The rest of the Regiment was not far behind. Pennycuick, at the head of his Brigade, was killed. Colonel Brookes, the Commanding Officer, fell, as soon as he reached the Sikh position. All members of the Colour Party were killed and the Colours temporarily disappeared from view. There had been tremendously heavy casualties and considerable confusion not unnaturally prevailed. The men set about spiking the Sikh guns, but there was little control and no proper consolidation.

An immediate Sikh counter-attack was launched and the survivors of the 24th gave way and made their way back to Chillianwalla, the Ghorchurras pursuing them a short way. The Regiment had lost 231 killed, and 236 wounded, of whom thirteen of the killed and ten of the wounded were officers. The great majority of these casualties occurred in only a few minutes; the time that elapsed between their breaking out of the jungle and being driven back into it again. Pennycuick's son, who was serving with the Regiment as an ensign, was among those killed; he was last seen standing over his father's body and defending it against the oncoming Sikhs. The Regimental Colour was brought out of action by a private soldier. The Queen's Colour was never found. One theory is that a private, who was subsequently killed, wrapped it round his body, the staff having broken, and that he was buried with the Colour still round him. Possibly it was at the bottom of a pond. There is no evidence that it fell into Sikh hands. Among other bodies found well forward later on was that of one of the regimental bhisties. The 24th was re-formed by Captain Blachford and advanced later in the day, but not in time to take any further part in the battle.

Both native regiments were also repulsed. The 25th, which seems to have gone in with rather more enthusiasm than the regiment on the left, hit the Sikh position not very long after the 24th had recoiled. An allegation that it did not 'come on' at all is belied by its casualties. It lost 3 officers and 201 other ranks, while the 45th lost 4 officers and 75 other ranks. The 25th lost both its Colours and the 45th, which had an extra honorary Colour, two out of the three. Both regiments fell back towards their start line. Captain Clarke kept the rifle company of the 25th together, and about 100 men of the 45th rallied round the remaining Colour and were later led forward and joined up with General Gilbert's Division. One little story about the brigade attack is worth relating. An officer was lying wounded, having been hit in the early stages of the advance. A horse which he had recently sold to a brother officer came by riderless and, recognizing him, stopped, allowing him to mount and get away.

Hoggan's Brigade had deployed with the 61st in the centre, the 36th Native Infantry on the right and the 46th on the left. The men of the 61st were wearing their flat Kilmarnock caps, but with white covers, thus being distinguishable from the native regiments which had no covers on their caps. The advance of the Brigade, which had about eight hundred yards to cover, was steadily controlled. Fortunately the jungle was not quite so thick as that which had faced the 24th. Visibility was a maximum fifty yards. Robertson's battery, which should have supported the Brigade, had disappeared and, although the advancing troops did not know it, had contributed to the easing of their task by helping to silence the big Sikh battery away to their left, which would have enfiladed them. They did receive considerable assistance from Mowatt's battery which, having lost Pennycuick, did its best to support Hoggan, Mowatt bringing his guns up on the flank to open fire within about 160 yards of the enemy. The Sikh guns opened up when the advancing line was about four hundred yards away, but fortunately, perhaps because their view was obscured by the trees, the gunners fired high and so inflicted few casualties. The 61st broke cover from the jungle about eighty yards from the Sikh line and found itself facing cavalry. It halted briefly, fired an effective volley, charged and carried the Sikh position, capturing a number of Sikh guns. The 36th Native Infantry on its right came up against Sikh infantry, met with a repulse and broke back to the rear, losing its Colours, which were dropped in the jungle. The Sikhs pursued for a short distance. It appears to have got behind the 61st and to have remained in a state of confusion shouting and firing in the air and taking no further part in the battle. Meanwhile the 46th Native Infantry on the left had reached the Sikh position and had promptly been attacked by cavalry, whom it most gallantly repulsed.

With the repulse of the 36th Native Infantry, the right flank of the 61st was uncovered and was promptly attacked by Sikh infantry. Colin Campbell wheeled the two right-hand companies to meet this threat and drove the Sikhs back. The same movement forced the withdrawal of those who were following up the

36th. Campbell himself was wounded at this point, but not seriously enough to leave the field. The whole regiment then wheeled to face right. It was attacked by further Sikh infantry, a part of Atar Singh's command, whose assault was met and repulsed. One of the regiments which made the attack was seen marching across the front of the 46th Native Infantry, as it wheeled into line, at about one hundred yards distance in perfect order and despite the regiment's fire. No sooner had the infantry been repulsed than a cavalry attack came in on the Brigade's original left. The 61st faced about and drove them off as they did a further attack a little later. The 46th Native Infantry, which had been holding its own splendidly against the Sikh cavalry, now joined up with the 61st and the two regiments swept along the Sikh front, clearing the part of the line from which Pennycuick had been repulsed. They eventually joined up with Brigadier Mountain's Brigade advancing from the opposite direction. The 61st had spiked and captured thirteen guns, although only three were actually brought off the field. Regimental accounts again speak of the gallantry of the Sikh gunners and mention is made of one gun which was harnessed up and got away when the advancing troops had almost reached it.

At about the time Hoggan made his junction with Mountain, Robertson's battery reappeared, together with Warner's horse battery and an escort of a Squadron of the 8th Bengal Light Cavalry, having been sent across by Thackwell. Shortly afterwards the whole of White's Cavalry Brigade followed and took post in the British centre in front of Chillianwalla and in rear of Hoggan's and Mountain's Brigades.

On the left of Gilbert's Division, just to the north of Chillianwalla, Mountain's Brigade had advanced with HM's 29th on the right, the 56th Native Infantry in the centre and the 30th on the left. The men of the 29th were, like the 61st, wearing their Kilmarnock caps and shell jackets and each company had two spikes with it to put the enemy guns out of action. The jungle was pretty thick, with a good deal of undergrowth and bushes about head high and with a number of trees scattered about. A number of casualties were caused by Sikh snipers in these trees. As the Brigade, which was well supported by

Dawes's battery, approached the clearing in front of the Sikh position it was met by a storm of grape and the centre of the Regimental Colour of the 29th was shot out. The regiment had come up against one of the main Sikh batteries. On clearing the jungle it paused for a moment, fired a volley and charged. As it approached, the Sikh infantry, who were in trenches, were seen throwing away their muskets and taking out their tulwars. The 29th charged home and the Sikh infantry fell back, turning to fire as they did so, but as usual the Sikh gunners fought with great gallantry, in many cases seizing their opponents bayonets with their bare hands. Two Sikh guns further to the left which enfiladed them were captured by separate parties of the regiment, one led by the Commanding Officer, Congreve, and another by a subaltern of the Light Company. The regiment claimed the capture of twelve guns.

At the time the 29th seemed isolated, for it had both flanks in the air. The 56th Native Infantry, having lost its Commander and a number of British officers, was charged and overrun by Sikh cavalry. The Grenadier Company stood fast, but the remainder fell away to the rear. They subsequently rallied and, moving to the right, joined Godby's Brigade. Meanwhile the 29th wheeled left, but it was almost immediately counter-attacked from its original right by Sikh infantry. Wheeling about it charged and drove off the attackers. No sooner had this been done than the regiment was attacked in rear by Sikh cavalry. It again faced about and dealt with this new threat. It then moved left to join up with the 30th Native Infantry and the Grenadier Company of the 56th and advanced along the Sikh position. The Brigade had also been joined by the 31st Native Infantry, which had somehow become detached from Godby, and it moved along the line of the Sikh defences until it met Hoggan's Brigade coming the other way. Both Brigades then faced their original front. Mountain's Brigade had suffered heavier loses than any other in the battle and both its native regiments had had higher casualties than had the 29th, those of the 56th being 330, and the 30th just under 300. The 56th lost both its Colours, and the 30th lost one.

Once his Division was fairly launched, General Gilbert had been compelled to give most of his attention to his right brigade.

Brigadier Pope's cavalry had met with a disaster and Gilbert's right flank was completely in the air as a result. Godby's Brigade had deployed with the 2nd Bengal Europeans in the centre, with the 70th Native Infantry on the right and the 31st on the left. It had advanced steadily, the visibility of the jungle being about twenty yards, and suffered less from Sikh artillery fire than did Mountain's Brigade. However, to meet the threat from his right Gilbert had to order Godby to refuse his flank. It seems that the 70th Native Infantry halted and formed square and that as the Brigade reached the enemy position, which it cleared successfully, the two right companies of the 2nd Europeans had to be thrown back to protect it from the threat in that direction. The Brigade had struck the Sikh line some little time later than Mountain and like him had received support from Dawes' battery. The Europeans were consolidating the position and collecting their wounded when they were suddenly fired on from their rear, the Sikhs from the flank having worked right round behind them. The regiment faced about and Dawes swung round his guns and scattered some Sikh cavalry, forming up to charge, with grape shot. At this point General Gilbert rode up and seeing Major Steele, who was commanding the 2nd Europeans, said to him very coolly, 'Well Major, how are you? Do you think you are near enough to give those fellows a charge?' Steele replied, 'By all means', and Gilbert then said, 'Well let us see how you can do it.' The Europeans charged with a will and after a short struggle overran their opponents. They then halted facing right and continued to fire steadily, aiming low, at other Sikh troops who threatened them, keeping them at a distance. The 70th Native Infantry, now on their right, remained in square and suffered only light casualties, not having been seriously attacked. One report by an officer of the 2nd Europeans describes the 70th as 'blazing away at anything and everything'. It will be remembered that the other regiment of this Brigade, the 31st Native Infantry, had somehow veered away to the left in the jungle and had joined up with Mountain.

Meanwhile Penny's Brigade had been ordered forward by the Commander-in-Chief to replace Pennycuick, but it lost direction in the jungle and arrived in the area in which Godby was fighting.

It was also attacked in the flank, in front and in the rear, but the ubiquitous Dawes, who always seemed to have his guns just where they were needed, arrived and assisted in driving off the enemy. Penny's Brigade seems to have made its way over the ground on which the 2nd Europeans had made their last attack and to have found that many of their wounded had been murdered by the Sikhs. This made the 2nd Europeans determined that they would take no Sikh prisoners for the rest of the campaign. Penny eventually reached the Sikh position to fill the gap which had now occurred between Mountain and Godby.

The sequence of events in the cavalry disaster which had uncovered Gilbert's right flank is perhaps the most difficult to establish in what was overall an extremely confusing battle. When something goes seriously wrong on the battlefield all those concerned are at pains to justify their actions and tend to throw the blame on somebody else. Thus in this instance, understandably, contemporary accounts vary widely. The most likely version of what actually happened appears to be as follows. Brigadier Pope, who had no experience at all of handling large bodies of cavalry, formed his Brigade in one single line with no supports or reserves at all. He had on the left four squadrons of the 14th Light Dragoons, whose right flank was to direct the advance. Then came one and a half squadrons each of the 1st and 6th Bengal Light Cavalry and on the right two squadrons of the 9th Lancers, these three last units having all detached a wing to operate towards Russool under Colonel Lane. The Brigade was supported by Christie's horse artillery battery, which was positioned on its left flank. The whole Brigade moved forward at a trot into the jungle, but it found the going very difficult and the trot soon became a walk. The advancing line somehow veered towards the left, got in front of Christie's guns and completely masked them. Possibly Pope was over-anxious to keep in touch with the advancing infantry, although he was in fact ahead of them. Realizing that he had masked his supporting guns, it seems that he gave the order 'threes right' in order to clear their front, his whole line at that moment having almost come to a halt. Just at this time a body of about fifty Sikh cavalry were seen ahead. The Commanding Officer of the 14th Light Dragoons urged Pope to charge the Sikhs. Then three things

19 The Maharajah Dhuleep Singh

20 Sikh Guns and Elephants

21 The Surrender of the Sikhs to the British

seem to have happened very quickly. Pope himself was wounded; some officers of the Bengal Light Cavalry, who had ridden about fifty yards ahead of the line, finding themselves close to the Sikh horse and unsupported, turned and came galloping back; and someone shouted the order 'threes about'. No one has ever established with certainty who first gave this order, but the majority of accounts agree that it appeared to come from the Light Cavalry. Whatever its origin the order was obeyed and the Brigade turned its back on the enemy, who promptly charged. In a moment the whole British line was galloping to the rear, some men apparently riding over Christie's guns, which fell into the hands of the pursuing Sikhs, Christie himself being mortally wounded. The cavalry came pounding back to their start line and, although the Europeans rallied in the administrative area, took no further part in the battle. The native regiments seem to have disappeared from the field entirely. A number of troopers were held up at pistol point by Gough's Chaplain and the Commander-in-Chief afterwards said he much regretted he could not 'make him a Brevet Bishop'.

Panic, which undoubtedly seized most of the Brigade on this occasion, is a most contagious thing, sometimes arising from quite inexplicable reasons. It is fortunately a rare occurrence in the British Army, but it does happen and sometimes surprisingly good regiments are affected. The officer commanding the wing of the 9th Lancers, Hope Grant, who does appear to have pulled his squadrons together pretty quickly, was to go on to have a most distinguished career and to be one of the heroes of the Indian Mutiny. The Commanding Officer of the 14th Light Dragoons unfortunately shot himself some months later, upset by quite unjustified slurs on his personal courage.

The cavalry away to the right under Lane took no part in the fighting. Their task was to watch the bodies of Sikh horse on the slopes above Russool and indeed these Ghorchurras twice endeavoured to launch an attack against them. One account speaks of them 'rushing down the hillside through the jungle like a mountain torrent'. In each case, however, their attack was broken up by Huish's horse artillery guns and the cavalry remained dismounted for most of the time. Lane has been severely criticized for not intervening more actively to protect

177

the right flank and particularly for not coming to the assistance of the hard pressed infantry after Pope's debacle. It is only fair to point out in his defence that he had been given the definite task of neutralizing the Sikhs about Russool and that he did this successfully. On the other hand, although the jungle probably hid from him the full extent of the disaster to Pope's Brigade, he must have realized that something had gone seriously wrong. He had already broken up an attempt by the Ghorchurras from Russool to advance and with a horse artillery battery and the equivalent of one and a half regiments of completely fresh cavalry available, it does seem that a commander with more initiative might have taken some positive action to relieve the pressure on Gilbert's men.

However serious the situation may have seemed to Godby's hard-pressed troops on the right, the battle had in fact already been won. Mountain's and Hoggan's Brigades were firmly established on the Sikh position and White's cavalry were in support of them. The main body of the Sikhs was withdrawing in some confusion to its original position along the banks of the Jhelum. Those facing Godby and Penny soon conformed, going off towards Russool and being shelled by Huish's horse artillery battery from Lane's detachment as they did so. Darkness was now coming on and there was no question of the exhausted British troops trying to follow them up.

Gough's inclination was to hold the ground he had won with a view to advancing as soon as possible next morning, but he was strongly advised by some of his officers and particularly Campbell to draw back to Chillianwalla to obtain water. He gave way on this point although he said firmly 'I am damned if I will move until all my wounded are safe' and the force did not move back to Chillianwalla until it was reported that all the surviving casualties had been found. When the troops had reached the ground on which it had been originally intended that they should bivouac, Gough rode round the various regiments and received a tremendous ovation from his men. The British losses were given as 2,331 of all ranks.

The decision to withdraw, which would have not been necessary if the administrative arrangements had been such that it was possible to bring forward water for the men, had unfortunate

178

results. Finding the British had gone, the Sikhs came forward again during the night and removed all the guns which they had lost as well as four of the six which had formed Christie's battery. The remaining two of Christie's guns were saved by the initiative of an artillery subaltern named Cookworthy, who took forward a party during the night and brought them back. At the time he did so the other four were still there. It is likely also that at this time the Sikhs secured some of the Colours which had been lost in the jungle. They also seem to have murdered some wounded, who had been overlooked in the darkness, and certainly when the British troops searched the battlefield next day, many of the dead were found stripped naked and some of their bodies were badly mutilated. It is possible, however, that this was done not by the Sikh troops but by local villagers. It is noteworthy that the Sikhs returned two privates of the 9th Lancers, who had got lost in the jungle and had been captured, unharmed after the battle. Shere Singh also allowed a Lieutenant Bowie, who had been captured in Derajat and was in his camp, to visit his compatriots on parole, just as his father Chuttur Singh had allowed George Lawrence to go to Lahore also on parole.

Gough's intention of resuming the battle next day was frustrated by tremendously heavy rain, which was to last for three or four days and which, apart from making everyone wretched, inhibited further movement. This was unfortunate, for the Sikh General, Elihu Baksh, who was to desert to the British a short time afterwards, expressed the opinion that the Sikhs were so shaken that any attack would undoubtedly have driven them into the Jhelum. As it was they drew off from their riverside position in the villages of Tupai, Lallianee and Moong and concentrated at Russool.

The news that the British had lost four guns and a number of Colours, and had had pretty severe casualties created a very bad impression both in India and at home. These facts, together with the realization that the Sikh Army was still in being and in the same area, caused people to assume that the battle had been a defeat, and that the blame rested squarely on the shoulders of the Commander-in-Chief. Once again it was said that he had thrown his unfortunate infantry on the enemy with no preparation and regardless of casualties. People remembered the 'We'll be at them with the bayonet' story. Lord Dalhousie wrote privately that 'the conduct of the battle was beneath the contempt even of a militiaman like myself'. The authorities at home at once took steps to replace Gough by Sir Charles Napier; but before the news of this decision reached the Army, the decisive battle of Gujerat had completely altered the situation.

Gough had been largely the victim of circumstances over which he had no control. The main fault which can justly be blamed on him is that he allowed his Army so nearly to walk into a trap and found himself in much the same situation as he had at Moodkee just over two years before. Once he was in that situation he had no option but to attack. The availability of daylight limited the length of his artillery preparation. He could hardly be held responsible for Campbell's failure to control his Division, for Pennycuick's impetuous unsupported advance, nor for the unfortunate 'no firing' order which contributed to its repulse. He could not foresee that Pope's Brigade would gallop from the field leaving his flank uncovered and he can hardly be blamed for the torrential rain which bogged down his intended advance on the morrow. Had these things not happened it is distinctly possible that Chillianwalla would have been decisive and brought the war to an end. One thing is certain. Whatever the critics might be saying in Calcutta or London, the men he led, especially his European infantry, upon whom as ever the brunt of the struggle had largely fallen, felt they had beaten the Sikhs at Chillianwalla and were confident that the old man in the white coat would lead them to victory again.

CHAPTER 14

Gujerat

THE three days of torrential rain after Chillianwalla having prevented Gough from following up the enemy, he was now determined to wait for the arrival of General Whish's troops from Multan before he engaged Shere Singh again. The Sikh leader had been joined by his father Chuttur Singh and thus had an even more marked superiority. Moreover his position at Russool was a very strong one. He suffered from one serious disadvantage, which Gough fully realized, in that he could not maintain his troops in the barren hills along the Jhelum and sooner or later he would have to break out and make for the more fertile areas near the Chenab. This would give Gough a chance to meet him in the open field. His political adviser, Major Mackeson, did urge him to attack, but Gough was firm in his decision. Mackeson may well have been influenced by the reports brought in by Elihu Baksh, the Sikh artillery commander, who, as already related, came over to the British about three days after the battle, bringing with him his two sons and one of the Sikh cavalry commanders, Amir Khan. All his party were, like himself, Mohammedans. They painted a picture of low morale in the Sikh army and gave as their reason for desertion the fact that they felt they were no longer trusted, which could be taken as a sign of a possible split between Sikh and Mohammedan elements.

The British threw up breastworks to defend their camp at Chillianwalla, there being the usual complaints from the European troops that the sepoys would not do their fair share of the digging, and waited upon events. There was a good deal

181

of cavalry skirmishing in which the British came off best, including one particularly successful action on 30 January, when a party of the 9th Bengal Irregular Cavalry under Lieutenant Chamberlain, the future Field-Marshal, killed sixteen of the enemy, Chamberlain himself being wounded. Shere Singh in his strong position, realizing his supply difficulties and knowing full well that Gough would be reinforced, was anxious to tempt the British to attack him. Early in February he moved a part of his army out of the hills to Khoree, which lay to the west and equally distant from Russool and Chillianwalla. From there he moved forward some troops to a place called Nur Jemal, whence they were in a position to threaten Dinghi, through which Gough's communications ran. The British Commander-in-Chief, however, contented himself by watching the Sikh movements with a screen of cavalry and declined to be tempted. Shere Singh thereupon withdrew his forward elements and made a demonstration towards the British camp. Again Gough contented himself by sending out a few squadrons of cavalry to contain the enemy. This was on 12 February and shortly afterwards Chamberlain's Irregulars brought off a very successful raid against the Sikhs, in which they got away with about eighty camels.

Early on the morning of 4 February Shere Singh evacuated Russool and moved off with his army to the south-east in the direction of Gujerat, which lay about six miles from the Chenab due north of Wazirabad. This was also the route to Lahore and it was the move which Gough had expected him to make in order to take advantage of the fertile country around Gujerat. If Shere Singh had any intention of making for Lahore, he had probably missed his chance of doing so immediately after the battle. He had, however, been convinced that Gough would attack him in his position at Russool and had been loath to take the offensive. He did send forward a detachment to probe the crossings over the Chenab in the Wazirabad area, but by that time there were British forces on the far bank and he could hardly take the risk of making an opposed crossing with Gough coming up in his rear. He was therefore content to offer battle in a defensive position in which Gough would have to attack him. By adopting this strategy he may have thrown away his

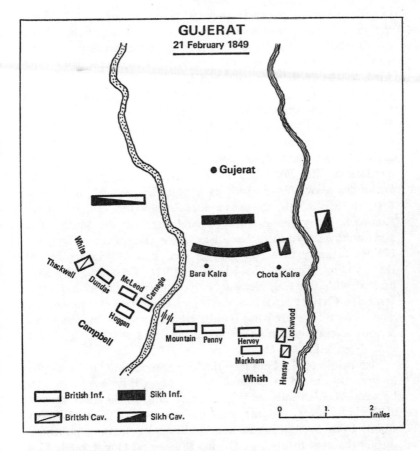

GUJERAT
21 February 1849

Gujerat

White

Thackwell

Dundas

McLeod

Carnegie

Hoggan

Campbell

Bara Kalra

Chota Kalra

Mountain   Penny   Hervey

Markham

Lockwood

Hearsay

Whish

British Inf.   Sikh Inf.

British Cav.   Sikh Cav.

0   1   2 miles

last possible chance of success; for he knew that Gough would soon be much stronger and that this was the final opportunity he had to meet him in the field with a distinct numerical advantage.

Shere Singh's departure seems to have taken Gough by surprise and it was some time before it was realized that the Sikhs had gone. At first it was not known for certain which direction they had taken—a further instance of the indifferent British reconnaissance, which had been apparent throughout the campaign. As soon as the situation clarified, the Commander-in-Chief took steps to secure the Wazirabad crossing, despatching

183

two regiments of irregular cavalry there and ordering General Whish, who had himself already arrived at Ramnuggar ahead of his troops, to send the 53rd with a native infantry regiment and one regiment of irregular cavalry to the same spot. The 53rd, less some detachments, had been moved up from Lahore to Ramnuggar at the beginning of February, having been relieved in the capital by the 98th, which had arrived from British India. There were also three regiments of native infantry and some irregular cavalry at Ramnuggar. At the time Whish arrived Wazirabad does not seem to have been properly garrisoned. The Sikhs had in fact selected the ford at Sudra, five miles above Wazirabad, as a possible crossing place. The first British troops to arrive there were the Guides under Lumsden. They found a few Ghorchurras on the south bank and rapidly drove them back across the river again. When the Guides Infantry came up they erected breastworks to defend the crossing. During the night of 15-16 February, the 53rd arrived with the 13th Bengal Native Infantry, the 12th Bengal Irregular Cavalry and two guns, and the crossing was secure. The Sikhs on the far bank numbered about 6,000, but made no serious attempt to cross when they realized that the ford was now defended.

Meanwhile on 15 February the Commander-in-Chief with the main army moved to Lassorie, which lay a little over half-way between Chillianwalla and Sadulapore and on the 16th arrived at the latter. Next day the leading elements of General Whish's troops from Multan joined him, additional columns coming up during the next three days. During this period Gough moved by short marches towards the Sikh position at Gujerat and by the evening of 20 February he was concentrated about Shadiwal, roughly three miles from the Sikhs. When he was about half-way to Chillianwalla Gough had sent back all the heavy baggage, thus getting rid of something like 8,000 camels. The men were in excellent heart and had been cheered, after spending some time in the barren country near the Jhelum, to find, as they approached Gujerat, intensive cultivation with fields of cotton and corn. The men from Multan were in equally good heart, although inevitably rather tired. They had not dawdled on the way, for they had covered 235 miles in eighteen days, fifty of them in the last two. They had met no opposition en route, although in the early stages of their march it had been thought that they might have to assault the fortified town of Cheniote, which was held by Narain Singh, who was a fervent supporter of Mulraj. The town had been blockaded for some time by the forces of Imam-ud-Din. The troops from Multan heard firing as they approached, but on their arrival Narain Singh surrendered without further trouble.

The Sikh army held a position about 3,000 yards from the walled city of Gujerat between two nullahs. That on their left, which ran down to the Chenab, was wet with a very boggy bottom, which made it difficult for cavalry to cross. That on the right was dry. Two villages were held as strong points, Bara (Big) Kalra, which lay rather forward of the main position and not far from the dry nullah and Chota (Small) Kalra, which was close to the wet nullah. The position was held by infantry interspersed with artillery, there being two big batteries emplaced close to Bara Kalra. The Sikh line was described by some observers as crescent shaped. The infantry do not appear to have dug in. There were some cavalry in rear of Chota Kalra, but the majority of the horsemen were on the far sides of the two nullahs with the main strength, including most of the Afghan horse under Akram Khan, on the right beyond the dry nullah. The ground in front of the position was well cultivated, being mainly young corn with little scattered patches of sugar cane.

There had been no changes among the Regiments Gough had brought with him from Chillianwalla, but some of the brigades had new commanders. Brigadier Godby had, to the very great regret of his Brigade, been sent to command in Lahore and Penny had taken over from him. In Campbell's Division Brigadiers Carnegie and McLeod had taken over from Penny and Pennycuick. General Whish had brought with him from Multan Markham's Brigade, with HM's 32nd and the 51st and 72nd Bengal Native Infantry, and Hervey's Brigade with HM's 10th and the 8th and 52nd Bengal Native Infantry. The Bombay Contingent under Dundas consisted of HM's 60th Rifles, the Bombay Fusiliers and the 3rd and 19th Bombay Native Infantry. The Scinde Horse and four other irregular regiments had been added to the cavalry. Brigadier Tennant now had ninety-six guns, eighteen of heavy calibre. For the first time Gough was superior in artillery to his opponent. Colonel Cheape had taken over as Chief Engineer to the force.

The British deployed with Lockwood's (formerly Pope's) Cavalry Brigade and the Irregular Cavalry Brigade of Brigadier Hearsay on the right, with their flanks resting on the wet nullah. Then came General Whish's Division, with Hervey's Brigade leading and Markham's in support. Next was Gilbert's Division with Penny's Brigade on the right and Mountain's on the left. Across the dry nullah came General Campbell's Division with Carnegie's Brigade on the right, McLeod's on the left and Hoggan's in reserve, with the task also of supporting the Bombay Contingent, which was on Campbell's left. General Thackwell himself commanded the cavalry on this flank, consisting of White's Brigade, which now had the 9th Lancers instead of the 5th Bengal Light Cavalry, and the two Regiments of Scinde Horse. The heavy battery of eighteen guns was positioned on Gilbert's left next to the dry nullah. Whish had with him Dawes's field battery and altogether five troops of horse artillery. There were two troops of horse artillery with the cavalry on the right. Across the dry nullah Campbell had the field batteries of Ludlow and Robertson, while Dundas had Blood's battery of Bombay Horse Artillery. There were two troops of horse artillery with the cavalry on the left. There was a force reserve of two regiments of Bengal Light Cavalry, two regiments of Bengal Native Infantry and a Bombay field battery in rear of the army.

On the morning of 21 February the British advanced against Shere Singh's army at 0730. An example of the spirit which animated the force was given by Lieutenant Sandford of the 2nd Europeans, who was sick and had himself carried in a doolie during the advance, taking his place with his company when the fighting started. It was a gloriously clear morning and as they moved forward the men could see in front of them the city of Gujerat and beyond it as a backcloth the white-capped mountains of the Himalayas. Not long before 0900 the Sikh batteries opened fire before the British were within range, and thus disclosed their positions. Gough at once halted his infantry and sent his guns forward to engage the enemy. This they did with a will and appropriately enough the first shot was fired by Dawes, the hero of Chillianwalla. Colonel Stephenson's heavy guns, which were all elephant drawn, were as boldly handled as any of the others. Everyone remarked upon the speed with which they got into action. Away to the left, Blood's Bombay battery, seen in action for the first time by most of the Bengal troops, also drew particular praise. The gunners suffered heavy casualties and indeed in this battle the proportion of losses among the artillery was higher than among the infantry. Fordyce's battery, which came up against the heavy Sikh guns around Bara Kalra, twice had to draw back to replenish men and horses. It appears also to have been threatened by parties of Sikh infantry, since one company from each of the battalions of Penny's Brigade was sent forward to support it. These troops seem to have suffered almost the only infantry casualties in this phase of the battle. At first the artillery contest appeared to be fairly even, but gradually the British guns got on top and battery after battery of the Sikh artillery was silenced. Shortly after 1100 Gough judged that the artillery preparation had been sufficient and indeed it was quite apparent that the British guns had at long last mastered those of the Sikhs. He thereupon gave the order for the whole line to advance and this they did with the gunners still moving ahead by bounds.

While the bombardment was in progress the Sikh cavalry on both sides of the wet nullah had moved forward to try and turn the British right flank. As they searched for places to cross the nullah they worked well down towards the Chenab and Hearsay's Irregular Brigade facing them was also drawn down towards the river. Lockwood's Brigade, which consisted of the 14th Light Dragoons, the 1st Bengal Light Cavalry and the 11th Bengal Irregular Cavalry, had the primary task of covering Brigadier Hervey's flank, and its horse artillery battery inflicted a number of casualties on those Sikhs who were on the near side of the nullah. The Sikhs did at one time get close enough to Hervey's infantry to be engaged with musketry, the two native regiments forming square, although the 10th remained in line; but they were soon forced away by the British cavalry. The British cavalry tactics were not to close with the enemy, but to cover all their possible lines of approach. The horse artillery kept them at bay. A small party of about thirty Afghan horsemen did break through the net and make straight for the point where the Commander-in-Chief was watching the progress of the battle. They were engaged by the troop of 5th Bengal Light Cavalry which was acting as his escort and it is claimed that none of them escaped to tell the tale.

On the right the advance of Hervey's Brigade was directed upon Chota Kalra and as it went forward it received splendid support from its gunners, constantly moving on to close the range. There was a moment of concern when it looked as if some of the Sikh cavalry might again slip in on the flank, but they were successfully dealt with by the artillery. The 10th stormed the village, ably supported by the 8th Bengal Native Infantry, and after a tough fight drove out the Sikhs. The line of advance had diverged from that of the right brigade of Gilbert's Division, directed upon Bara Kalra, and this left a gap through which it was feared the Sikhs might infiltrate. The 52nd Bengal Native Infantry was 'refused' to meet this danger, until Markham's Brigade could be brought up to fill the gap. Immediately after it arrived, Markham's Brigade was able to help deal effectively with a Sikh counter-attack. Anderson's battery, which was native manned, had behaved splendidly but had suffered such heavy casualties that for a short time it had to be withdrawn from Chota Kalra after its capture and the 10th had to provide men to help work its guns when it went forward again. Fordyce's battery, which had positioned itself between Chota Kalra and Bara Kalra, did excellent service, again with heavy losses.

The attack of Penny's Brigade on Bara Kalra was led by the 2nd Europeans well supported by the 70th Bengal Native Infantry. The Sikhs fought desperately and held out to the last man in some of the mud houses in the village. In many cases the attackers got on to the roofs and knocked holes into the rooms below. The village was finally cleared, three Sikh standards being captured. The 31st Bengal Native Infantry had been ordered to remain in reserve until the village was actually taken and it suffered considerably from the fire of a Sikh battery, which had not yet been knocked out, and particularly from two guns firing grape. When it was ordered forward, it stormed the battery which had been giving it so much trouble. The Regiment had suffered 140 casualties. The Brigade had not long been established in Bara Kalra when the Sikhs were seen forming up for a counter-attack, just at the moment when Fordyce's battery, which had been so useful to it, had been withdrawn in order to replenish its ammunition. However Fordyce galloped back just in time and broke up the Sikh attack before it could come in.

What was intended to be the main Sikh counter-attack was designed to come roughly down the line of the dry nullah, directed approximately at the point of junction of Gilbert's and Campbell's Divisions. The Sikhs had massed in the nullah, where they were caught by the guns of Campbell's Division, suffering many losses, and the attack never got going. Very few of Campbell's men fired a shot during the battle.

The cavalry on the Sikh right flank seem to have been less offensively minded than those on their left and some accounts infer that it was only the Afghan elements who showed real fight. A few of the latter did make a determined dash for our heavy guns, but were broken up by artillery fire. Some got close enough to Campbell's waiting infantry to be engaged with musketry by HM's 24th, a few individuals even getting through only to be killed, although one of them succeeded in first killing a political officer. At one stage the 3rd Light Dragoons 'presented a front' to a body of Sikhs, who were escorting a battery of six guns, and retired, drawing them on till they were well within range of the 60th Rifles. Unaware of the presence of the riflemen, they went into action, but were promptly swept with a storm of fire from the 60th and all the gunners were knocked out. The Light Dragoons then trotted forward and spiked the guns. The Sikh cavalry on this flank was still hovering in a threatening manner when it was charged by the Scinde Horse, with a squadron of the 9th Lancers on its flank and another in support. The charge crashed into a mass of mainly Afghan horse, considerably superior to the attackers in number. For about two minutes there was a fierce melee and then the Afghans broke and, with the main body of cavalry on this flank, went galloping back through the Sikh camp, hotly pursued by the Scinde Horse, which had captured two standards in its charge, and by White's Brigade. The 9th Lancers also claimed two standards and had the satisfaction of recapturing a British gun which had been lost at Chillianwalla.

By 1230 the battle was over and the whole Sikh line was in retreat. The infantry withdrew from the field in orderly fashion, though later many units lost cohesion. They had fought well, but they had been shaken by the British bombardment and overborne by the well-supported attack. It appears that once again the Sikh leaders were among the first to quit the field. Going over the battlefield later one British officer remarked that there were a large number of enemy dead lying about, nearly all of them Sikhs and many of them elderly men. Some of the infantry endeavoured to put up a show of resistance in Gujerat and about two hundred threw themselves into a walled garden, which was stormed by the 10th and the 52nd Bengal Native Infantry, but the city was pretty soon cleared. There were some unfortunate accidents such as occurred when some soldiers of the 2nd Europeans joined some sepoys sitting on an ammunition limber and one of them lit his pipe. The whole party was destroyed in the explosion.

The infantry advanced about two miles from the field of battle and were then halted, leaving the cavalry to continue the pursuit, which they did with considerable enthusiasm, taking no prisoners—the murder of British wounded at Chillianwalla had determined them to allow no quarter to their enemy. Thackwell personally led the cavalry on the left flank, which covered about twelve miles. On the other flank the 14th Light Dragoons captured a standard and the 1st Bengal Light Cavalry overran a battery of nine guns which was withdrawing. Hearsay's Irregulars seem to have got rather further than anyone else and to have pursued the enemy for fifteen miles before halting. Gough has been criticized for not pushing the pursuit further and in particular for not ordering the cavalry to go on that night; but in fact events subsequently proved that it was hardly necessary. It was just as well to halt and get everything properly organized for the pursuit on the morrow. The total British losses in the battle were given as five officers and ninety-one other ranks killed and twenty-four officers and six hundred and forty-six other ranks wounded, eighty-two of this number being among

190

the artillery. The gunners had only lost fifty at Chillianwalla, including the figures for Christie's Battery. No less than fifty-three Sikh guns were captured. One need hardly add that as Gough rode round his army that evening he was once more loudly cheered by all his troops.

General Gilbert was given the task of pursuing the main Sikh army, for which he had his own Division, now commanded by Brigadier Mountain, to which had been added the 53rd, and the Bombay contingent under Brigadier Dundas. There has been criticism of the decision to use the Bombay troops as, although they had seen no serious fighting since Multan, they were still footsore after their long march. Gilbert also had with him the 14th Light Dragoons, the 11th Bengal Irregular Cavalry and Fordyce's and Dawes's Batteries. He set out to the north-west early on the 22nd. At the same time General Campbell's Division was directed northwards towards Bhimbar, as it was thought part of the Sikh Army had retired towards the foothills. In fact it had not done so and Campbell in due course returned and followed in the wake of Gilbert's Division. Gilbert pressed on hard and on 24 February was at Naurangabad. He was just too late to intercept the Sikhs crossing the Jhelum. As he came up to the river there were some Sikh guns on the far bank, which opened fire but soon made off. He had then marched fifty miles in seventy-two hours. He was joined by Hearsay's Irregular Cavalry Brigade. There was delay in getting his troops across the Jhelum, as the fords were very difficult, and he did not complete his crossing until the 28th. It was shortly after this that Brigadier Mountain met with an unfortunate accident, his pistol going off in its holster and wounding him. Meanwhile George Lawrence, who to the admiration of the Sikhs had obeyed the terms of his parole and returned to join them, arrived in the capacity of an emissary from Shere Singh, asking for terms. Gough was not prepared to offer anything but unconditional surrender. Gilbert pressed on and on 8 March was within thirty miles of Rawalpindi, to which point the Sikh army had retired, and here with Sikhs returned all the prisoners whom they held. There were some further negotiations, but the Sikh army, which had suffered from the hostility of the Mohammedan villagers during its retreat and was desperately short of supplies,

191

was in no condition to fight. On 14 March at Rawalpindi the Khalsa finally surrendered. General Gilbert insisted upon a formal ceremony and the Khalsa regiments marched out and laid down their weapons before the British troops. Gilbert had sound psychological reasons for insisting on this procedure, for it was a clear demonstration to everyone that the vaunted Khalsa had finally been defeated. Observers who watched the surrender greatly admired the bearing of the Sikh soldiers, who still carried themselves with pride. They were tired and hungry, but their spirit was by no means broken. It was noticed that many of the older men threw down their tulwars with a gesture of disgust, some exclaiming as they did so 'Now Ranjit Singh is dead'.

There remained the problem of the Afghans and the day after the surrender Gilbert started for Attock. On 16 March he had arrived at Wah, which was some thirty miles off. Next day he made a forced march to try and save the bridge of boats, using cavalry with some horse artillery. He arrived just as the Afghans were about to cut the bridge and the Guides, who were as usual the first on the spot, always claim it was their fire which made the Afghans botch the job, so that the bridge drifted virtually intact to the near side of the river. Although there was a delay it was not as great as it might have been. The fort at Attock had been abandoned and the whole column passed over the Indus on the 19th. On 21 March it entered Peshawar, which two days previously the Afghans had evacuated and withdrawn through the Khyber Pass. The British troops pursued as far as Jamrud at the mouth of the pass and there halted. The second Sikh War was over, and the Afghans were back beyond their mountains. The problem that remained was the peaceful future settlement of what had been Ranjit Singh's Empire.

CHAPTER 15

The Second Sikh War in Retrospect

$\mathbf{T}$HERE were a number of marked differences between the two Sikh Wars. The first was a much more clear-cut affair than the second. It was fought by the British against the Sikh nation as a whole and it started with a formal declaration of war against the Lahore Government when the Khalsa invaded British India. The second grew out of an internal rebellion, which was not in the first place purely anti-British and in which British troops were not initially employed. Indeed the actual time at which the war started cannot be irrefutably fixed. It can be argued that it commenced when Shere Singh went over to Mulraj at Multan, but it can equally be said that the rebellion against the Durbar did not turn into war until he left Multan to march north. There was no formal declaration of war, and although Dalhousie might speak of war with the Sikh nation, in theory the British were still suppressing a revolt against the authorities in Lahore, whom they were supporting. Indeed, quite apart from those members of the Durbar like Tej Singh who remained in office in Lahore, there were some prominent Sikh leaders, such as Shumser Singh and Uttar Singh, who refused to rally to the Khalsa. It was noteworthy too that the newly-raised regiments of Sikh Local Infantry remained loyal to the British and were actually used on operations.

An important factor was that many of the Mohammedans in the Punjab regarded the British as liberators, and much had been done under Sir Henry Lawrence's régime to win them over.

Under Sikh rule they had tended to be regarded as second class citizens, and they saw that this would no longer be so if the British controlled the Punjab. The effect of this was that the Sikh army, although operating in its own country, was apt to find itself among a hostile populace, while the British found the inhabitants friendly and helpful. This anti-Sikh attitude was most marked in the lands beyond the Indus—the situation would have been very different had the Pathan tribesmen made common cause with the Khalsa. It is significant that the Mohammedan Imam-ud-Din, who had endeavoured to resist the implementation of the Treaty of Bhyrowal, was the one Durbar general, apart of course from Van Cortlandt, who consistently and actively rendered good and loyal service to the British cause.

It will always be a moot point whether the Mulraj rebellion could have been contained. Edwardes, who was nearest to the scene of the trouble, maintained that it could, had the British authorities reacted more promptly. He may have been right, but he did not see the broader picture nor realize Lord Gough's difficulties in getting an army into the field in the hot weather, nor the political advantages of making the Lahore Durbar put its own house in order. Edwardes himself admitted that in the long term it was better that events took the course they did, for the spirit of the Khalsa was still very much alive and, like the Phoenix, would be sure to rise again. This is the view taken by those Sikh authorities who claim that the British held back deliberately to tempt the Khalsa to rise and then smash it. It is possible that, had no clash taken place, good government in the Punjab would have won over the Sikh people and eroded support for the diehards of the Khalsa until it was too weak to strike again; but this does not seem very likely and it is difficult to envisage such a situation arising before the crisis of 1857 came. The temptation for the men of the Khalsa to make common cause with the Mutineers would then have been well nigh irresistible.

The hero of the Mulraj rebellion from the British point of view was undoubtedly Herbert Edwardes. The story of how a young British subaltern not only maintained order in his own recently conquered district but organized and kept loyal an army of irregulars and moreover led them to victory against an

194

enemy of superior strength is one of the finest episodes in the story of the establishment of British rule in India. Throughout his operations he showed a sound strategic and tactical sense, and there can be no serious criticism of the way he conducted his actions at Kineyree and Suddoosam. He must have been possessed of a magnetic personality and outstanding powers of leadership. In praising Edwardes one must also pay tribute to that wily old warrior Van Cortlandt, who supported him so well, to Lake who led the Daudpatras, and to Edwardes' loyal Pathan lieutenant, Foujdar Khan. Edwardes was the captain of the team, but he could not have won his victories without their help.

The war included one major siege and two major battles preceded by two intensive engagements. The first siege of Multan was really part of the attempt to suppress the Mulraj rebellion but, except for minor operations under Wheeler in the north, which played their part and should not be forgotten, was also the first occasion on which British troops were involved; the second siege was a side-show, an essential but annoying delay before the besiegers could be released to join the main army. Ramnuggar was a none-too-well managed cavalry affair and Sadulapore a battle which hardly happened, a tactical failure to press home a strategical success. Chillianwalla was one of the bloodiest engagements in the history of British India, comparable to Ferozeshah in the first war, the British losses being about the same in each, but it did not, like the latter, end in a clear-cut defeat for the Sikhs. Indeed, it was such a Pyrrhic victory that it shattered the morale of everyone concerned with the war, except those who mattered most—the soldiers of the Army of the Punjab. Gujerat was one of the most decisive and cheaply won battles in the history of the British Army.

As in the first war the solid base of the British Army was provided by the European infantry regiments. A cavalry officer writing from Dinghi just before the move forward to Chillianwalla bemoaned the fact that there were not more of them, as it was they who decided the issue in battle. At Multan it was the British infantry who did most of the work and led the successful assaults. At Chillianwalla one regiment met with a disastrous repulse, but this could be blamed on bad handling rather than on the troops themselves; and the other three European infantry regiments covered themselves with glory and indeed turned a possible defeat into victory. At Gujerat only two of the European regiments were seriously involved, and they both carried their objectives in fine style. No one could question the leadership of the officers of the British regiments; but there were times in both wars when perhaps it was not as skilful as it might have been, notably in the case of the 24th at Chillian- walla. There was a risk inherent in the purchase system in the Queen's regiments, since it meant that the more competent and certainly the more experienced could be passed over by men who were less fitted for promotion but had more money. Curiously enough, one of the most extraordinary examples of the working of the system occurred in the 24th at this time. Not long before the war there was a major's vanacy. The senior captain, who had waited a long time for promotion, had the money to purchase the step in rank but elected to stand aside and buy the vacancy for his son, who was also a captain in the Regiment, presumably because the latter would be well placed for a promising career, while his ageing parent could hardly hope to go much further. The son was promoted, but was killed at Chillianwalla and his father, who survived, filled the vacancy caused by the death of his son.

The native regiments had a better overall record than in the first war. The 46th Bengal Native Infantry did splendidly at Chillianwalla and the sepoys gave excellent support to their European comrades in the assaults on the two Kalras at Gujerat; but they were hardly of the same quality as the European regiments and they could only be relied on to fight well when alongside one of them. The troubles in the Bengal Army caused by elderly British and native officers, caste difficulties and lack of a close relationship between officers and men, all apparent in the first war, were still there. It is noteworthy that nearly all contemporary accounts, and even some from members of the Bengal Army, praise the higher quality of the Bombay regiments, where the dead hand of sheer seniority did not apply. Apart from questions of training and organization, it may not be entirely without significance that ninety years later when the non-Gurkha units of the Indian Army were recruited very

196

largely from the Punjab and the North-West Frontier Province, there were hardly any Hindustanis, but still a number of Mahrattas and other races from the area from which the Army of Bombay drew its soldiers.

Anyone writing a 'popular' history of the British cavalry would, one feels, tend to pass quickly over the Second Sikh War. Once again the 3rd Light Dragoons did everything that could be expected of them, but the panic at Chillianwalla, which the historian of the 9th Lancers calls 'the blackest day in the history of the Regiment', although they were only partly involved, overshadows the whole scene. The descendants of the 14th Light Dragoons still commemorate their gallantry at Ramnuggar, but it is no use pretending that it was anything but an ill-managed affair. As in the earlier war, reconnaissance was weak. The British were surprised at Chillianwalla when well-handled cavalry should have given Gough warning that the Sikhs had moved forward, just as at Sadulapore they should have been able to warn Thackwell that the enemy was approaching. It should certainly have been possible for patrols to find out beforehand whether the fords which Thackwell needed to cross to carry out his turning movement were practicable. Nor can it be said that the cavalry showed much drive in following up Shere Singh when he withdrew from the Chenab.

The regular regiments of Bengal Light Cavalry appear, as in the first war, to have been less effective than the irregular regiments. Perhaps the finest cavalry feat during the war was the charge of the Scinde Horse, an irregular cavalry regiment of the Bombay Army, which was at that time of the same composition as many of the Bengal units, at Gujerat.

The artillery once more earned universal praise. Seldom can a battery have been in the right place at the right time so often in so short a period as was Dawes's at Chillianwalla. The native-manned batteries fully lived up to the standard of their European comrades. No gunners could have served their guns more faithfully than did Anderson's men at Gujerat. It was at Gujerat that the artillery really came into its own. For the first time it had the edge on the Sikhs and it was the gunners who had the major share in that decisive victory.

The Army of the Punjab suffered from bad staff work just

197

as the Army of the Sutlej had done. The hopeless muddle which delayed Thackwell's start from Ramnuggar was one particularly bad case; the failure to get forward food, fodder and tentage when the army first concentrated before moving on Ramnuggar was another. The mysterious staff officer who ordered away Robertson's battery at Chillianwalla reminds one of similar happenings at Ferozeshah.

For the British Commander-in-Chief the second Sikh War had much in common with the first. He was again prevented by political considerations from taking all the steps he thought necessary to prepare for the conflict. Although he no longer had his political master sitting on top of him when operations started, the Governor-General was not very far away and showed a tendency to send him instructions which on occasion hampered his plans. He kept firmly to his aim of destroying the Sikh Army in the field. He won a victory so costly that public opinion became alarmed and steps were taken to remove him from command. But finally he won a decisive victory. Where things went wrong it was usually because he was let down by his subordinates. He could not be blamed for the mishaps at Ramnuggar. He had intended to use his cavalry to make a reconnaissance in force and it did so. He must bear some blame for the weakness in intelligence and staff work which delayed the turning movement before Sadulapore, in that as Commander-in-Chief he was responsible for the efficiency of the staff; but the concept of the operation was sound. At Chillianwalla he should not, remembering what had happened at Moodkee, have allowed himself to be surprised by the presence of the Sikhs, but there was nothing he could do to foresee the two disasters brought about by his subordinates, nor could he be blamed for the rain which prevented him exploiting his success next day. At Gujerat he fought a set-piece battle with complete success.

His actions throughout the campaign go a long way to disprove the theory that he was reckless, bull-headed and careless of men's lives. He declined, despite Campbell's urgings, to bring up his infantry at Ramnuggar and risk getting involved with the Sikhs on commanding ground across the river. He eventually manoeuvred them out of their position. He declined to attack Shere Singh in his strong position at Russool until it was

198

apparent that the Sikhs would receive reinforcements which would more than offset the advantages the Multan troops would bring to him. Chillianwalla was forced upon him when he had intended to fight next day, he could not afford a long artillery preparation and still leave himself enough daylight; and the night withdrawal which resulted in the loss of captured guns was only ordered very reluctantly on the strong advice of his senior officers. After Chillianwalla he resisted every attempt of Shere Singh to bring him to battle before General Whish's troops had arrived. At Gujerat, with a superiority in artillery for the first time, he made proper use of his guns and did not launch his infantry until the bombardment had done its work. Indeed the more one peers through the mists of contemporary criticism and Victorian prejudice, the more one admires this much maligned general and understands why, despite his faults, his soldiers loved him.

Lord Dalhousie, the Governor-General, back at Ambala did not of course have nearly so much influence on events as did Hardinge in the first war. He was young and full of self-assurance, but he was very self-opinionated and he did not know India. His knowledge of military affairs was negligible. This would not have mattered had he been prepared fully to trust his Commander-in-Chief. He seems, however, to have been under the influence of the 'anti-Gough lobby'. He was slow to take his Commander-in-Chief's advice about preparations for the campaign and he did not make things easier for his military subordinate by never making it clear whether he was suppressing a rebellion on behalf of the Durbar or whether he was at war again with the Sikh nation. His instruction to Gough permitting him to cross the Chenab, but only to fight the Sikhs if they stayed where they were, was hardly one which any politician should have given to a soldier in the field. It is something of a contrast between the two men that while the Commander-in-Chief loyally carried out all Dalhousie's instructions, and as far as we know never said anything against him, Dalhousie was taking steps behind Gough's back to secure his replacement.

Of the other British generals, Colin Campbell stands out in the same way that Harry Smith did in the first war. He was the junior divisional commander and would not have commanded a division at all had Cureton not been killed and Thackwell taken his place in command of the cavalry. At the time Campbell was still a substantive lieutenant-colonel in the 98th Regiment. The fact that he subsequently became a Field-Marshal and was Commander-in-Chief during the Indian Mutiny, and mainly responsible for its suppression, tends to make writers consider his views before those of other people and perhaps exaggerate the part he played in this campaign. Indeed, had Campbell been killed in the closing stages at Chillianwalla he would probably have been written down as a first-rate brigadier who was not much good at commanding a division. It was his Division which caused the delay at the start of Thackwell's turning movement to Sudalapore and, when the fords were found to be impracticable, it was Campbell who wanted to give up, while Thackwell wanted to push on and finish the job. He completely failed to control his Division at Chillianwalla, although Gilbert succeeded in controlling his. He must accept a large share of the responsibility for Pennycuick's unfortunate advance and the repulse of the 24th. He made matters worse by his 'no firing' order and it seems also that he did not give proper orders to his gunners. In practice he took over command of Hoggan's Brigade, which he handled extremely well, but that was not his job.

Thackwell, as commander of the cavalry, must accept some responsibility for certain weaknesses in that arm to which attention has been drawn. He was the only general of the Army of the Punjab to be entrusted with an important independent role, namely the turning movement across the Chenab which led to the action at Sudulapore. He showed determination in sticking to his task, despite delay, and in getting his force across the river at Wazirabad, but he can fairly be accused of lacking the initiative required for an independent commander when presented with the problem which he faced as he approached the Sikhs. A general with more drive would have realized much earlier that the troops to reinforce him were going to have the greatest difficulty in getting across the Ghuriki ford and that Gough's instructions inhibiting an attack without them no longer applied.

General Gilbert continued to command his Division as soundly as he had during the first war and his conduct of the pursuit after Gujerat cannot be faulted.

General Whish does not give the impression of being a ball of fire. He seems to have been content to do very little after Shere Singh deserted until the Bombay troops arrived and it is often argued that he could have made the latter's departure from Multan very much more difficult for him. It is hard to justify his decision to assault Multan so late in the afternoon and thus ensure that his troops were committed to street fighting in the dark. He seems to have been better on the administrative side than some of the other leaders and he certainly moved fast to the assistance of the main army after Multan fell.

The Sikh army was not the same Khalsa which had taken the field in 1845. It contained a high proportion of irregulars and a number of newly raised units which had not been properly trained. Individually its men were as brave and determined as ever, but whereas in 1845 they were supremely confident of victory and sure of themselves, in 1849 they had already tasted defeat. They were of course fighting in their own country and for many of them it was a war of liberation, as well as an effort to wipe out the stain of defeat on the honour of the Khalsa, but they were by no means as united as they had been. The fact that many of the Mohammedan peasants were openly hostile must have caused distrust of the Mohammedan elements in the army, a feeling intensified when Elihu Baksh deserted after Chillianwalla. Accounts of the final British advance in France and Flanders in 1918 have often pointed out that, gallantly as they fought, the Germans at that time were not the Germans of the Somme two years before. It is probably a fair simile to apply to the Sikhs in 1845 and 1849. Infantry and artillery both fought well, but once again the cavalry was singularly ineffective. In the artillery some slackening of discipline may have been the cause of the fact that both at Chillianwalla and at Gujerat they opened fire prematurely with, from their point of view, unfortunate results.

The Sikh side of the picture is dominated by Shere Singh. He was in a difficult position. There is ample evidence that he took up the sword reluctantly. Edwardes always maintained that until just before he went over to Mulraj he had every intention of remaining loyal to the Durbar and it was only when the pressure put to bear on him as 'a son and a Sikh' became irresistible that he took the final plunge. As a general he proved over-cautious and not the man to lead a rebellion against potentially superior forces. He probably missed his main chance of doing real damage to his enemies when he left Multan and failed to make straight for Lahore. He had a reasonable chance of getting there before the Army of the Punjab could come up and he might well have set the whole Sikh heartland ablaze. It is also difficult to see why he did not seize the chance to strike a blow at Sudalapore instead of retreating so precipitately to the Jhelum. He had the Army of the Punjab divided by a wide and difficult river and he might well have been able to concentrate a superior force against the detached wing.

In the closing stages of the campaign, when he must have realized that the dice were loaded against him, he might well have risked all on a dash to Lahore or at least have attacked Gough before he could be reinforced by the troops from Multan. He appears to have been sounder tactically then strategically and it is to his credit that he very nearly succeeded in leading the British into a trap at Chillianwalla; but yet again he elected to fight a battle with a wide river at his back, a surprising decision in view of what had happened at Aliwal and Sobraon. Like most of the other Sikh generals he appears to have been obsessed with the desire to fight on the defensive, placing his faith in his artillery. His handling of his army may have been influenced to some degree by its high proportion of poorly trained troops. Another factor to bear in mind is that he must have had some doubts as to the correctness of the course he was taking, although it has never been suggested that once he had called upon the Khalsa to support him he did not lead it to the best of his ability. Nevertheless a doubting general is hardly of the same value as one passionately devoted to the cause.

In 1848 the Khalsa endeavoured to reverse the decision which had been reached two years before. It failed and in failing signed its own death warrant. The last remnants of the edifice built by Ranjit Singh had been kicked away and from then on only the British could be paramount in the Punjab.

CHAPTER 16

The Aftermath

$\mathbf{N}$ow that the war was over most people considered that annexation was virtually inevitable, for the attempt to support a native government friendly to the paramount power had been a failure. However, the method by which British rule was to be applied was very debatable and there was a conflict of opinion between Lord Dalhousie and Sir Henry Lawrence. Their differences were accentuated by a clash of personalities. Dalhousie, much the younger man and a peer of the realm, was not prone to take advice or to brook opposition. He saw himself as being there to give orders in his capacity as Governor-General and his subordinates as existing to carry them out. He believed in the maximum amount of centralization. In a sense he reflected the views of many of his countrymen at the time that the British Empire was God's gift to the peoples of Asia and it behoved them to do what they were told and be thankful for their blessings. Sir Henry Lawrence, with his much longer experience of the country, understood the people of India and respected their feelings. He was a great believer in personal contact rather than in rule by regulations laid down by a distant Government. He liked to decentralize as much as possible and preferred to give his subordinates instructions as to the general policy and to leave them as much initiative as he could, rather than tie them down by rigid orders from above.

Lord Dalhousie took the view that the Sikhs had risen in rebellion against a benevolent Government, which had treated them leniently after their first offence, and that it would be unsafe to trust them again. He considered that the Sikhs had asked for trouble and deserved all they would get. In particular he thought it essential that the Sikh sirdars should be stripped of all power, so that they would not in future have the resources to cause trouble. He regarded annexation as a thoroughly sound plan.

Lawrence took a diametrically opposite view. He would have liked to avoid complete annexation and regarded it at best as a regrettable necessity. He considered that many of the Sikh sirdars had been forced into active or passive support for Shere Singh and his associates by the weakness of the Durbar, the strength of the Khalsa and to some degree by the tactlessness of the British. He thought that British ineptitude in the handling of the Mulraj affair had to some extent led to the late conflict. He therefore felt that it would be unwise to be too hard on the leaders of the Sikh community and that it would pay a far better dividend in the long run if they were treated leniently. Whereas Dalhousie believed that the time had come to crush the Sikhs completely, Lawrence considered that, having beaten them in the field, the best British policy was to treat them with fairness and justice and to convert them into firm friends as a bulwark for British authority in the future.

The clash between the two men came to a head even before the war was over. Lawrence had arrived back in Lahore on 18 January and was promptly asked by Lord Dalhousie to prepare a proclamation of annexation. He drew up a document in accordance with his own ideas to which the Goveror General took the strongest objection, as it held out hopes of leniency which he himself had no intention of allowing. In his comments on the document to Sir Henry Lawrence he referred to it as being 'objectionable both in matter and manner'. He further added the rather unnecessary remark 'I can allow nothing to be said or done which would raise the notion that the policy of the Government of India or its intentions depend on your presence as Resident of the Punjab'. This was hardly the language to use to a man who had been virtual dictator of the Punjab in the period between the wars and had made an outstanding success of administering it. Relations between the two men continued to deteriorate. Dalhousie began discussing problems with John Lawrence, whose views were much nearer to his own than were his elder brother's. Complete annexation was decided upon and Henry Lawrence offered to submit his resignation. However, with his immense prestige Dalhousie could not afford to let him go. He eventually persuaded him to stay on by using the argument that he was better placed to look after the interests of the Sikhs by remaining in Lahore. The actual proclamation was issued in full Durbar on 30 March and formally placed the country under British sovereignty. Young Dhuleep Singh was given a pension of £50,000 per annum with leave to reside wherever he wished, provided he left the Punjab and did not return.

Had relations between Dalhousie and Henry Lawrence been easier it might have seemed logical, now that the Punjab was a province of British India, to make Lawrence, so successful as Resident under the former régime, its Governor. This solution, however, did not appeal to the Governor-General. It was therefore decided to set up a Board of Control of which Lawrence would be the President and his brother John and a Mr Mansell the members. Sir Henry would retain the main responsibility for political affairs, while John would deal with financial matters and be responsible for the important revenue department, and Mansell would deal with all judicial and legal questions. The Board as a whole would have responsibility for all matters of major policy. Initially the arrangement worked quite well. The Lawrences often had differences of opinion. John's views were much closer to Dalhousie's and, as a trained civil servant, he gave great emphasis to the importance of revenue and was not as inclined as his brother to listen kindly to the excuses of those who did not comply with the tax regulations. Mansell with his judicial training took a detached philosophical view of things and was able to act as a peacemaker between the brothers.

Meanwhile, another strong personality had entered the scene. Sir Charles Napier, who had taken over from Gough as Commander-in-Chief, was a blunt soldier who loathed committees and had the average soldier's hearty dislike for politicians and civil servants. He would have preferred the Punjab to be placed under military government, as Sind had been when he conquered it in the war of 1843. He had no use at all for Lord Dalhousie, whom he referred to as 'the laird of Cockpen' and

205

went on to describe as 'a young Scotch lord with no head for governing an Empire'. He was soon to find the general situation too frustrating for him and in 1850 he resigned and went home.

The Province was divided into seven districts, each under its own commissioner with the appropriate number of subordinate officials. Henry Lawrence selected his men carefully, many of them already having served under him when he was Resident. Robert Montgomery, who was shortly to replace Mansell on the Board, was given Lahore, and among others to fill important positions were Edwardes, Abbott, Nicholson, Robert Napier, Hodson, Alex Taylor and Neville Chamberlain. These were the men who were to establish the new order in the land of the five rivers and they did it so successfully that when the great test of the Indian Mutiny came in 1857 the Punjab remained loyal.

Sir Henry Lawrence's methods are well summed up in a letter he wrote to one of his subordinates. 'In a new country, especially a wild one lacking in accessibility, brevity and kindliness are the best engines of Government. Have as few forms as possible and as are consistent with the brief record of proceedings. Be considerate and kind, not expecting too much from ignorant people. Make no change unless certain that it will result in a decided improvement.'

To Chamberlain, on his first appointment as an assistant commissioner, Sir Henry gave the following advice: 'He is the best officer who best manages the following two items—interferes with the people as little as possible and is as prompt as he can be in disposing of cases. Keep the peace and collect the revenue and Utopia will be gained. Our assessment should be so light as to require no compulsion in the collection and we should be rather protectors of the taxed than tax-masters. We should try to induce the heads of villages to look after their own affairs and not interfere with them except by advice.'

Lawrence himself was always on tour, but at the same time he interfered with his commissioners as little as possible. The fact that he was so seldom in his office in Lahore infuriated Dalhousie and tended to throw much of the routine administration on to his brother John.

The problem facing the Board of Control was a serious one.

Much of the new province was in a state of chaos and lawlessness was rife. There were numbers of disbanded soldiers of the Khalsa about and many bands of dacoits were roaming the countryside. Thuggee, the ritual murder of travellers for gain under a semi-religious cloak, was not uncommon. The collection of revenue had completely broken down and some method had to be devised to replace the Sikh system of gathering taxes, which had frequently been done by force. Infanticide was widespread in the Punjab, where girl children were considered a liability. There were many relics of the despotic rule of Ranjit Singh, including the savage punishments, which would have to be abolished if the new province was to be brought into line with the rest of British India.

An early step to increase stability was the raising of no less than five regiments of Punjab Infantry, largely from the men of the disbanded Khalsa. This was to prove a wise measure, for not only did it solve to some degree the problem of unemployed soldiery, but these regiments were to prove completely loyal in the dark days ahead and in more recent times were grouped together to form the Frontier Force Rifles. Between 1849 and 1856 five regiments of cavalry were also raised in the Punjab.

To cope with internal lawlessness an efficient armed police force was formed, consisting of about some 2,700 mounted and 5,000 unmounted men. Steps were taken to disarm the civil population and this was done not by sudden raids or by cordoning and searching villages, but through the village headmen themselves. Sir Henry Lawrence made it clear to them that they were there to enforce the law. His subordinates were instructed always to deal with them. When they realised that the new police, and indeed the new order of things, would allow them to remain safe in their villages, the headmen made no difficulties in co-operating. At the same time their position in authority had been established. Feeling that they were trusted they returned that trust with loyalty.

The system of arms control could not be applied similarly in the frontier districts, those areas which in due course were to become the North-West Frontier Province. It was impossible for the army, even with the new regiments of the Punjab Irregular

207

Force, to guarantee the safety of the villages near the frontier, which were liable to be raided by their fellow Pathans from across the mountains, who were outside British jurisdiction. The villagers in these areas were therefore allowed to keep their weapons and indeed encouraged to form what were really home guard units to look after their own homes. The headman was, however, still responsible to British authority. He was given an important role to play in the structure which the Raj set up in that desolate area.

On the financial side the aim was to make the new province self-supporting, and this was soon achieved as far as the Punjab proper was concerned. The basic Sikh principle for taxation had been to tax everything possible as much as possible. Under the new régime taxes were removed from many articles and most of those remaining had their assessments reduced. The result was a considerable upsurge in the economy and an overall increase in the money coming in to the treasury. The same applied to land. In the days of Ranjit Singh half the gross product had been claimed for the state. Under the new system the amount was reduced to a quarter or sometimes an eighth and again the effect was to increase the revenue, mainly because the tax collector, who had acted as a middle man and taken his share, was cut out. Between 1849 and 1857 the revenue of the Punjab was to rise from 134 lakhs of rupees to 205.

Generally speaking the Mohammedans of the Punjab welcomed the British as deliverers from their Sikh overlords, while the Sikhs were smarting under their defeat and resentful of their conquerors. There was a far amount of intrigue in which both Shere Singh and Chutter Singh were found to be involved and were sent into exile. When the Bengal Fusiliers were stationed in Lahore in 1850 they found the Sikh population universally sullen and it was not unusual for Europeans to be insulted in the streets. However, they were under strict orders, to adopt a modern phrase, 'to play it cool'. There was a case in which six Sikh fanatics suddenly attacked the married quarters compound of the Fusiliers and succeeded in wounding eleven soldiers before they were killed. In this instance the men's wives went out to help their husbands fight off the raiders, but since they were women the Sikhs refused to harm them. Gradually the atmosphere began to improve and before long there were very few overt signs of Sikh hostility to their new masters.

A rift finally came in the British administration over the question of the Jaghirdars. These were the Sikh sirdars who held grants of land from the government free of any obligations save for the responsibility of rendering military service if required. The problem of fitting these people into the new system was a difficult one, complicated by the fact that it was possible to quibble over the legality of many of the grants. It was a case of having to judge each individual Jaghir on its merits. Lawrence was anxious to make things as easy as possible for the Jaghirdars and to leave them with the resources which would enable them to continue as men of authority. John Lawrence, with his eye on any chance to increase the revenue, inclined to Lord Dalhousie's view that they should be stripped of all power. When Montgomery took over from Mansell he tended to take John's view. Thus the policy of a hard line towards the Jaghirdars was adopted. This made relations between the two brothers even less easy and in 1852 when the Residency at Hyderabad became vacant both of them applied for the post. Henry's application was accepted, although in fact he ultimately went to Rajputana, and John was left in charge of the Punjab. With hindsight it can be said that the elder brother was almost certainly right in his approach. When the Indian Mutiny broke out the Sikh sirdars were all loyal, but hardly any of them were still in a position to call out their retainers to help the Raj, which they would have been had Henry's policy been followed.

After the war the Bengal Army, which now had a large number of units stationed in the Punjab and on the Frontier, continued to show the defects which had already become apparent. Nothing was done to rectify the dead hand of promotion by seniority among both officers and other ranks. The evils of the caste system and the influence of the Brahmins continued unabated. Worse still the formation of many new units in the Punjab and the proliferation of further political jobs increased the drift of officers away from regimental duty. They included many of the best and left units more than ever understaffed. The gap between officers and men tended to widen. There were a number of straws in the wind and indeed in 1850 one regiment,

209

the 66th Bengal Native Infantry, became so disaffected over the question of batta or allowances resulting from its service in the Punjab that it had to be disbanded.

It is interesting to note what happened to the regiments engaged in the two Sikh wars when the Mutiny did break out Bodyguard remained loyal. Of eight regiments of light cavalry in 1857. Of the regular cavalry, only the Governor-General's involved, five mutinied and three were disarmed to prevent their mutinying. The Irregular Cavalry had a better record. Of fourteen regiments which took part in the two campaigns, five remained loyal; three mutinied; four partially mutinied and were disarmed; one which partially mutinied was allowed to continue in the service and the remaining one was disarmed and disbanded. These figures do not include the Guides, who remained loyal, as did all the Punjab cavalry raised after the war. Of the regiments of Bengal Native Infantry engaged in the campaigns, twenty-three mutinied; eleven were disarmed and then disbanded; five partially mutinied, their loyal portions going to form new regiments which continued in the service; three were disarmed but continued in the service; two remained loyal; one partially mutinied and was later disbanded and one which partially mutinied was allowed to remain on in the service. The Gurkha Regiments were all loyal. Among the Sikh regiments raised after the first war, the Regiment of Ferozepore remained completely loyal; the Regiment of Ludhiana was partially affected but recovered itself and rendered good service. It was noteworthy that of the Bengal native regiments which mutinied at Lucknow a high proportion of those who remained true to their salt and helped to defend the Residency, later forming a new regiment, were in fact Sikhs. All the Punjab Infantry raised during or immediately after the second Sikh war, the ancestors of the Punjab Frontier Force, remained completely loyal. No less than eighteen new regiments of Punjab Infantry were raised in the Province during the Mutiny and fourteen of these remained in the army after 1861 when it was reorganized on a long term basis. All of these regiments were still in existence when independence was granted to India in 1947. The Indian Army, which was to earn such a splendid name for itself over the next hundred years, especially in the 1914–1918 and

1939–1945 wars, drew a far higher percentage of its men from the territory once ruled by Ranjit Singh than from any other part of India. The Punjabi Mussulman (Mohammedan) provided a larger proportion of the army than any other class. There were large numbers of Sikhs, Dogras from the hills and of course Pathans from the Frontier. In 1939 there were, apart Army and forty-nine of these were recruited exclusively from the Punjab and the North West Frontier Province, while the from the Gurkhas, seventy-six battalions of infantry in the Indian ubiquitous Punjabi Mussulman was represented in ten of the remainder.

John Lawrence was still in charge at Lahore when the Mutiny broke out. Britain was to owe a great deal to his management of affairs, although the foundations of the loyalty of the Province had undoubtedly been laid by his brother Henry, and by the many men like Nicholson, Montgomery and Chamberlain, whom Henry had chosen. To these men Britain owes the fact that the country, which went to war with the Raj in 1845 and only finally accepted defeat in 1849, was only eight years later the province which rallied most strongly to the cause of its new rulers in the dark days of the Mutiny and continued its loyal support for many years to come.

APPENDIX I

Regiments involved in the Sikh Wars

Titles in 1845   *Subsequent History*

3rd (Kings Own) Light Dragoons   3rd (King's Own) Hussars 1861.
                                     3rd The King's Own Hussars
                                     1921. Amalgamated with the 7th
                                     Queens Own Hussars as The
                                     Queens Own Hussars 1958.

9th (Queens) Royal Lancers   9th Queens Royal Lancers 1921.
                                     Amalgamated with 12th Royal
                                     Lancers as the 9th/12th Royal
                                     Lancers (The Prince of Wales's)
                                     1960.

14th Kings Light Dragoons   14th (Kings) Hussars 1861. 14th
                                     Kings Hussars 1921. Amalga-
                                     mated with the 20th Hussars as
                                     14th/20th Hussars 1922. 14th/
                                     20th Kings Hussars 1936.

16th (The Queens) Lancers   16th The Queens Lancers 1921.
                                     Amalgamated with the 5th
                                     (Royal Irish) Lancers as the
                                     16th/5th Lancers 1922. 16th/
                                     5th The Queens Royal Lancers
                                     1954.

9th (East Norfolk) Regiment)   Norfolk Regiment 1881. Royal
                                     Norfolk Regiment 1935. Amal-
                                     gamated with the Suffolk Regi-
                                     ment to form the 1st East
                                     Anglian Regiment 1959. Absor-
                                     bed into The Royal Anglian
                                     Regiment 1964.

10th (North Lincoln) Regiment   Lincolnshire Regiment 1881.
                                     Royal Lincolnshire Regiment
                                     1946. Amalgamated with the
                                     Northamptonshire Regiment as
                                     the 2nd East Anglian Regiment
                                     1960. Absorbed into the Royal
                                     Anglian Regiment 1964.

24th (2nd Warwickshire) Regiment   South Wales Borderers 1881.
                                     Amalgamated with Welch Regi-

29th (Worcestershire) Regiment — 1st Battalion the Worcestershire Regiment 1881. Amalgamated with the Sherwood Foresters (Nottinghamshire and Derbyshire Regiment) as the Worcestershire and Sherwood Foresters Regiment 1970.

31st (Huntingdonshire) Regiment — 1st Battalion East Surrey Regiment 1881. Amalgamated with the Queens Royal Regiment (West Surrey) as the Queens Royal Surrey Regiment 1959. Absorbed into the Queens Regiment 1966.

32nd (Cornwall) Regiment — 32nd (Cornwall) Light Infantry 1858. 1st Battalion Duke of Cornwalls Light Infantry 1881. Amalgamated with the Somerset Light Infantry as the Somerset and Cornwall Light Infantry 1959. Absorbed into the Light Infantry 1968.

50th (The Queen's Own) Regiment — 1st Battalion Queens Own (Royal West Kent) Regiment 1881. Queens Own Royal West Kent Regiment 1921. Amalgamated with the Buffs (Royal East Kent Regiment) as the Queens Own Buffs, the Royal Kent Regiment, 1961. Absorbed into the Queens Regiment 1966.

53rd (Shropshire) Regiment — 1st Battalion The Kings (Shropshire Light Infantry) 1881. Kings Shropshire Light Infantry 1921. Absorbed into the Light Infantry 1968.

60th (Kings Royal Rifle Corps) — Kings Royal Rifle Corps 1881. Absorbed into the Royal Greenjackets 1966.

61st (South Gloucestershire) Regiment — 2nd Battalion the Gloucestershire Regiment 1881.

62nd (Wiltshire) Regiment — 1st Battalion The Duke of Edinburgh's (Wiltshire Regiment) 1881. Wiltshire Regiment (The Duke of Edinburghs)

213

	1921. Amalgamated with the Royal Berkshire Regiment as The Duke of Edinburghs Royal Regiment (Berkshire and Wiltshire) 1959.
80th (Staffordshire Volunteers) Regiment	1st Battalion South Staffordshire Regiment 1881. Amalgamated with the North Staffordshire Regiment as the Staffordshire Regiment (The Prince of Wales's) 1959.
98th Regiment	98th (Prince of Wales's) Regiment 1876. 2nd Battalion The Prince of Wales's (North Staffordshire Regiment) 1881. North Staffordshire Regiment (The Prince of Wales's) 1921. Amalgamated with The South Staffordshire Regiment (see 80th Regiment) 1959.

Note: After the 1939–1945 War the 1st and 2nd Battalions of British infantry regiments were amalgamated.

EAST INDIA COMPANY EUROPEAN REGIMENTS

1st Bengal European Light Infantry	1st Bengal European Fusiliers 1846. 1st Bengal Fusiliers 1858. 101st (Royal Bengal) Fusiliers 1861. 1st Battalion Royal Munster Fusiliers 1881. Disbanded 1922.
2nd Bengal European Regiment	2nd Bengal European Fusiliers 1850. 2nd Bengal Fusiliers 1858. 104th (Bengal) Fusiliers 1861. 2nd Battalion Royal Munster Fusiliers 1881. Disbanded 1922.
1st Bombay European Fusiliers	1st Bombay Fusiliers 1858. 103rd (Royal Bombay) Fusiliers 1861. 2nd Battalion Royal Dublin Fusiliers 1881. Disbanded 1922.

INDIAN UNITS

The Governor-Generals Bodyguard	To India as the President's Bodyguard in 1947.
1st Bengal Light Cavalry	Mutinied at Lucknow 1857.

3rd Bengal Light Cavalry	Mutinied at Meerut 1857.
4th Bengal Light Cavalry	Disarmed in 1857.
5th Bengal Light Cavalry	Disarmed at Peshawar in 1857. Later disbanded.
6th Bengal Light Cavalry	Mutinied at Jullundur 1857.
7th Bengal Light Cavalry	Mutinied at Lucknow 1857.
8th Bengal Light Cavalry	Disarmed at Meean Mir 1857.
11th Bengal Light Cavalry	2nd Bengal Light Cavalry 1850. Mutinied at Cawnpore 1857.
2nd Bengal Irregular Cavalry	2nd Bengal Cavalry 1861. 2nd Bengal Lancers 1890. 2nd Lancers (Gardners Horse) 1903. Amalgamated with the 4th Cavalry 1922, retaining its title. 2nd Royal Lancers (Gardners Horse) 1935. To India 1947.
4th Bengal Irregular Cavalry	3rd Bengal Cavalry 1861. 3rd Bengal Cavalry (Skinners Horse) 1901. 3rd Skinners Horse 1903. Amalgamated with the 1st Duke of Yorks Own Lancers (Skinners Horse) as the 1st Duke of Yorks Own Skinners Horse 1922. Skinners Horse (1st Duke of Yorks Own Cavalry) 1927. To India 1947.
7th Bengal Irregular Cavalry	5th Bengal Cavalry 1861. 5th Cavalry 1901. Amalgamated with the 8th Cavalry as the 3rd Cavalry 1922. To India 1947.
8th Bengal Irregular Cavalry	Mostly mutinied at Bareilly 1857, but loyal part became the 6th Bengal Cavalry in 1861. 6th (Prince of Wales's) Bengal Cavalry in 1863. 6th Prince of Wales's Cavalry 1903. 6th King Edwards Own Cavalry 1906. Amalgamated with the 7th Hariana Lancers to form the 18th King Edwards Own Cavalry 1922. To India 1947.
9th Bengal Irregular Cavalry	Partly mutinied in 1857 and remainder disbanded in 1861.
11th Bengal Irregular Cavalry	Disarmed at Berhampore and then mutinied in 1857.
12th Bengal Irregular Cavalry	Partly mutinied at Segowli. Loyal portion disbanded 1861.

215

13th Bengal Irregular Cavalry	Mutinied at Benares 1857.
14th Bengal Irregular Cavalry	Mutinied at Nowgong and Jhansi 1857.
15th Bengal Irregular Cavalry	Mutinied at Sultanpore 1857.
16th Bengal Irregular Cavalry	Disarmed at Rawalpindi 1857.
17th Bengal Irregular Cavalry	7th Bengal Cavalry 1861. 7th Bengal Lancers 1900. 7th Lancers 1903. 7th Hariana Lancers 1906. Amalgamated with the 6th King Edwards Own Cavalry to form the 18th King Edwards Own Cavalry 1922. To India 1947.
Corps of Guides (Cavalry)	Queens Own Corps of Guides, Punjab Frontier Force 1875. Queens Own Corps of Guides (Lumsdens) 1901. Queen Victorias Own Corps of Guides, Frontier Force (Lumsdens) 1911. 10th Queen Victorias Own Corps of Guides Cavalry, Frontier Force 1922. To Pakistan 1947.
1st Bombay Light Cavalry	1st Bombay Lancers 1880. 1st (Duke of Connaughts Own) Bombay Lancers 1890. 31st Duke of Connaughts Own Lancers 1903. Amalgamated with the 32nd Lancers to form the 13th Duke of Connaughts Own Lancers 1922. 13th Duke of Connaughts Own Bombay Lancers 1923. 13th Duke of Connaughts Own Lancers 1927. To Pakistan 1947.
1st Scinde Irregular Horse	1st Scinde Horse 1860. 5th Bombay Cavalry (Jacob-Ke-Risalla) 1885. 5th Bombay Cavalry (Scinde Horse) 1888. 35th Scinde Horse 1903. Amalgamated with the 36th Jacobs Horse to form the 14th Prince of Wales's Own Scinde Horse 1922. Scinde Horse (14th Prince of Wales's Own Cavalry) 1927. To Pakistan 1947.

216

2nd Scinde Irregular Horse	2nd Scinde Horse 1860. 6th Bombay Cavalry (Jacob-Ke-Risalla) 1885. 6th Bombay Cavalry (Jacobs Horse) 1888. 36th Jacobs Horse 1903. Amalgamated with the 35th Scinde Horse (see above) 1922.
Bengal Sappers and Miners	Bengal Sappers and Pioneers 1847. Bengal Sappers and Miners 1851. A number of companies mutinied in 1857. 1st Sappers and Miners 1903. 1st Prince of Wales's Own Sappers and Miners 1906. 1st King Georges Own Sappers and Miners 1923. King George Vs Own Bengal Sappers and Miners 1927. Mainly to Pakistan in 1947.
Bombay Sappers and Miners	3rd Sappers and Miners 1903. 3rd Royal Bombay Sappers and Miners 1921. Royal Bombay Sappers and Miners 1923. To India 1947.
1st Bengal Native Infantry	Mutinied at Cawnpore 1857.
2nd Bengal Native Infantry	Disarmed at Barrackpore 1857.
3rd Bengal Native Infantry	Mutinied at Phillour 1857, but loyal portion formed part of the Loyal Purbeah Regiment.
4th Bengal Native Infantry	Disarmed 1857 and disbanded 1861.
7th Bengal Native Infantry	Mutinied at Dinapore 1857.
8th Bengal Native Infantry	Mutinied at Dinapore 1857.
12th Bengal Native Infantry	Mutinied at Jhansi and Nowgong 1857.
13th Bengal Native Infantry	Mutinied at Lucknow 1857 but loyal portion helped form the Regiment of Lucknow.
14th Bengal Native Infantry.	Mutinied at Jhansi 1857.
15th Bengal Native Infantry.	Mutinied at Nasirabad 1857.
16th Bengal Native Infantry.	Disarmed at Meean Meer 1857.
18th Bengal Native Infantry	Mutinied at Bareilly 1857.
20th Bengal Native Infantry	Mutinied at Meerut 1857.
22nd Bengal Native Infantry	Mutinied at Fyzabad 1857.
24th Bengal Native Infantry	Disarmed at Peshawar 1857.
25th Bengal Native Infantry	Disbanded in 1857.
26th Bengal Native Infantry	Mutinied at Meean Meer 1857.

29th Bengal Native Infantry	Mutinied at Moradabad 1857.
30th Bengal Native Infantry	Mutinied at Nasirabad 1857.
31st Bengal Native Infantry	31st Bengal Light Infantry 1856. Greater part remained loyal in 1857. 2nd Bengal Light Infantry 1861. 2nd (Queens Own) Bengal Native Light Infantry 1876.* 2nd (Queens Own) Regiment Rajput Bengal Light Infantry 1897. 2nd (Queens Own) Rajput Light Infantry 1901. 2nd Queen Victoria's Own Rajput Light Infantry 1911. 1st (Queen Victoria's Own Light Infantry) Battalion, 7th Rajput Regiment 1922. To India 1947.
33rd Bengal Native Infantry	Disarmed in 1857. 4th Bengal Native Infantry 1861.* 4th (Prince Albert Victor's) Bengal Infantry 1890. 4th (Prince Albert Victor's) Rajput Regiment Bengal Infantry 1897. 4th (Prince Albert Victor's) Rajput Infantry 1901. 4th Prince Albert Victor's Rajputs 1903. 2nd Battalion (Prince Albert Victor's) 7th Rajput Regiment 1922. To India 1947.
36th Bengal Native Infantry	Mutinied at Jullundur 1857. Loyal portion went to form the Loyal Purbeah Regiment.
37th Bengal Native Infantry	Mutinied at Benares 1857.
41st Bengal Native Infantry	Mutinied at Sitapur 1857.
42nd Bengal Native Light Infantry	Partly mutinied at Saugor 1857. 5th Bengal Native Light Infantry 1861.* 5th Light Infantry 1903. Disbanded 1922.
43rd Bengal Native Light Infantry	Disarmed at Barrackpore 1857. 6th Bengal Native Light Infantry 1861.* 6th Jat Regiment, Bengal Light Infantry 1897. 6th Jat Light Infantry 1903. 6th Royal Jat Light Infantry 1922. 1st Royal Battalion (Light Infantry) 9th Jat Regiment 1922. To India 1947.
45th Bengal Native Infantry	Mutinied at Ferozepore 1857.

46th Bengal Native Infantry	Mutinied at Sialkot 1857.
47th Bengal Native Infantry	Partially disarmed at Mirzapur but remained loyal 1857. 7th Bengal Native Infantry 1861. 7th (Duke of Connaught's Own) Bengal Native Infantry 1883.* 7th Rajput (Duke of Connaught's Own) Regiment of Bengal Infantry 1897. 7th Duke of Connaught's Own Rajputs 1903. 3rd Battalion (Duke of Connaught's Own) 7th Rajput Regiment 1922. To India 1947.
48th Bengal Native Infantry	Mutinied at Lucknow 1857 but loyal portion became part of The Regiment of Lucknow.
49th Bengal Native Infantry	Disarmed at Meean Mir in 1857 and later disbanded.
50th Bengal Native Infantry	Mutinied at Nagode 1857.
51st Bengal Native Infantry	Disarmed at Peshawar 1857.
52nd Bengal Native Infantry	Mutinied at Jubbulpore 1857.
53rd Bengal Native Infantry	Mutinied at Cawnpore 1857.
54th Bengal Native Infantry	Mutinied at Delhi 1857.
56th Bengal Native Infantry	Mutinied at Cawnpore 1857.
59th Bengal Native Infantry	Disarmed at Amritsar 1857. 8th Bengal Native Infantry 1861.* 8th Rajput Regiment Bengal Infantry 1897. 8th Rajput Infantry 1901. 8th Rajputs 1903. 4th Battalion 7th Rajput Regiment 1922. To India 1947.
63rd Bengal Native Infantry	Disarmed at Berkampore 1857. 9th Bengal Native Infantry 1861.* 9th (Gurkha Rifles) Regiment Bengal Infantry 1894. 9th Gurkha Rifles 1901. To India 1947.
68th Bengal Native Infantry	Mutinied at Bareilly 1857.
69th Bengal Native Infantry	Disarmed at Multan 1857.
70th Bengal Native Infantry	Disarmed at Barrackpore 1857. 12th then 11th Bengal Native Infantry 1861.* 11th (Rajput) Regiment Bengal Infantry 1897. 11th Rajput Infantry 1901. 11th Rajputs 1903. 4th Battalion 7th Rajput Regiment 1922. To India 1947.

219

71st Bengal Native Infantry	Mutinied at Lucknow 1857 but loyal portion became part of the Regiment of Lucknow.
72nd Bengal Native Infantry	Mutinied at Neemuch in 1857.
73rd Bengal Native Infantry	Two companies mutinied at Dacca in 1857, but rest remained loyal. Ultimately disbanded.
Infantry of Shekhawati Brigade	Shekhawati Battalion 1847. 14th then 13th Bengal Native Infantry 1861. 13th (Shekhawati Regiment) Bengal Native Infantry 1884.* 13th Rajputs (The Shekhawati Regiment) 1903. 10th (Shekhawati) Battalion, 6th Rajputana Rifles 1922. To India 1947.
Nasiri Battalion	66th or Gurkha Regiment of Bengal Native Infantry 1850. 66th or Gurkha Light Infantry 1858. 11th Bengal Native Infantry and then 1st Gurkha Regiment of Light Infantry 1861. 1st Gurkha (Rifle) Regiment 1890. 1st Gurkha Rifles 1901. 1st Gurkha Rifles (The Malaun Regiment) 1906. 1st King Georges Own Gurkha Rifles (The Malaun Regiment) 1910. 1st King George Vs Own Gurkha Rifles (The Malaun Regiment) 1937. To India 1847.
The Sirmoor Battalion	The Sirmoor Rifle Regiment 1858. 17th Bengal Native Infantry and then 2nd Gurkha Regiment 1861. 2nd Gurkha (Sirmoor Rifles) Regiment 1864. 2nd (Prince of Wales's Own) Gurkha Regiment (The Sirmoor Rifles) 1876. 2nd King Edwards Own Gurkha Rifles (The Sirmoor Regiment) 1906. 2nd King Edwards VII Own Gurkha Rifles (The Sirmoor Rifles) 1927.
Corps of Guides (Infantry)	Corps of Guides, Punjab Irregular Force 1851. Corps of

Guides, Punjab Frontier Force 1865. The Queens Own Corps of Guides, Punjab Frontier Force, 1876. Queens Own Corps of Guides (Lumsdens) 1904. Queen Victorias Own Corps of Guides (Frontier Force) (Lumsdens) Infantry 1911. 5th Battalion (Queen Victorias Own Corps of Guides) 12th Frontier Force Regiment 1922. 5th Battalion 12th Frontier Force Regiment (Queen Victorias Own Corps of Guides) (Lumsdens) 1927. To Pakistan 1947.

1st Sikh Local Infantry

1st Sikh Infantry, Punjab Irregular Force 1857. 1st Sikh Infantry, Punjab Frontier Force 1865. 1st Sikh Infantry 1901. 51st Sikhs (Frontier Force) 1903. 51st (Prince of Wales's Own) Sikhs (Frontier Force) 1921. 1st Battalion (Prince of Wales's Own) (Sikhs). 12th Frontier Force Regiment 1922. To Pakistan 1947.

2nd or Hill Regiment Sikh Local Infantry

2nd, or Hill, Sikh Infantry, Punjab Irregular Force 1857. 2nd, or Hill, Sikh Infantry Punjab Irregular Force 1865. 2nd, or Hill, Sikh Infantry 1901. 52nd Sikhs (Frontier Force) 1903. 2nd Battalion (Sikhs), 12th Frontier Force Regiment 1922. To Pakistan 1947.

3rd Bombay Native Infantry

3rd Bombay Native Light Infantry 1871. 103rd Mahratta Light Infantry 1903. 1st Battalion/5th Mahratta Light Infantry 1922. To India 1947.

4th Bombay Native Infantry

4th Regiment, 1st Battalion Rifle Regiment, of Bombay Infantry 1889. 4th Bombay Rifles 1901. 104th Welleslevs Rifles 1903. 1st Battalion

221

	(Wellesleys) 6th Rajputana Rifles 1922. To India 1947.
9th Bombay Native Infantry	109th Infantry 1903. 4th Battalion 4th Bombay Grenadiers 1922. Disbanded 1930.
19th Bombay Native Infantry	119th Infantry (The Mooltan Regiment) 1903. 2nd Battalion (Mooltan Regiment), 9th Jat. Regiment 1922. To India 1947.
Marine Battalion Bombay Native Infantry	21st Bombay Native Infantry (The Marine Battalion) 1861. 21st Bombay Pioneers and then 121st Pioneers 1903. 10th Battalion 2nd Bombay Pioneers (Marine Battalion) 1922. 1st (Marine) Battalion, Corps of Bombay Pioneers 1929. Disbanded 1933.

* The word 'native' was omitted from regimental titles from 1885.

Note 1: The Bengal and Bombay Artillery ceased to exist after the Indian Mutiny.

Note 2: The Regiment of Lucknow became the 20th and then 16th Bengal Native Infantry in 1861. 16th (The Lucknow Regiment) Bengal Native Infantry 1864. 16th (The Lucknow) Rajput Regiment, Bengal Infantry 1897. 16th (Lucknow) Rajput Infantry 1901. 16th Rajputs (The Lucknow Regiment) 1903. 10th Battalion (The Lucknow Regiment) 7th Rajput Regiment 1922. To India 1947.

Note 3: The Loyal Purbeah Regiment became the 21st and then 17th Bengal Native Infantry in 1861. 17th (Loyal Purbeah) Regiment Bengal Native Infantry 1864. 17th (The Loyal) Regiment Bengal Infantry 1898. 17th Mussulman Rajput Infantry (The Loyal Regiment) 1902. 17th The Loyal Regiment 1903. Disbanded 1922.

APPENDIX II

Battle casualties of European Regiments

K = Killed   W = Wounded   M = Missing

Note: The figures quoted from different sources seldom agree. Where possible I have followed regimental records. Where missing are shown it indicates that the figures are based on reports made soon after the battle and probably means 'body not found'. At Bhudewal some of the missing were prisoners who returned later.

1ST SIKH WAR

Regiment	Strength in initial battle (Officers and other ranks)	Moodkee	Ferozeshah	Bhudewal	Aliwal	Sobraon
3rd Light Dragoons	27 & 518	K 3 & 58 W 3 & 32	K 3 & 57 W 7 & 67	K 0 & 9		K 0 & 4 W 5 & 22
9th Lancers	33 & 539					K 0 & 1 W 0 & 1
16th Lancers	23 & 539			K 0 & 2 W 0 & 1	K 2 & 57 W 6 & 77	
9th Regiment	30 & 874	K 1 & 2 W 1 & 49	K 3 & 67 W 6 & 197 M 0 & 18			K 0 & 5 W 1 & 28
10th Regiment	36 & 742					K 1 & 29 W 2 & 101

1ST SIKH WAR

Regiment	Strength in initial battle (Officers and other ranks)	Moodkee	Ferozeshah	Bhudewal	Aliwal	Sobraon
29th Regiment	28 & 765		K 3 & 52 W 3 & 185			K 1 & 35 W 13 & 139
31st Foot	31 & 844	K 1 & 34 W 8 & 126 M 0 & 6	K 2 & 59 W 5 & 97 M 0 & 18	K 0 & 7 W 0 & 14 M 0 & 19	K 0 & 1 W 1 & 14	K 0 & 33 W 8 & 112 M 0 & 2
50th Foot	31 & 675	K 1 & 21 W 6 & 94 M 0 & 4	K 0 & 24 W 3 & 89 M 0 & 2	K 0 & 4 W 0 & 13 M 0 & 8	K 1 & 8 W 9 & 59	K 1 & 37 W 11 & 184
53rd Foot	27 & 861			K 0 & 36 W 2 & 12 M 0 & 4	K 0 & 3 W 0 & 7 M 0 & 1	K 1 & 4 W 8 & 105 M 0 & 3
62nd Foot	24 & 768		K 7 & 88 W 10 & 161	W 0 & 2		K 1 & 3 W 1 & 43
80th Foot	26 & 795	K 0 & 5 W 1 & 20	K 4 & 39 W 4 & 73	K 0 & 6 W 0 & 1		K 0 & 13 W 5 & 74
1st Bengal European Light Infantry			K 4 & 51 W 4 & 164			K 5 & 33 W 9 & 152

2ND SIKH WAR

Regiment	Multan	Ramnuggar	Sadulapore	Chillianwalla	Gujerat
3rd Light Dragoons		K 0 & 1 W 0 & 5		K 0 & 24 W 2 & 14	W 0 & 1
9th Lancers			W 0 & 1	K 0 & 4 W 0 & 8	
14th Light Dragoons		K 2 & 12 W 4 & 31		K 1 & 1 W 1 & 14 M 0 & 2	K 1 & 0 W 2 & 4
10th Foot	K 1 & 13 W 4 & 113				K 0 & 7 W 1 & 53
24th Foot			K 0 & 2 W 0 & 4	K 11 & 193 W 10 & 266 M 0 & 38	
29th Foot				K 0 & 31 W 4 & 203 M 0 & 3	W 0 & 6
32nd Foot	K 2 & 17 W 11 & 104				K 0 & 1 W 1 & 4

2ND SIKH WAR

Regiment	Multan	Ramnuggar	Sadulapore	Chillianwalla	Gujerat
60th Rifles	K 1 & 10 W 2 & 28				W 0 & 1
61st Foot*			K 0 & 2 W 0 & 9	K 0 & 11 W 3 & 100	W 0 & 9
2nd Bengal Europeans				K 0 & 6 W 2 & 59	K 1 & 9 W 3 & 135 M 0 & 3
Bombay Fusiliers	K 1 & 16 W 6 & 86				

* The 61st had 3 other ranks killed and 2 wounded in operations in the Jullundur Doab.

BIBLIOGRAPHY

Published Works—General

Despatches of Lord Hardinge, Lord Gough and Sir Harry Smith and other Documents (Oliver and Ackerman, 1846).

History of the Sikhs, W. G. McGregor, MD (John Medden, 1846).

The Second Sikh War 1848–1849, E. J. Thackwell (Richard Bentley, 1851).

Journal of the Sutlej Campaign 1845–1846, James Coley-Smith (Elder, 1856).

Memoirs and Letters of Lt Col A. S. H. Mountain, Edited Mrs A. S. H. Mountain (Longmans Green, 1858).

The Mutinies in Oudh, M. R. Gubbins (William Bentley, 1859).

The Punjab Frontier 1848–1849, Maj Herbert Edwards (Beatty, 1861).

From Sepoy to Subedar, Sita Ram. Edited Lt Col Norgate (Victoria Press, 1873).

Commentaries on the Punjab Campaign 1848–1849, Capt J. H. Laurence-Archer (W. H. Allen, 1878).

The Life of Colin Campbell Lord Clyde, Lt Gen Shadwell (William Blackwood, 1881).

Memorials of the Life and Letters of Maj Gen Sir Herbert Edwardes, Lady Edwardes (Keegan Paul, Trench, 1886).

Memoirs of Colonel Alexander Gardner, Ed Major Hugh Fraser (Blackwood, 1898).

The Sikhs and the Sikh Wars, Gough and Innes (A. D. Innes, 1897).

Hodson of Hodson's Horse, Capt L. J. Trotter (J. M. Dent, 1901).

Physician and Friend, George Smith (John Murray, 1902).

The Life and Campaigns of Hugh First Viscount Gough, R. S. Raitt (Constable, 1903).

Autobiography of Sir Harry Smith, Edited G. C. Moore Smith (John Murray, 1903).

The Services of the Bengal Native Army, F. G. Cardew (Govt Press Calcutta, 1903).

The Military Memoirs of Lt Gen Sir Joseph Thackwell, John Murray (1908).

Life of Field Marshal Sir Neville Chamberlain, G. W. Forrest (Wm Blackwood, 1909).

227

The First and Second Sikh Wars, Lt Col R. G. Burton (Govt Press, Simla, 1911).
'Chillianwalla', G. F. MacMunn, *United Services of India Journal* (1911).
History of the British Army, Hon. J. W. Fortescue (MacMillan, 1927).
'The Revolt in Kashmir—1846', R. Z. Sethi, *Journal of Society of Army Historical Research* (1932).
The Lure of the Indus, Lt Gen Sir George MacMunn (Jarrolds, 1934).
The Journal of General Sir Sam Browne (Wm Blackwood, 1937).
The Hero of Delhi, Hesketh Pearson (Collins, 1939).
The Army of Ranjit Singh, Sita Ram Kohll.
Havelock, Leonard Cooper (Bodley Head, 1957).
'Autobiography of an Indian Soldier (Sita Ram)', Sir Patrick Cordell, *Journal of Army Historical Research*.
The Bengal Native Infantry, Amiya Bharat, (Mukhopadayay, Calcutta, 1962).
The Military System of the Sikhs, Fauja Singh Bajwa (Motizal Banarsidass, Delhi, 1964).
A History of the Sikhs, Khushwant Singh (Princeton University Press, 1966).
Victorian Military Campaigns, Edited Brian Bond (Hutchinson, 1967).
At Them with the Bayonet, Donald Featherstone (Jarrolds, 1968).
Six Battles for India, George Bruce (Arthur Barker, 1969).
The Military System of the Sikhs, Lt Col B. N. Majumdar (New Delhi, 1965).
'Notes on the Armies of India', The Marquis of Anglesey, *Journal of the Society of Army Historical Research* (1969–1970).
From Sepoy to Subedar, Sita Ram. Ed Maj Gen James Lunt (Routledge and Keegan Paul, 1970).
The Invasion of Nepal, John Pemble (1971).
Dictionary of National Biography. History of the World, W. N. Weech (Odhams Press).

Published Works—Regimental

Historical Records of the 3rd Light Dragoons, Cannon (Wm Clowes, 1837). Later additions.
The Galloping Third, Hector Bolitho (John Murray, 1963).
Sergeant Pearman's Memoirs, Ed Marquis of Anglesey (Jonathan Cape, 1968).
The Ninth (Queen's Royal) Lancers 1715–1903, Frank H. Reynard (Blackwoods, 1904).
The Ninth (Queen's Royal) Lancers 1715–1936, Maj E. W. Shepherd (Gale and Polden, 1938).

Journal of a Cavalry Officer, W. W. W. Humbley, 9th Lancers (Longmans, 1854).

Historical Records 14th (King's) Hussars, Col H. B. Hamilton (Longmans Green, 1901).

'The 14th Light Dragoons at Chillianwalla', Thompson and Chetwynd. *Royal United Services Institute Journal* (1895).

History of the Sixteenth Queen's Light Dragoons (Lancers) 1759-1912, Col Henry Graham (1912).

Historical Records of the 9th Foot, Cannon, Horse Guards (1847).

History of The Norfolk Regiment, F. Lorraine Petre (Jarrolds, 1925).

The Royal Norfolk Regiment, Tim Carew (Hamish Hamilton, 1967).

Historical Record of 10th Foot, Cannon (1847).

History of the 10th Foot, Albert Lee (Gale and Polden, 1911).

Historical Records 24th Regt, Regimental Committee (1892).

The South Wales Borderers, Jack Adams (Hamish Hamilton, 1968).

History of Thos Farringtons Regiment subsequently designated The 29th (Worcestershire) Foot, Major H. Everard (Littlebry & Co, Worcester, 1891).

The Worcestershire Regiment, Gen Sir Richard Gale (Leo Cooper Ltd, 1970).

Historical Records of the 31st Foot, Cannon, Horse Guards (1850).

History of the East Surrey Regiment, Col H. W. Pearse (1916).

Personal Adventures and Anecdotes of an old Officer, J. P. Robertson (Formerly 31st) (Edward Arnold, 1906).

Historical Records of the 32nd Light Infantry, Col G. C. Swiney (Simpson, Marshall, Kent, 1873).

The Memoirs of Private Waterfield, Ed. Arthur Swanson and Donald Scott (Cassels, 1968).

The Duke of Cornwall's Light Infantry, R. F. K. Goldsmith (Leo Cooper, 1970).

History of the 50th (Queen's Own) Regiment, Col. Fyler (Chapman and Hall, 1895).

Historical Records 53rd Foot, Cannon (1848).

Historical Records of the 53rd Foot, Col W. Rogerson (Simpson Marshall, 1889).

The Annals of The King's Royal Rifle Corps, H. T. Wood (Hamish Hamilton, 1967).

Cap of Honour, D. S. Daniel (Harrap, 1951).

'Journal of Lt A. G. Bace 61st Regiment, Edited Col R. H. Grazebrook, *Journal of Society of Army Historical Research* (1952).

'The Sisted Letters, India 1844-1858', Lt Gen G. N. Molesworth, *Journal of Society of Army Historical Research* (1963).

Historical Memoirs—62nd Foot (1865).

Historical Records of the Wiltshire Regiment, G. B. O'Connor (1885).

229

The Story of The Wiltshire Regiment, Col N. C. E. Kenrick (Gale and Polden, 1963).

The Wiltshire Regiment, Tom Gibson (Leo Cooper, 1969).

Reminiscences of a Veteran, Lt Col Thomas Bunbury (James Street, 1861).

Moodkee, Ferozeshah and Sobraon, Letter from S. A. Kershaw 80th (published privately 1899).

The Night of Ferozeshah 21–22 December 1845, Letter of Capt John Comming 80th. Edited Sir C. Oman (*Orkney Herald*, 1910).

History of The South Staffordshire Regiment (1705–1923), J. P. Jones (Whitehead Press (Wolverhampton)).

The Adventures of Commander Aylmer RN. (otherwise John Cumming), (Mackintosh, Kirkwall, 1930).

'Col Thomas Bunbury', Col M. B. Savage. Article in *United Empire* (1934).

History of The South Staffordshire Regiment, Col W. L. Vale (Gale and Polden, 1969).

The History of the Bengal European Regiment, Lt Col P. R. Innes (Sampson Low, 1885).

History of the Royal Munster Fusiliers, Capt S. McCann (Gale and Polden, 1927).

Crown and Company, A. H. Mainwaring (Arthur Humphrey, 1911).

Leaves from the Journal of a Subaltern, D. S. Sandford, 2nd Bengal Europeans (Blackwoods, 1899).

'Pte John O'Callaghan's Account of the Battle of Chillianwalla', *Journal of Society of Army Historical Research* (1963).

The Bengal Artillery, Capt E. Buckle (W. H. Allen, 1852).

History of the Bengal Artillery, F. W. Stubbs (W. H. Allen, 1895).

The Bengal Horse Artillery, Maj Gen B. P. Hughes (Arms and Armour Press, 1971).

Memoirs of Maj Gen Sir Henry Tombs, Royal Artillery Institute Woolwich (1913).

The Indian Sappers and Miners, Lt Col E. W. C. Sands (Institute of Royal Engineers Chatham, 1948).

Lumsden of the Guides, Lumsden and Elmslie (John Murray, 1899).

The Story of the Guides, Col G. J. Younghusband (MacMillan, 1908).

The History of the Guides (Gale and Polden, 1938).

Short History of the 13th (DCO) Lancers.

The Prince of Wales's Own, The Scinde Horse, Col E. D. Maunsell (published privately, 1926).

The 2nd Bengal Light Infantry (published Julpigoree, 1872).

History of the 3rd Battalion 7th Rajput Regiment, H. G. Rawlinson (Oxford University Press, 1941).

Historical Record 5th/7th Rajput Regiment, Capt P. E. Scudamore (Pioneer Press, Allahabad, 1925).

230

History of Wellesley's Rifles, Lt Col F. H. James (Gale and Polden, 1938).
The Rajputana Rifles, Major M. G. Abayankar (Orient Longmans, Bombay, 1961).
King George's Own Gurkha Rifles (RUSI, 1925).
History of 2nd King Edward's Own Gurkha Rifles, Col W. L. Shakespeare (Gale and Polden, 1929).
History of the 9th Gurkha Rifles, Lt Col B. S. Poynel (RUSI, 1937).

Unpublished Sources

Indian Military Proceedings.
Letter Book of 2nd Division, Army of the Punjab.
Letter Book of the 5th Brigade, Army of the Punjab.
Autobiography of Maj Gen J. R. Pughe.
Letters of Brigadier A. S. H. Mountain.
The Diary of General Sir Edward Holdich.
Miscellaneous letters covering period 1848–51 (Army Museum Archives).
Record of Service of the 3rd or King's Own Light Dragoons.
Record of Service of 9th Lancers.
Letter of Capt Charles Delmar—9th Lancers—1848–49.
Letters of Pte George Tookey—14th Light Dragoons.
Record of Service of the 9th (East Norfolk) Regiment.
Letter from Frederick Abbot. Battle of Sobraon.
Diary of Assistant Surgeon W. Furlong 24th Foot.
Record of Service 29th Foot.
Letters of Lt Col George Congreve—29th Foot.
Letter of Major Way—29th Foot.
Contemporary Press Cuttings based on accounts of an officer (29th) in Bengal—1846.
Letter written by Capt E. A. Noel—31st Regt—20 Dec 1845.
Muster Rolls—31st Foot.
Record of Service—50th Foot.
Record of Service—53rd Foot.
Record of Service—61st Foot.
Recollections of Sgt Grenan—late 61st Foot.
Journal of Sgt J. D. Halliday—61st Foot.
Journal of Lt W. J. Hudson—61st Foot.
Letters of Lt Col McLead, CB—61st Foot.
Letter from Lt H. E. H. Burnside—61st Foot.
Narrative of Sgt J. Ford—61st Foot.
Account of Chillianwalla—Henry Balmer (later RSM) 61st Foot.
Letters of Robt Haviland—62nd Foot.
Account of Mr M. Morris—late 62nd Foot.
Letter of Col Matthias—62nd Foot.

Record of Service of 80th Foot.
Nominal Rolls—80th Foot.
Record of Service of 98th Foot.
Letters of F. L. Stokes covering Gujerat.
Letter from George Pocock. Chillianwalla.
Journal of Lt George Pearse, Madras Artillery, later Lt Gen, Comdt RHA.
Documents of W. W. H. Greathed, RE.
Letter from Lt G. Biddulph.
Autobiography of Maj Gen J. R. Pughe.
Letter of Lt Ryder—14th Bengal Native Infantry.
Letter of Major Tulloch—33rd Bengal Native Infantry.
Journal of Gen Sir Arthur Becher.

GENERAL INDEX

235

REGIMENTAL INDEX